COMMENTARY ON

PAÑCADAŚĪ

Vol : 1

(Chapters 1 to 5)

by

Swami Anubhavananda

Be Happy

मौज में रहो

Be Happy Inc. USA

Yo Veda Inc. Australia

Sat Bhavana Trust, India

Happy Folks of South Africa

Indra Publishing House

www.indrapublishing.com

Published by:

Indra Publishing House

E-5/21, Arera Colony,
Habibganj Police Station Road,
Bhopal-462016
Phone : +91 755-4059620, 6462025
Telefax : +91 755-4030921
Email : manish@indrapublishing.com
pramod@indrapublishing.com
Web. : www.indrapublishing.com

First Indian Print 2010
ISBN : 978-93-80834-07-8

₹ : 250/-

Printed By: Repro India Limited, Navi Mumbai
& published by Mr. Manish Gupta for Indra Publishing House,
E-5/21, Arera Colony, Habibganj Police Station Road,
Bhopal 462016 INDIA

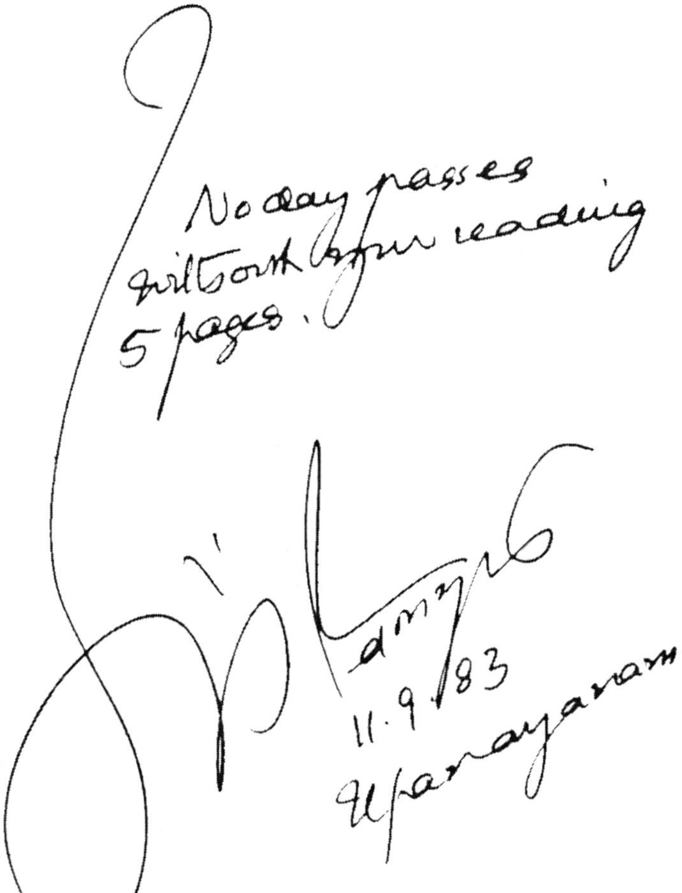

With His blessings, we continue.....

Dedicated To The Ever Shining Presence of Pujya Gurudeva

The Last Word

In the beginning was 'Silence'. When it broke, sound manifested. Meaning given to the sound created the world of names and forms. Thus begins the *samsara*. In this world of relative existence, a lot of efforts are put to go beyond by creating more and more words, sentences, books, CDs, cassettes and there is no limit to it. Although the intention is good, it leads to entanglement in the relative world and not freedom from the publications, talks, reading, discussing about the world and the Absolute. This creates the world of absolute chaos and subsequently getting lost in the world through words.

The Lord, out of His compassion relieved us of this entanglement through the deluge masterminded on 26th July, 2005 in Mumbai which took away the cause of absolute chaos through the relative world. Hence it was accepted as His will and no more publications of books in particular will be produced in large quantities by the Sat Bhavana Trust.

For the information of the seekers, let it be known that our books are now taken up for publishing by the Indra Publishing House, Bhopal and will be available through us and their outlets.

This huge work of restructuring the publications is attributed to a collective contribution of a team of devoted seekers of Truth to whom we remain ever indebted.

Swami Anubhavananda

CONTENTS

FOREWORD

Pañcadaśī is a book of categories dealing with the different aspects of *Vedāntic* philosophy. The major emphasis of this book is to help the sincere seekers in getting the perfect vision of the Truth without any doubt whatsoever, in the philosophical aspects of the Truth. The author indicates very distinctly in the beginning of his composition, that this text is composed for the sincere seekers of Truth who have pure minds with single-pointed devotion for knowing the Truth. Any student of *Vedāntic* philosophy is incomplete in his studies without a thorough study of *Pañcadaśī*.

There are many commentaries in different languages on this text. However, the commentary of *Srī Rāmakrishna* is considered to be the most authentic and to the point. *Srī Rāmakrishna* was a direct disciple of the two authors of *Pañcadaśī* namely *Srī Vidyāraṇya Svāmī* and His *Guru Srī Bhārati Tīrtha.*

The scheme of the thought presentation is divided under three categories namely:

1. Chapters dealing with discrimination.
2. Chapters dealing with illumination.
3. Chapters dealing with bliss.

The first five chapters mainly deal with the discrimination, predominantly on '*Sat*' aspect of the Truth. The second five chapters deal with the '*Cit*' aspect of the Truth while the remaining five chapters deal with the *'Ānanda'* aspect of the Truth.

In the above classification, there is no exclusion of the other two aspects of the Truth while dealing with a predominantly particular aspect of the Truth.

It is believed by the different commentators that the first six chapters were written by *Srī Vidyāraṇya Svāmī* and were presented to His *Guru, Srī Bhārati Tīrtha* and the latter added the remaining nine chapters to make it into a volume of 15 chapters. Hence the name *Pañcadaśī*.

The present publication on *Pañcadaśī* is brought out in the Chinmaya style of commentaries wherein the original *śloka* or verse is followed by transliteration, word-to-word meaning, running translation of the *Saṁskṛta śloka* and a short commentary on different words and the thoughts. We have used the international transliteration symbols for writing the *Saṁskṛta* words in Roman script. However, the splitting of the transliteration is strictly on the basis of the phonetic sounds rather than the breaking of *Saṁskṛta* words as per the grammar rules. This was done for a simple purpose that a student who is not able to read the *Devanāgari* script is able to join the chorus chanting along with other students who are chanting the original text in a *Vedāntic* class-room. This has been the tradition of imparting knowledge in our Chinmaya style wherein every verse is chanted by the teacher and the student joins the chorus chanting of the same verse.

The present book is an outcome of the Grace of *Parama Pūjya Gurudev (Svāmī Chinmayānanda)* who encouraged me in many ways and also blessed the commentary that was shown to Him during Dehra Dun *Yajña* in October 1992.

This book is the result of the sincere efforts put forth by the students at Delhi Chinmaya Mission who were very regular in attending the classes in spite of the difficulties. The lectures were recorded, transcribed, edited and finally given the shape of a book. Those who were involved in the preparation of the manuscript need special thanks. Without their untiring efforts, this book would never have come out. To name them, I remember the following with special reverence, Mrs. Saraswati Doraiswami and Mrs. Gayatri Balakrishnan.

The students who were instrumental in encouraging me to take up this text need and deserve the foremost appreciation.

The computer composition of the entire text was done by Mrs. Uma Kumar, Sri. Gopalkrishnan and staff of CCMT. The proof-reading was rendered by Sri Vishwamitra Puri who took pains to go through the total manuscript.

Parama Pūjya Svāmī Tejomayānanda was kind enough to go through the manuscript and suggested some changes which has given the book a better look. His blessing is a continuation of *Param Pūjya Gurudev's 'saṅkalpa'* for the completion of this book. I have no words to express my gratitude for His encouraging suggestions and guidance.

This commentary is brought out in five volumes :

Vol **1** : Chapters 1 to 5
Vol **2** : Chapter 6
Vol **3** : Chapter 7
Vol **4** : Chapters 8 to 10
Vol **5** : Chapters 11 to 15

Swami Anubhavananda

TRANSLITERATION GUIDE FOR *SAṀSKṚTA* WORDS

a	as *o* in son	अ *	ṛ	as *r* in Krishna	ऋ
ā	as *a* in master	आ (ा)*	ś	as *sh* in shut	श्
b	as *b* in book	ब्	ṣ	as *sh* in show	ष्
c	as *ch* in check	च्	s	as *s* in sit	स्
d	as *d* in father, than	द्	t	as *t* in french sound	त्
ḍ	as *d* in do	ड्	ṭ	as *t* in touch	ट्
e	as *a* in evade	ए(े)*	u	as *u* in full	उ (ु)*
g	as *g* in good	ग्	ū	as *oo* in boot	ऊ (ू)*
h	as *h* in hard	ह्	v	as *w* in want, avert	व्
ḥ	as *h* in oh!	:	y	as *y* in yak	य्
i	as *i* in if	इ (ि)*	ai	as *y* in my	ऐ (ै)*
ī	as *ee* in feel	ई (ी)*	au	as *ow* in now	औ(ौ)*
j	as *j* in jar	ज्	bh	as *bh* in abhor	भ्
k	as *k* in kite	क्	ch	as *chh* in catch him	छ्
l	as *l* in Lord	ल्	dh	as *theh* in breathe	ध्
m	as *m* in man	म्	ḍh	as *dh* in godhood	ढ्
ṁ	as *m* in simple, hum	(ं)	gh	as *gh* in ghost	घ्
n	as *n* in nose	न्	jh	as *dgeh* in hedge	झ्
ṅ	as *n* in monkey	ङ्	kh	as *kh* in khāki	ख्
ñ	as *n* in lunch	ञ्	ph	as *ph* in photo	फ्
ṇ	as *n* in under (hard)	ण्	th	as *th* in thumb	थ्
o	as *o* in over	ओ (ो)*	ṭh	as *th* in ant-hiṭ	ठ्
p	as *p* in put	प्	‘	as unwritten ‘*a*’ sound	ऽ
r	as *r* in run	र्	“	as -do- ‘*aa*’ sound	ऽऽ

Also letters ḷ and ṝ represent ऌ * and ॠ* respectively and F,Q,W,X and Z are not called to use.

In *saṁskṛta* consonants represented with a stroke below e.g. as in क् cannot be pronounced except in conjunction with a vowel marked* e.g. क् (k) + अ (a) = क (ka).

For easy pronounciation while reading or reciting, in some publications, the break-up of the transliteration is based on the phonetic sounds and not on the basis of *saṁskṛta* grammar rules or words.

Abbreviations used in this volume -

Ait.Ā	Aitereya Āraṇyaka
Anu.G.	Aṇu Gītā
Apb.	Aparokṣānubhūti
B.G.	Bhagavad Gītā
Bj.G.	Bhaja Govindaṁ
B.G.B.	Saṅkara's Bhagavad Gītābhāṣya
B.S.	Brahmasūtra-s
B.U.	Bṛhadāraṇyaka Upaniṣad
C.U.	Chāndogya Upaniṣad
G.D.S.	Gautama dharmasūtra-s
I.U.B.	Śaṅkarācārya's Īśavāsya Upaniṣad Bhāṣya
Jal.U.	Jābāla Upaniṣad
K.U.	Kaṭha Upaniṣad
Kai.U.	Kaivalya Upaniṣad
Ke.U.	Kenu Upaniṣad
Manu.	Manu Smṛti
M.B.	Mahābhārata
M.U.	Muṇḍaka Upaniṣad
Mk.U.	Muktikopaniṣad
Nar.Pari.U.	Nārada Parivrājaka Upaniṣad
Nrpt.U.	Narasimha Purvatāpaṇi Upaniṣad

P.U.	Praśna Upaniṣad
R.V.	Ṛg Veda
Śānti	Śāntiparva
Ś.U.	Śvetāśvatara Upaniṣad
Sk.	Skandha
T.A.	Taittirīya Āraṇyaka
T.B.	Taittirīya Upaniṣad Bhāṣya of Śaṅkara
T.S	Taittirīya Saṁhitā
T.U.	Taittirīya Upaniṣad
Vana	Vanaparva
V.P	Viṣṇu Purāṇa
V.C.	Vivekacūḍāmaṇi

* * *

1

१५

Chapter I

TATTVA VIVEKA

or

DIFFERENTIATION OF THE REAL PRINCIPLE

Tattva (Tat - That, *tva* - ness) *viveka* is the study of, enquiry into and inner-realisation of That which is all-pervading, self-determined and which exists without cause and effect. At the end of that enquiry comes the realisation that *'Tat'* is *'Tvam'* - 'That thou art'. Thus, the identity between the unmanifest and the manifest, between the Absolute and the limited, between spirit and matter is established.

Such a deep and intense study results in doubtless knowledge. When followed by constant reflection and single-pointed (*ekatānatā*) contemplation, it leads to a total understanding of the Truth from all four angles of *jīva, jagat, Īśvara* and the Absolute.

When contemplation is *puruṣa pradhāna* and not *prakṛti* (matter) *pradhāna* and it is continuously practised over a length of time, then by the grace of a *Brahmaniṣṭha Puruṣa* or a sage and that of the Lord, there is a possibility of one getting absorbed in one's own being, where meditation is a state of being and not doing.

How to carry out this analysis of that Great Principle, what are the obstacles, how to overcome them and the ultimate goal to be reached by this *jīva*, constitute the subject matter of this chapter in capsule form. The fourteen chapters that follow are elaborations of each facet of this *viveka*.

नमः श्रीशंकरानन्द गुरुपादाम्बुजन्मने ।
सविलासमहामोह ग्राहग्रासैककर्मणे ।।१।।

Namaḥ Śrī Śaṅkarānanda Gurupādāmbujanmane
Savilāsamahāmoha grāhagrāsaikakarmaṇe (1)

सविलास - alongwith with manifest effects; **महामोहग्राह** - the shark of primordial ignorance; **ग्रासैक कर्मणे** - whose only undertaking is to destroy; **श्री शंकरानन्द पादाम्बुजन्मने** - to the lotus feet of *Śrī Śaṅkarānanda*; **नमः**- salutations.

Salutations to the lotus feet of *Śrī Śaṅkarānanda* whose only undertaking is to destroy the primordial shark of delusion along with its manifest effect. (1)

Namaḥ Śrī Śaṅkarānanda Gurupādāmbujanmane : Salutations to the Lotus Feet of *Guru Maharāja Śrī Śaṅkarānanda - Śaṅkara,* who brings all auspiciousness in our lives, who is *aiśvarya yukta* i.e., who is able to transfer glory of Self to those who surrender at His feet.

I salute in all humility, in a spirit of total surrender. Surrender is, dropping all efforts born out of individuality, sense of doership and ego. To whom is this surrender?

Savilāsa mahāmoha grāha grāsaika karmaṇe - To that *Śaṅkara,* whose only pastime and work is to devour *grāha*, the shark of illusion. Destroyer of primal ignorance of our own essential nature is *Śrī Śaṅkara*; and *ānanda*- auspicious, plentiful and blissful. In this self, I absorb myself by destroying and transcending my individuality born out of ignorance.

For whom and for what purpose is this text written?...

तत्पादाम्बुरुहद्वंद्व सेवानिर्मलचेतसाम् ।
सुखबोधाय तत्त्वस्य विवेकोऽयं विधीयते ।।२।।

Tatpādāmburuhadvaṁdva Sevānirmalacetasām
Sukhabodhāya tattvasya viveko'yaṁ vidhīyate (2)

तत् पादाम्बुरुह द्वंद्व - The pair of lotus feet of the *Guru*; सेवा - service; निर्मल - without impurities; चेतसाम् - those (with such) mind; सुख बोधाय - for effortless comprehension; अयम् - this; तत्त्वस्य - of the reality; विवेकः- discrimination; विधीयते - is designed.

This discrimination of the Reality is designed for the effortless comprehension of the Truth, for those, who have cleaned their mind of all impurities by serving the lotus feet of the *Guru*. (2)

Ayaṁ tattvasya vivekaḥ vidhīyate: This *tattva viveka* is being expounded for those - *tat pādāmbu ruha dvaṅdva sevā nirmala cetasām* -whose hearts have been purified by the devoted service to the pair of the Lotus Feet of the *Guru*.

Highest spiritual *sādhanā* is *sevā bhāva,* an attitude of sevice. Through such *sevā,* the mind gets purified and cleansed of three major *mala-s,* the impurities namely, *ālasya* or laziness which robs the seeker of much valuable time and opportunity; *pramāda* - inadvertence; and *nidra* - excessive sleep. Such a purified *antaḥkaraṇa* will be calm, contemplative and vigilant so as not to slip from the chosen path.

Sukha bodhāya: For such a person, this enquiry will bring the dawn of wisdom effortlessly. The real spiritual bliss is in wanting nothing, not even joy!

शब्दस्पर्शादयो वेद्या वैचित्र्याज्जागरे पृथक् ।
ततो विभक्ता तत्संवित् ऐकरूप्यान्न भिद्यते ।।३।।

Śabda sparśā dayo vedyā vaici tryāj jāgare pṛthak
Tato vibhaktā tat saṁvit aika rūpyānna bhidyate (3)

जागरे - In the waking state; वेद्याः- the objects of knowledge;शब्द स्पर्श आदयः– sound touch etc.; वैचित्र्यात् - being many; पृथक् - are different ;ततः - from them; विभक्ता - separated out; तत् संवित् - the consciousness; ऐकरूप्यात् – being undifferentiated; न – not; भिद्यते - get differentiated.

In the waking state, the objects like sound, touch etc., are many and different from each other. The Consciousness establishing their differences, being one, is not different (like the objects) (3)

Jāgare śabda sparśādayaḥ vedyaḥ pṛthak : In the waking state, the consciousness gets identified with the gross body and the world is born! The 'I' perceives a multiplicity of objects of knowledge as seen, heard, felt, tasted, smelt etc., depending on the senses through which perception takes place. And all these objects of knowledge differ from each other by their specific characteristics.

Tato vibhaktā tat saṁvit aikya rūpāt na bhidyate : However, that consciousness (*saṁvit*) which is different from these pluralistic world of objects of knowledge, is only one, it does not become many.

Through all the great changes of perceptions, the Consciousness remains one and only one. To withdraw the mind from the multiplicity of sounds, sights etc., and fix it on this *saṁvit* which is illuminating this plurality, is a potent method of contemplation.

What about dream state?

तथा स्वप्नेऽत्र वेद्यं तु न स्थिरं जागरे स्थिरम् ।
तद्भेदोऽतस्तयोः संवित् एकरूपा न भिद्यते ।। ४।।

Tathā svapne'tra vedyaṁ tu na sthiraṁ jāgare sthiram
Tad bhedo' tastayoḥ saṁvit ekarūpā na bhidyate (4)

तथा - Similarly; अत्र - in case of; स्वप्ने - dream state; वेद्यम् - the objects of knowledge; तु - indeed; न - not; स्थिरम् - are stable; जागरे - in waking state; स्थिरम् - are stable; अतः- therefore; तद् भेदः- these two states differ; तयोः- of these two; संवित् - consciousness; एकरूपा - of the nature of oneness; न - not; भिद्यते - differ.

Similar is true with reference to dream state; although the objects seem to be stable in waking and not in dream, and this difference between the dream and waking state seems to be true, but the consciousness is ONE and does not differ in two states. (4)

Tathā atra svapne vedyaṁ tu : Similar is the situation in the dream state. In each state, the trio viz., the waker, the waking world, the waking experience; the dreamer, the dream world and the dream experience happen simultaneously and not sequentially.

Na sthiraṁ jāgare sthiraṁ : The difference between the dream state and waking state is that in the former, the objects of the dream world keep changing while those of the waking world seem to be permanent, in comparison to the dream state.

Tat tayoḥ bhedaḥ saṁvit eka rūpā na bhidyate : Thus, there is a difference between the two states. However, the consciousness is only one, witnessing both states and it does not become divided into many.

Now regarding the deep sleep state...

सुप्तोत्थितस्य सौषुप्त तमोबोधो भवेत्स्मृतिः ।
सा चावबुद्धविषयाऽवबुद्धं तत्तदा तमः ।।५।।

Suptot thitasya sauṣupta tamo bodho bhavet smṛtiḥ
Sā cāva buddha viṣayā'vabuddhaṁ tattadā tamaḥ (5)

सुप्तोत्थितस्य - To a person awakened from deep sleep; सौषुप्त तमोबोधः- the knowledge of the ignorance of deep sleep; स्मृतिः- memory; भवेत् - is; च - and; सा - that (the memory); अवबुद्धविषया - is of the known object; तत् तमः- that ignorance; तदा - in deep sleep; अवबुद्धम् - was known in deep sleep;

For a person awakened from deep sleep, the ignorance of deep sleep is known in the form of memory. This memory is that of the object (ignorance) experienced during deep sleep. Therefore, the Consciousness alone illumined the ignorance in deep sleep. (5)

Suptot thitasya sauṣupta tamo bodhāḥ bhavet smṛtiḥ : One who has come out of the deep sleep state, he is able to remember the ignorance of the deep sleep state.

Sā ca avabuddha viṣayāḥ : This memory is that of experience of the object called ignorance.

Avabuddhaṁ tat tadā tamaḥ : Thus even in deep sleep, absence of knowledge is experienced.

This experience of ignorance is illumined by the Consciousness which is in unmanifest form in the deep sleep state. The same

Consciousness illumines the experiences of the waking state, the dream state and the absence of everything in the deep sleep state.

This Consciousness that is illuminating the differences of waking, dream or deep sleep states, is One Without A Second...

स बोधो विषयाद्भिन्नो न बोधात्स्वप्नबोधवत् ।
एवं स्थानत्रयेऽप्येका संवित्तद्वद्दिनान्तरे ।।६।।

Sa bodho viṣayād bhinno na bodhāt svapna bodha vat
Evaṁ sthāna traye'pyekā saṁvit tadvad dinān tare (6)

स बोधः- that knowledge of ignorance in deep sleep; विषयात् - from the object; भिन्नः- is different; न - not; बोधात् - from consciousness; स्वप्न बोधवत् - like that of dream knowledge; एवम् - in this way; स्थान त्रये अपि - in three planes of Consciousness; संवित् - the Consciousness; एका - is one; तद्वत् - similarly; दिनान्तरे - in all the days.

The knowledge (of deep sleep) is different from object (i.e., ignorance) but not from the Consciousness, but is the same that illumined the dream experience. In this way, the Consciousness is one in all the three planes. So is true for all time to come! (6)

Sa bodhaḥ viṣayāt bhinnaḥ na bodhāt svapna bodha vat : That knowledge of ignorance in the deep sleep state is different from the object viz., the ignorance but not from itself. As we saw in the dream state, the knowledge aspect does not change.

Evaṁ sthāna traye api saṁvit ekā : Thus, in all the three planes of Consciousness, the Consciousness remains one and the same --- the illuminator of the knowledge and the ignorance.

Tad vat dināntare : In the same way, Consciousness also does not change with time. *Deśa, kāla, vastu bedha* (The differences on account of place, time or objects) does not make any change in the Consciousness.

"The Consciousness is changeless" is further emphasized...

मासाब्दयुगकल्पेषु गतागम्येष्वनेकधा ।
नोदेति नास्तमेत्येका संविदेषा स्वयंप्रभा ।।७।।

Māsābda yuga kalpeṣu gatā gamye ṣvane kadhā
Nodeti nāsta metyekā saṁvi deṣā svayaṁ prabhā (7)

अनेकधा - in many ways; गतागम्येषु - in the past and future; मास - month; अब्द - year; युग - *yuga*; कल्पेषु - in the cyle of time; संवित् - the Pure Consciousness; एका - is but ONE; न उदेति - neither born; न अस्तम् एति - nor become non-existent; एषा - this Consciousness; स्वयंप्रभा - is Self-effulgent.

In the same way, in and through all the past and future, months, years, *yuga*-s, *kalpa*-s to come, the pure Consciousness is but ONE; which is self-effulgent, neither was it ever born nor does it ever become non-existent. (7)

Anekadhā gatā āgamyeṣu māsa abda yuga kalpeṣu : In the same way, in and through all the past and future months, years, *yuga-s*, (time cycles) *Svayaṁprabhā saṁvit ekā* : the Pure Self-effulgent Consciousness is but ONE. *Na udeti na astaṁ eti* : The Pure Consciousness, the *saṁvit cetanā*, is neither born (*na udeti*); nor does it ever end *na astaṁ eti* i.e., it has no beginning and no end. It is Self-existing i.e., *Sat svarūpa.*

It is also *Svayaṁ-prabhā*, Self effulgent, *Cit-svarūpa.*

The Consciousness is only One (*ekā*). That which is Existence, *Sat* is itself Consciousness, *Cit*. That *Sat* and *Cit* are not two, they are one and the same Consciousness. It requires no other authority to prove its existence, nor any other light to illumine it.

Having dealt with the *Sat* and *Cit* aspect of the Truth, the third aspect of *Ānanda* is now taken....

इयमात्मा परानन्दः परप्रेमास्पदं यतः ।
मा न भूवं हि भूयासमिति प्रेमात्मनीक्ष्यते ।।८।।

Iya mātmā parā nandaḥ para premās padaṁ yataḥ
Mā na bhūvaṁ hi bhūyā sam iti premāt manī kṣyate (8)

इयम् - refers to *saṁvit* in the last verse; आत्मा - Self-Effulgent self; परानन्दः- is of the nature of Supreme Bliss; यतः- because; परप्रेमास्पदं - being loved most; प्रेम - this love; आत्मनि - in the Self; हि - indeed; मा न भूवम् - may I not cease to be; भूयासम् - may I always be; इति - in this way; ईक्ष्यते - is seen.

This Pure Consciousness referred in last verse is one's own Self. The nature of which is Supreme Bliss. Because we love ourselves the most. This love for the Self (*Ātmā*) is seen to express as "May I never cease to be, may I ever be present." (8)

Yataḥ para premāspadaṁ iyaṁ ātmā parānandaḥ : Because we love ourselves the most, (anything that gives us the maximum happiness is loved by us). Therefore, this *ātmā* 'I' is of the nature of Supreme bliss.

This *pratyag Ātmā*, this 'I', how is it experienced by everyone?

Mā na bhūvaṁ bhūyāsaṁ, "May I never cease to be". No one wants one's own absence, because one loves oneself the most.

May I always be present. Everyone wants continuous presence, because continuous presence is Existence, and Existence itself is Consciousness which is itself *ānanda.*

This is *Tattva viveka.*

In this way, it has been shown in the last six verses, that the Consciousness, the *saṁvit* is one through all the multiplicity of the three planes of Consciousness and the world of objects and experiences; it is not born nor does it ever die; and it is *Sat, Cit* and *Ānanda svarūpaṁ.* This is 'I'.

In this way, *Tattva darśana* has been discussed with reference to 'I' the Pure Being, who is not conditioned by the waking state although it supports the waker, the waking world and the waking experience. Where the *bhoktā, bhogya* and *bhoga* - experiencer, experienced and experience trio does not exist, that Pure One is referred to here as *iyaṁ ātmā parānandaḥ*. This *Ātmā* is of the nature of Supreme Bliss.

How do you say that? The teacher now quotes the scriptures and also makes some logical deductions to substantiate our own experience in this regard...

तत्प्रेमात्मार्थमन्यत्र नैवमन्यार्थमात्मनि ।
अतस्तत्परमं तेन परमानन्दताऽऽत्मनः ।।९।।

Tat premāt mārtham anyatra naiva manyārtham ātmani
Atastat paramaṁ tena paramā nandatā''tmanaḥ (9)

अन्यत्र - For others; प्रेम - love; तत् आत्मार्थम् - is for the sake of the Self; एवम् - similarly; आत्मनि - for the Self; अन्यार्थम् - for others; न - not; अतः- therefore; तत् - that love; परमम् - Supreme; तेन - therefore; आत्मनः- of the Self; परमानन्दता - the nature of Supreme Bliss (is proved).

The love for the other things and beings is for the sake of Self; but the love for the Self is not for the sake of others, thereby it is said that the love for the Self is Supreme. Therefore, the Self is of the nature of Supreme Bliss. (9)

Anyatra prem tat ātmārtham : Love for objects in locations other than oneself, such as love for wife, husband, children, wealth, property, health etc., all that love is in the ultimate analysis, for one's own sake.

(Re: B.U. where it says "*Ātmanastu kāmāya sarvaṁ priyaṁ bhavati*". Everything is not dear for the sake of that object, but for one's own sake). 'I' is the central figure with reference to whom liking and disliking operates.

Evaṁ ātmani anyārthaṁ na : To say that one loves oneself not for one's own sake but for the sake of others is not possible, it will only be a hypocritical statement, because the love for the Self is the Supreme love.

Tena ātmanaḥ paraṁ ānandatā : Therefore, one can conclude logically that everything in this world is because of this *Ātmā*, this self, which is of the nature of *Param Ānandā.*

Continuing this thought further, the teacher proceeds to establish *Brahma-ātmā-aikya-bodha*, by explaining that this *Sat-cit-ānanda*, the essential nature of 'I', the *Ātmā*, is also the nature of the *Brahman* which is referred to in the scriptures...

इत्थं सच्चित्परानन्द आत्मा युक्त्या तथाविधम् ।
परं ब्रह्म तयोश्चैक्यं श्रुत्यन्तेषूपदिश्यते ।।१०।।

Itthaṁ saccitparānanda ātmā yuktyā tathāvidham
Paraṁ brahma tayoś caikyaṁ śrutyan teṣū padiśyate (10)

इत्थम् - in this way; युक्त्या - by proper logic; आत्मा - the Self; सच्चित्परानन्दः - (is of the nature of) *Sat-cit* supreme *ānanda*; परम् ब्रह्म – the *Param Brahma*, तथा विधम् - is of similar nature; च - therefore; तयोः- of the two (i.e., *tvaṁ* and tat); ऐक्यं - oneness; श्रुत्यन्तेषु - in the *Vedānta Śāstra*; उपदिश्यते - is expounded.

In this way, the Self is proved to be *Sat-cit-ānanda.* The *Upaniṣads* declare that the *Param Brahman* is also of the nature of *Sat-cit-ānanda.* Therefore, the identity between the *Self* and the *Param Brahman* is expounded in the (*mahāvākya* of) *upaniṣad.* (10)

Itthaṁ yuktyā ātmā sat-cit-parānandaḥ : In this way, through logical deduction, it has been concluded that the *Ātmā* is of the nature of Pure Existence, Pure Knowledge and Supreme Bliss.

Tathā vidhaṁ śruti anteṣu paraṁ brahma upadiśyate : In the *upaniṣads* also, it is explained and declared that the *Param Brahma* is also of the same nature, namely *Satyaṁ, Jñānaṁ, Anantaṁ Brahma* i.e., *Sat-cit-ānanda*).

Tayoḥ ca aikyaṁ : Therefore, the oneness in the *tvaṁ pada* and *tat pada* is explained and established in the *Vedānta Śāstra.*

The *tvaṁ pada* in the *Mahāvākya, Tat-Tvaṁ-Asi* is with reference to our essential nature, *Sat-cit-ānanda.* The *Tat-pada* also refers to the nature of *Brahman* and is also *Sat-cit-ānanda.*

In this way, what has been said earlier by logical deduction gets the authority of the *upaniṣadik* declarations.

Now some seeming contradictions are pointed out in the statement that "the *Ātmā* is *Paramānanda svarūpa*", and they are answered...

अभाने न परं प्रेम भाने न विषये स्पृहा ।
अतो भानेऽप्यभाताऽसौ परमानन्दतात्मनः ।।११।।

Abhāne na paraṁ prema bhāne na viṣaye spṛhā
Ato bhāne' pyabhātā' sau paramā nandatā tmanaḥ (11)

परम् प्रेम - Supreme love; अभाने - for the unknown; न - not; भाने - having known (the self); विषये - for the objects; स्पृहा - desire and attachment; न - not; अतः- therefore; असौ - this Self; भाने अपि - although Consciousness; अभाता - is unknown; परमानन्दता - Supreme Bliss, आत्मनः- of the Self.

There cannot be supreme love for an unknown (Self) and if known, there cannot be desire for the objects. Therefore, (is it not a contradiction that) the Self is yet unknown and although of the nature of Supreme Bliss, is not experienced! (11)

Abhāne na paraṁ prema : One can only love someone whom we know; we cannot love an unknown person; and it has been said that *Ātma tattva* cannot become the object of knowledge. Therefore, *abhāne,* that which cannot be known, *Na paraṁ prema*, it is not possible to love it the most, it cannot possibly be *parama premāspada.*

Furthermore, *Viṣaye bhāne spṛhā na* : When one sees the world of objects, one should not have any desire for them (because one loves oneself the most), but it is common knowledge that one does have desire for worldly objects. These seem to contradict the statement that the *Ātmā* is *Parama-ānanda-svarūpa* and *parama premāspada.*

Ataḥ bhāne api asau abhātā : These two contradictions are now resolved. This *Ātmā* is very peculiar: it is, yet it is not known; and *Paramānandatā,* although it is of the nature of Supreme Bliss, that Bliss is not known.

Is this not playing with words? No. That the *Ātmā* is *Paramātma svarūpa* and yet is not known can be made clear by an example...

अध्येतृवर्गमध्यस्थ पुत्राध्ययनशब्दवत् ।
भानेऽप्यभानं भानस्य प्रतिबन्धेन युज्यते ।।१२।।

Adhyetṛ varga madhya stha putrā dhyayana śabda vat
Bhāne' pyabhānaṁ bhānasya prati bandhena yujyate (12)

अध्येतृ वर्ग मध्यस्थ पुत्र - The son among his classmates; अध्ययन शब्द वत् - like the words of chanting; भाने अपि - although known to be; अभानम् - is not known; भानस्य - of the knowledge; प्रतिबन्धेन - due to obstacles; युज्यते - is possible.

Although, *Ātmā* is present, remains unknown due to some obstacle, like the words of one's son are hidden in the collective chanting of a class. (12)

Bhāne api bhānasya abhānaṁ : Although (the *Ātmā*) is manifest, yet it remains uncognised. This is possible. How? An example is given...

Adhyetṛ varga madhyastha putra adhyayana śabda vat : In a *Gurukul*, all the children are chanting the Veda-s. Can a father recognise his son's voice alone in the midst of the collective chanting of all the children?

Prati bandhena yujyate : Because the collective chanting of the group acts as *pratibandha* or obstacle in the way of his distinguishing and singling out the voice of his son alone.

In the same way, although the *Ātmā* is of the nature of absolute *ānanda*, Supreme Bliss, there is a possibility that we may not realize this because of some obstacle or *pratibandha*.

What is the nature of this *pratibandha* (obstacle) is explained in the next verse...

प्रतिबन्धोऽस्ति भातीति व्यवहारार्हवस्तुनि ।
तन्निरस्य विरुद्धस्य तस्योत्पादनमुच्यते ।।१३।।

Prati bandho' sti bhātīti vyavahārārha vastuni
Tanni rasya viruddhasya tasyot pādanam ucyate (13)

व्यवहारार्हवस्तुनि - in case of an object under discussion; अस्ति - is; भाति - is known; इति - thus; तम् - that real nature; निरस्य - denying; विरुद्धस्य - of the opposite (i.e., is not and is not known); तस्य - of that; उत्पादनम् - the cause of this opposite knowledge; प्रतिबन्धः- an obstacle or hindrance; उच्यते - is called.

When an existing object which can be known, yet it is hidden from cognition, resulting into opposite knowledge (i.e., the object does not exist, and therefore it cannot be known), the hindrance because of which this happens is called as *pratibandha* or obstacle (13)

Vyavahārārha vastuni asti bhāti iti : That object where the knower-known transaction can take place (in objective perception, it is possible to speak in terms of this object 'is' and this object 'is known'). In all transactions in the world, *asti, bhāti* (existence and knowledge) are abundantly present, simultaneously. Every experience, every knowledge is the manifestation of subjective acceptance of an object as is and is known.

Taṁ nirasya tasya viruddhasya utpādanaṁ pratibandhaḥ ucyate : However, an obstacle can obstruct the object from being known. For example, when the sun is hidden by the clouds (which constitute the *pratibandha*), we know the sun is, although we do not know exactly where it is. When the clouds move away, the sun will be revealed (not created). In the same way, it is as if, the truth has been revealed to us. Although this *Ātmā* is *paramānanda svarūpa*, we are not able to know because of some obstacle which is veiling the vision of this essential nature of ours. Not only does it veil the vision of the Truth but it creates or produces contrary knowledge (*viruddha*) such as :-

a) the fear of extinction of That which is eternal; (*Sat*)

b) the fear of deception for That which is of the nature of Knowledge (*Cit*)

c) the fear of suffering for That which is of the nature of bliss (*ānanda*)

When the *pratibandha* (hindrance) is removed, the contrary knowledge caused by it will also go and the *Ātmā* which is *Paramānanda svarūpa* will be Self-effulgently revealing itself to our cognition.

What is the nature of this *Pratibandha* which causes such contrary knowledge? And how is this *pratibandha* got rid of?

तस्य हेतुः समानाभिहारः पुत्रध्वनिश्रुतौ ।
इहानादिरविद्यैव व्यामोहैकनिबन्धनम् ।।१४ ।।

Tasya hetuḥ samānābhi hāraḥ putra dhvaniśrutau
Ihā nādira vidyaiva vyāmo haika niban dhanam (14)

पुत्रध्वनि श्रुतौ - in hearing, the voice of the son; तस्य - of that obstacle; हेतु - cause; समानाभिहारः- like simultaneous chantings by all the students; इह - here, in not knowing the presence of blissful conscious Self; व्यामोह - opposite knowledge; निबन्धनम् - obstacle; एक - alone; अनादि - beginningless; अविद्या - ignorance; एव - indeed.

The cause for hiding the voice of the son is the concealment in the simultaneous chanting by all students; and here in the present topic, that although the *Ātmā* is abundantly present, is concealed by intense delusion alone. (14)

Putra dhvani śrutau (In the example given in verse 12) : If the father wants to hear the voice of his son alone, *tasya hetu samānābhihāraḥ* : he has to remove the cause (*hetu*) or *pratibandha*, namely all the other voices because of which he could not hear his son's voice. Once all other children stop chanting, then his son's voice, which had been hidden in the many voices, becomes cognizable.

Samānā iha : In the same way, in the subject under discussion, viz., that although the *Ātmā* is of the nature of *Sat-cit-ānanda*, we are not able to know and experience it because of the contrary knowledge. The remedy is to remove the obstacle which is veiling this essential nature of ours.

What is this *pratibandha*?

Vyāmoha eka nibandhanaṁ : *Moha* itself indicates a confused state, *vyāmoha* is *viśeṣa moha*, where confusion is worst confounded. It is not only the inability to understand but also the projection of a wrong perception, as if it is wisdom. The classic example is that of Arjuna at the start of the war against the Kaurava-s. He took a wrong angle in perceiving his duty and found himself in a state of utter confusion, *vyāmoha* (ref. B.G. Ch.1). The *Muṇḍaka upaniṣad* likens such a person to the blind leading the blind (M.U. 1,2,8)

Thus, *vyāmoha* which is a deadly combination of absence of correct perception and the projection of a wrong perception; is the one and only one obstacle to be removed for the revelation of one's own essential nature.

What is the cause of this *vyāmoha*?

Anādi avidyā eva : The cause is *avidyā* - ignorance. Since when? It is beginningless (*anādi*). Ignorance has no beginning for the simple reason that it does not exist! *Avidyā* means a combination of two things --- non-existence and non-knowledge resulting in wrong knowledge.

The *Paramātmā* was also described as beginningless (vide verse 7 ante): The difference is that ignorance which is beginningless can end at some point, whereas *Paramātmā* never ends (*na astameti*).

Having said that *avidyā* or ignorance is the cause for non-experience of the *Sat-cit-ānanda* nature of this Pure 'I', the teacher goes on to explain the nature of this *avidyā,* so that it can be removed (*apaharaṇa kāraṇāt*).

चिदानन्दमयब्रह्मप्रतिबिम्बसमन्विता ।
तमोरजस्सत्त्वगुणा प्रकृतिर्द्विविधा च सा ।।१५।।

Cidā nanda maya brahma prati bimba saman vitā
Tamo rajas sattva guṇā prakṛtir dvividhā ca sā (15)

चिदानन्दमय ब्रह्म प्रतिबिम्ब - the reflection of the blissful conscious *Brahman*, समन्विता - along with; तमोरजः सत्त्व गुण - the *tamas*, *rajas*, *sattva guṇa;* प्रकृति - *prakṛti;* सा - *that prakṛti*; च - and; द्विविधा - two types.

The *prakṛti* in association with the reflection of *Brahman* which is of the nature of Conscious bliss, is made up of *sattva, rajas and tamas guṇa-s* and is of two types. (15)

Brahma cidānanda-maya : *Cidānanda* is *Brahmamaya*. There are no limitations in *Cit*, Consciousness and in *Ānanda*. And *Brahman* is that which has transcended all limitations of time, space, objects; *vyaṣṭi-samaṣṭi*, individuality and duality.

Pratibimba samanvitā prakṛti : When *prakṛti* or matter (*avidyā, māyā*) is associated with the *śuddha Brahma*, then the Consciousness, the *puruṣa* or *Brahman* gets reflected in the *prakṛti* ('Reflection' is not to be understood to be like a reflection in the mirror but more like a person's character being reflected in his behaviour).

What is the nature of this *prakṛti*?

Tamaḥ rajaḥ sattva guṇaḥ : *Prakṛti* is *triguṇātmikā*, made up of the three *guṇa-s*. *Dvividhā ca sā* : It is also of two types.

What are they?

सत्त्वशुद्ध्यविशुद्धिभ्यां मायाऽविद्ये च ते मते ।
मायाबिम्बो वशीकृत्य तां स्यात्सर्वज्ञ ईश्वरः ।।१६।।

Sattva śuddhya viśuddhi bhyāṁ māyā' vidye ca te mate
Māyā bimbo vaśī kṛtya tāṁ syātsarvajña īśvaraḥ (16)

सत्त्वशुद्धि - Knowledge predominance of *sattva guṇa*; अविशुद्धिभ्याम् - and impure aspect (*rajas* and *tamas*); ते - these two *prakṛti-s*; मायाऽविद्ये - *māyā* and *avidyā*; मते - are, च - and; मायाबिम्बः- the reflection of Consciousness in *māyā*, ताम् - to that *māyā*, वशीकृत्य - keeping under control; सर्वज्ञः- omniscient; ईश्वरः - *Īśvara*, स्यात् - is known.

When the *prakṛti* is predominantly *sattva pradhāna*, it is called as *māyā*, while contaminated with *rajas* and *tamas*, it is called as *avidyā*. The reflected Consciousness keeping the *māyā* under its control is called the Omniscient (Lord) *Īśvara*. (16)

Sattva śuddhi aviśuddhibhyāṁ : The two types of *prakṛti* are *śuddha sattva* and *aśuddha sattva.*

Te ca māyā avidyā mate : When the *Cidānanda Brahma* gets reflected in the *śuddha prakṛti,* it results in *māyā;* when it is reflected in *aśuddha prakṛti,* it is called *avidyā.*

Māyā biṁbaḥ vaśīkṛtya tāṁ syāt sarvajña Īśvara : Now *Īśvara* is defined. When the *Prakṛti* is *sattva guṇa pradhāna* (dominant) and (where the three *guṇa-s* are in a state of equilibrium, it is called *prakṛti-samyāvasthā*) reflects the *Cidānanda Brahman,* that reflected *Brahman* keeps the *māyā* under its own control (*vaśīkṛtya*). That reflection identified with the *māyā* is called *Īśvara.*

As a corollary, it follows that *jīva* is that same *Paraṁ brahma Paramātmā* coming under the influence of *prakṛti* --- not in equilibrium. The conditioned expression of the Absolute through the relativity or individuality is called *jīva.*

This is defined in the next verse...

अविद्यावशगस्त्वन्यस्तद्वैचित्र्यादनेकधा ।
सा कारणशरीरं स्यात्प्राज्ञस्तत्राभिमानवान् ।।१७।।

Avidyā vaśaga stvanya stad vaicitryāda nekadhā
Sā kāraṇa śarīraṁ syāt prājñas tatrā bhimāna vān (17)

अविद्या वशगः- (the reflection in *avidyā*) is controlled by *avidyā*; तु - unlike the *māyā* reflection; अन्यः- the other i.e., *jīva*; तत् - of the *avidyā*; वैचित्र्यात् - differences; अनेकधा - (the *jīva* is classified) in different types; सा - that (ignorance); कारणशरीरं - the causal body; स्यात् - is called; तत्र - there in that causal body; अभिमानवान् - identified with; प्राज्ञः- this *jīva* is known as *prājñaḥ.*

The other, namely the *jīva*, under the influence of *avidyā* on account of differences of many kinds, are many. This *avidyā* is called causal body. The *jīva* identified with the causal body is called *prājñaḥ* (17)

Anyaḥ avidyā vaśagaḥ : The other, namely the *jīva*, comes under the control of *avidyā*.

Vaicitryāt anekadhā manifests in strangely different ways depending upon which of the three *guṇa-s* is predominant at any one time.

Sattva guṇa pradhānatā may manifest in *deva yoni*, *rajo guṇa* predominance in *manuṣya yoni*, and *tamo guṇa* dominance in *jaḍa yoni* etc..

Sā kāraṇa śarīraṁ syāt : This *avidyā* (or imbalance in the mix of three *guṇa-s*) is called causal body or *kāraṇa śarīra*.

Abhimānavān prājñaḥ : When the *jīva* gets identified with the ignorance or *avidyā*, it is called *prājña*, one who is extremely ignorant.

Thus, *Tatra abhimānavān prājñaḥ* : When the *jīva* gets identified with the causal body (*avidyā*), it is called *prājña*.

When *avidyā* is called causal body, the question naturally arises, cause of what? What are the effects of this cause? This is now dealt with in the next few verses...

तमःप्रधानप्रकृतेस्तद्भोगायेश्वराज्ञया ।
वियत्पवनतेजोऽम्बुभुवो भूतानि जज्ञिरे ।।१८।।

Tamaḥ pradhāna prakṛte stadbho gāye śvarā jñayā
Viyat pavana tejo' mbu bhuvo bhūtāni jajñire (18)

तद्भोगाय - For the experience of that *prājña jīva*, तम प्रधान - predominantly *tamo guṇa* aspect; प्रकृतेः- from this *prakṛtiḥ*; ईश्वराज्ञया - by the will of *Īśvara*; वियत् - space; पवन - air, तेजः- fire; अम्बु - water; भुवः- earth; भूतानि - elements; जज्ञिरे - are manifested.

For the experience of the *jīva*, the *tamoguṇa* aspect of *prakṛti* creates, by the will of *Īśvara*, the five great elements viz., space, air, fire, water and earth. (18)

Tat bhogāya : For the enjoyment of this *jīva* who is *prājña* associated with ignorance; *Tamaḥ pradhāna prakṛteḥ* : From the *prakṛti* which is predominantly of *tamo guṇa, Īśvara ājñayā viyat pavana tejaḥ ambu bhuvaḥ bhūtāni ete jajñire* : by the Lord's will, the five great elements, namely, the space, air, fire, water and earth are created.

To summarise the thought thus far - The Reality is *Sat-Cit-Ānanda*. But one does not realize it because of the *pratibandha* of *vyāmoha* i.e., obstacle of delusion which is caused by ignorance or *avidyā* or *māyā*. *Avidyā* is of the nature of the three *guṇa-s*. When the three *guṇa-s* are in equilibrium, the *Cidānanda Brahman*, which though functioning through the *māyā*, keeps it under control, it is called *Īśvara*. When the *Cidānanda Brahman* comes under the influence of *māyā* or *avidyā*, in which the equilibrium of the three *guṇa-s* is disturbed, it becomes the *jīva*. For the *bhoga* or enjoyment of this *jīva*, the world of objects made of the *pañca mahā bhūta-s* is created by the Lord from the tamo-*guṇa* aspect of *prakṛti*.

Up to now, the general creation was explained. Now the teacher explains the specific creation with reference to the individuality.

After the *apañcīkṛta tanmātra-s* (the five great elements) have been created for the bhoga of the *jīva*, the next step is to provide the instrument of experience for this *jīva*. This instrument of experience is called the subtle body. This subtle body needs a 'case' or *āyatanaṁ* to be safely kept in. This 'case' is the *annamaya kośa*.

The nature of the subtle body is explained from verse 19...

सत्त्वांशैः पञ्चभिस्तेषां क्रमाद्धीन्द्रियपञ्चकम् ।
श्रोत्रत्वगक्षिरसनघ्राणाख्यमुपजायते ।।१९।।

Sattvā ṁśaiḥ pañcabhi steṣāṁ kramād dhīn driya pañcakam
Śrotra tvagakṣi rasana ghrāṇākhyam upajāyate (19)

तेषाम् - of these; पञ्चभिः- from the five elements; सत्त्वांशैः- by the *sattva guṇa* aspect; श्रोत्र - ear; त्वक् - skin; अक्षि - eye; रसन - tongue; घ्राण - nose; आख्यम् - known as; धी इन्द्रिय - the senses; पञ्चकम् - five; क्रमात् - in that sequence; उपजायते - are born.

From the *sattva guṇa* aspect of these five elements are born the five senses viz., ear, skin, eyes, tongue and nose respectively. (19)

Sattvāṁśaiḥ pañcabhiḥ teṣāṁ dhī indriya kramāt upajāyate : The *sattva* aspect of the five *mahābhūta-s* is taken and the five sense organs are created respectively (i.e., in decreasing order of subtlety as enumerated further) :

Śrotra, tvak, akṣi, rasana and ghrāṇa : The ears, the skin, the eyes, the tongue and the nose respectively. The quality of *ākāśa* or space is *śabda* and hence the ears or the faculty of hearing. Next lower in subtlety is the air from which the organ of touch, the skin is born; from *agni* or *teja*, eyes are born; from water, the organ of taste; and out of *pṛthvī* or earth, the grossest of the five *mahābhūta-s* (which has the quality of *gandha* or smell), the organ of smell, the nose is born. In this way, out of the *sattva guṇa* aspect i.e., the knowledge aspect of the *pañca mahābhūta-s*, the five sense organs are created.

This is the independent expression of each *pañca mahābhūta* in the subtle body. Knowledge of the five types of sense perceptions- *śabda, sparśa, rūpa, rasa, gandha* is received through the five reception centres called the sense organs. But if there is no co-ordination in the five perceptions, the result will be chaotic. The co-ordinating agent is the *antaḥkaraṇa* or the organ of inner perception which makes the collective expression of the *pañca mahābhūta-s* possible in the subtle body.

This is indicated in verse 20...

तैरन्तःकरणं सर्वैर्वृत्तिभेदेन तद्द्विधा ।
मनो विमर्शरूपं स्याद्बुद्धिः स्यान्निश्चयात्मिका ।।२०।।

Tai rantaḥ karaṇaṁ sarvai vṛtti bhedena tad dvidhā
Mano vimarśa rūpaṁ syād buddhiḥ syān niśca yātmikā (20)

तैः- By these; सर्वैः- all elements from their *sattva guṇa*; अन्तःकरणम् - the inner instruments (is born); तद् - that (inner instrument); वृत्तिभेदेन - depending upon the difference of thoughts; द्विधा - is two fold; विमर्श रूपम् - of the nature of doubt; मनः- mind; स्यात् - is; निश्चयात्मिका - of the nature of firm conviction; बुद्धिः - intellect; स्यात् - is.

From the *sattva guṇa* aspect of all the five elements together, is formed the inner instrument. Depending on functional differences, it exists in two ways. When the thoughts are in a state of doubt, it is called mind while in a decisive state, it is called intellect. (20)

Taiḥ sarvaiḥ antaḥ karaṇaṁ : By a combination of the *sattva guṇa-s* of all the *pañca mahābhūta-s* arises the *antaḥkaraṇaṁ* or the organ of inner perception.

Vṛtti bhedena tad dvidhā : The *antaḥkaraṇaṁ* is of the nature of the thoughts (*vṛtti rūpeṇa*). Due to the differences in the functions of these *vṛtti-s*, they are divided into two types; one is the mind or *manaḥ*, the other is the *buddhi* or intellect.

Manaḥ vimarśa rūpaṁ syāt : The mind thrives on doubts or cognitions. *Buddhiḥ syāt niścayātmikā* : When the thoughts which are vacillating at the level of the mind reach a state of decision (right or wrong), that state is called the *buddhiḥ*.

In this way, in verses 19 and 20, the effects or the *kārya* of the *sattva guṇa* of the *pañca mahābhūta-s* have been explained.

The effect of the *rajoguṇa* on the five great elements is now taken up...

रजोंऽशैः पञ्चभिस्तेषां क्रमात्कर्मेन्द्रियाणि तु ।
वाक्पाणिपादपायूपस्था भिधानानि जज्ञिरे ।।२१।।

Rajoṁ'śaiḥ pañcabhi steṣāṁ kramāt karmendriyāṇi tu
Vāk pāṇi pāda pāyūpastha abhi dhānāni jajñire (21)

तेषाम् - of these elements; पञ्चभिः- of these five; रजोंऽशैः- by the *rajoguṇa* aspect; वाक् - speech; पाणि - hand; पाद - leg; पायु - organs of excretion; उपस्थ - organs of reproduction; अभिधानानि - known as; कर्मेन्द्रियाणि - organs of action; तु - indeed; क्रमात् - respectively; जज्ञिरे - are created.

From the *rajoguṇa* aspect of the five elements are created the five organs of action, viz., speech, hands, legs, anus and organs of procreation respectively. (21)

Rajo aśāiḥ pañcabhiḥ teṣāṁ kramāt karmendriyāṇi : From the *rajoguṇa* aspects of the five great elements respectively, the organs of action are created.

Vāk, pāṇi, pāda, pāyu, upastha jajñire : They are the organs of speech, hands, legs, organs of excretion and organs of procreation. It must be remembered that the five great elements are still in the nascent, *tanmātra* stage, where they have not yet undergone any grossification. They are still in their pure state.

As in the case of the *Sattva guṇa,* where there was an individual independent manifestation, as well as a collective manifestation, so also in the case of the *rajo guṇa,* the *karmendriya*-s represent the independent manifestation of the *rajo guṇa* of the five great elements.

The second manifestation is the collective one, which is described in the next verse...

तैः सर्वैः सहितैः प्राणो वृत्तिभेदात्स पञ्चधा ।
प्राणोऽपानः समानश्चोदानव्यानौ च ते पुनः ।।२२।।

Taiḥ sarvaiḥ sahitaiḥ prāṇo vṛtti bhedāt sa pañcadhā
Prāṇo'pānaḥ samā naśco dāna vyānau ca te punaḥ (22)

तैः सर्वैः- By all these elements; सहितैः- together; प्राणः- the vital air; सः- this (vital air); वृत्तिभेदात् - on account of functional differences; पञ्चधा - is of five types; ते - these; पुनः- further; प्राणः- *prāṇah;* अपानः- *apānaḥ*; समानः- *samānaḥ;* च - *and;* उदानः- *udānaḥ;* व्यानः- *vyānaḥ*; च - and.

The *rajo guṇa* aspect of all the five elements together manifest as *prāṇa śaktiḥ* or vital air. This *prāṇa* gets further differentiated in five ways namely - *prāṇa, apāna, samāna, udāna and vyāna.* (22)

Taiḥ sarvaiḥ sahitaiḥ prāṇaḥ : When the *rajo guṇa* aspect of all the five great elements are put together (*sahitaiḥ*), they manifest as the *prāṇa śakti or Kriyā śakti. Te vṛtti bhedāt pañcadhā te punaḥ :* The *prāṇa śakti* is of five types, again depending on the functions performed viz., *prāṇa, apāna, samāna, udāna and vyānaḥ.*

In this way, the evolution of the *sattva* and *rajo guṇa* aspects of the five great elements can be summarized as follows :

SUMMARY OF THE EVOLUTION OF THE *SATTVA* AND *RAJO GUṆA* ASPECTS OF THE FIVE GREAT ELEMENTS

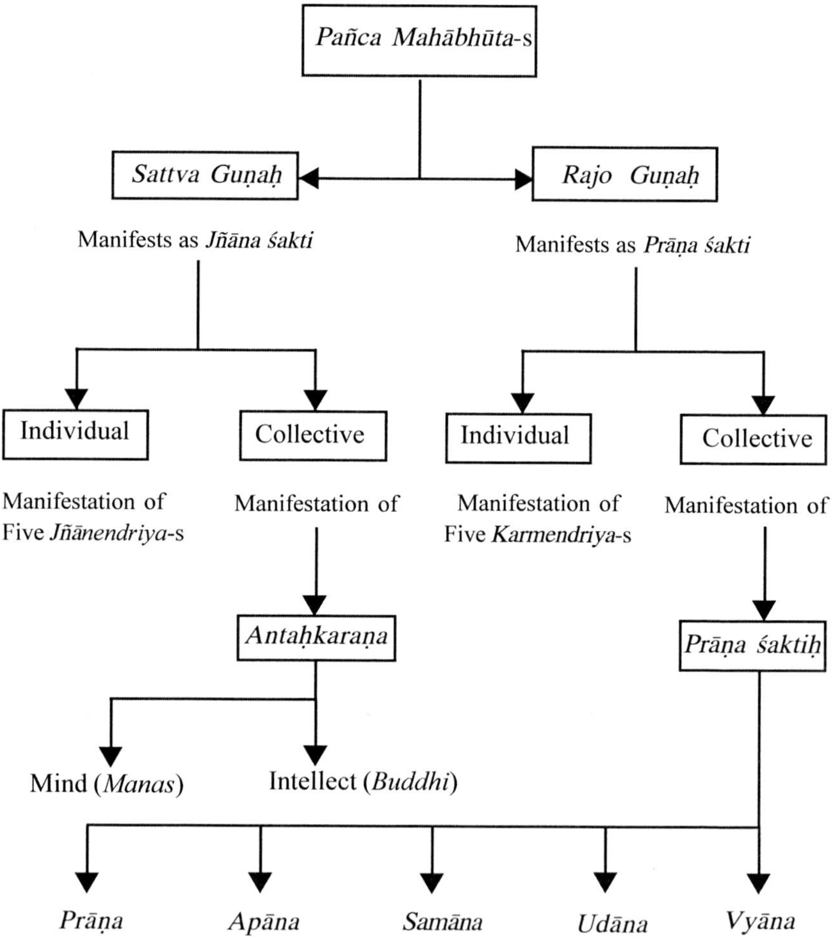

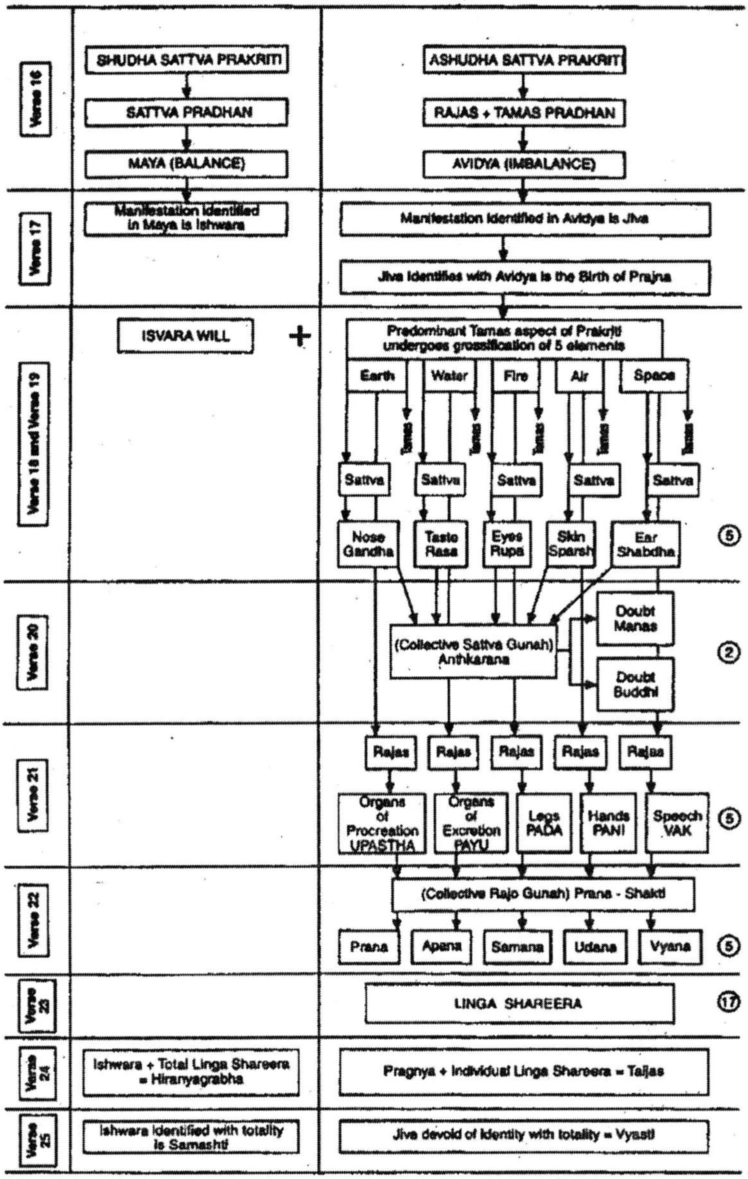
Verse 16
SHUDHA SATTVA PRAKRITI
SATTVA PRADHAN
MAYA (BALANCE)
ASHUDHA SATTVA PRAKRITI
RAJAS + TAMAS PRADHAN
AVIDYA (IMBALANCE)
Verse 17
Manifestation identified in Maya is Ishwara
Manifestation identified in Avidya is Jiva
Jiva identifies with Avidya is the Birth of Prajna
Verse 18 and Verse 19
ISVARA WILL
+
Predominant Tamas aspect of Prakriti undergoes grossification of 5 elements
Earth
Water
Fire
Air
Space
Tamas
Sattva
Nose Gandha
Taste Rasa
Eyes Rupa
Skin Sparsh
Ear Shabdha
⑤
Verse 20
(Collective Sattva Gunah) Anthkarana
Doubt Manas
Doubt Buddhi
②
Verse 21
Rajas
Organs of Procreation UPASTHA
Organs of Excretion PAYU
Legs PADA
Hands PANI
Speech VAK
⑤
Verse 22
(Collective Rajo Gunah) Prana - Shakti
Prana
Apana
Samana
Udana
Vyana
⑤
Verse 23
LINGA SHAREERA
⑰
Verse 24
Ishwara + Total Linga Shareera = Hiranyagrabha
Pragnya + Individual Linga Shareera = Taijas
Verse 25
Ishwara identified with totality is Samashti
Jiva devoid of identity with totality = Vyasti

In the next verse, the total result of these above described manifestations is summarised...

बुद्धिकर्मेन्द्रियप्राणपञ्चकैर्मनसा धिया ।
शरीरं सप्तदशभिः सूक्ष्मं तल्लिङ्गमुच्यते ।।२३।।

Buddhi karmendriyaprāṇa pañcakair manasā dhiyā
Śarīraṁ sapta daśabhiḥ sūkṣmaṁ talliṅga mucyate (23)

बुद्धिः- Five organs of knowledge; कर्मेन्द्रिय - five organs of action; प्राणपञ्चकैः - five vital airs; मनसा - with mind; धिया - with intellect; सप्तदशभिः- these seventeen together; सूक्ष्मम् शरीरम् - subtle body; तत् - that; लिङ्गम् - *liṅga śarīra*; उच्यते - is called.

The five senses, five organs of action, five *prāṇa-s*, mind and intellect, thus seventeen of them together constitute the subtle body which is called as *liṅga śarīra* (also). (23)

After this *liṅga śarīra* is formed, the further evolution is explained...

प्राज्ञस्तत्राभिमानेन तैजसत्वं प्रपद्यते ।
हिरण्यगर्भतामीशस्तयोर्व्यष्टिसमष्टिता ।।२४।।

Prājña statrā bhimānena taijasatvaṁ prapadyate
Hiraṇya garbhatā mīśas tayor vyaṣṭi samaṣṭitā (24)

प्राज्ञः- The *prājña jīva*, तत्र - in that (individual subtle body); अभिमानेन - being identified; तैजसत्वं - known as *taijasa*; प्रपद्यते - attains; ईशः- the *Īśvara*; हिरण्यगर्भताम् - being identified with total subtle body attains *Hiraṇyagarbha* state; तयोः- of these two i.e., *taijasa* and *Hiraṇyagarbha*, व्यष्टि - individuality; समष्टिता - totality.

The *prājña (jīva)* being identified with the subtle body is called as *taijasa* and the *Īśvara* identified with total *liṅga śarīra* is called

Hiraṇyagarbha. By these two, the individuality and totality is referred. (24)

Prājñaḥ tatra abhimānena taijasatvam prapadyate : The *jīva* which got identified with the *kāraṇa śarīra,* when it gets further degraded and becomes identified with the *liṅga śarīra,* he takes on another name called *taijasa.*

Īśaḥ hiraṇyagarbhatāṁ : *Īśvara* also undergoes a parallel manifestation when he gets identified with the total *sūkṣma śarīra* and he is now called *Hiraṇyagarbha. Tayoḥ vyaṣṭi samaṣṭitā :* When *Paramātmā* is referred with reference to the totality, it is called *samaṣṭi;* when referred with reference to an individual, it is called *vyaṣṭi.*

In this way, the concept of totality v/s individuality is born. *Samaṣṭi* means all inclusive and *vyaṣṭi* means individually, along with its components.

समष्टिरीशः सर्वेषां स्वात्मतादात्म्यवेदनात् ।
तदभावात्ततोऽन्ये तु कथ्यन्ते व्यष्टिसंज्ञया ।।२५।।

Samaṣṭi rīśaḥ sarveṣāṁ svātma tādātmya vedanāt
Tada bhāvāt tato'nye tu kathyante vyaṣṭi saṁ jñayā (25)

ईशः- the *Hiraṇyagarbha*; सर्वेषां - all the individual *taijasā,* स्वात्म तादात्म्य वेदनात् - being identified and knowing this; समष्टिः- totality; ततः- from this *Hiraṇyagarbha*; अन्ये - other i.e., *jīva*; तु - on the contrary; तत् - that (totality of identification and knowledge); अभावात् - absence of; व्यष्टि - individuality; संज्ञया - by this name; कथ्यन्ते - is called.

Being identified with the totality, the *Īśvara* is called *samaṣṭi* while the *jīva* being devoid of identity with totality, is called *vyaṣṭi.* (25)

Īśaḥ samaṣṭiḥ : This *Īśvara* is referred to as totality or *samaṣṭi* because he is identified with totality and because he keeps *māyā* under His control.

When the *jīva* gains control over *prakṛti*, matter, only then can he realize his own nature as *Sat-cit-ānanda Brahma.* Hence, the need for spirirtual *sādhanā*, to be able to come out of the clutches of *Prakṛti.*

Prakṛti is dvandvātmikā - of the nature of pairs of opposites. Overcoming *Prakṛti* is to accept the world which exists in the pairs of opposites. Such a *sādhanā* should lead to unconditional and reasonless love for every one without a trace of bitterness.

Therefore, to come out of the *dvandva* and accepting everyone and everything without comment and without rejection, is to conquer one part of *Prakṛti* - the external. When the external *Prakṛti* is brought under control with no *rāga-dveṣa* causing perpetual agitations, then only can one deal with the inner *Prakṛti*, the Mind.

Īśvaratva is therefore, *tadātmya vedanāt*, it is to know that the total waking state, the total dream state is because of me, the Consciousness. These states appear and disappear alternatively.

Tataḥ anye tu tat abhāvāt vyaṣṭi samaṣṭi kathayante : In the *jīva* (*anye*), such an identification with the totality is absent. Therefore, the *jīva* is called *vyaṣṭi.*

Having thus explained the creation of *samaṣṭi* and *vyaṣṭi,* the third stage in creation is now taken up viz., the location of the instruments of experience (*bhoga sādhanaṁ*) and the objects of experience. This is the effect or *kārya* of the *tamo guṇa...*

तद्भोगाय पुनर्भोग्यभोगायतनजन्मने ।
पञ्चीकरोति भगवान्प्रत्येकं वियदादिकम् ।।२६।।

Tad bhogāya punar bhogya bhogā yatana janmane
Pañcīkaroti bhaga vān pratyekaṁ viyadā dikam (26)

भगवान् - the Almighty Lord; पुनः- then; तद्भोगाय - for the experience of; भोग्य - the object of experience; भोगायतन् - the gross body to have experiences; जन्मने - for creating these; वियदादिकम् - the space etc..; प्रत्येकं - every element; पञ्चीकरोति - makes them grossified.

For the experience of the *jīva* and also for creating the objects of experience and the house for living for the *jīva*; the Lord grossifes each of the five elements like space etc.. (26)

Tat bhogāya : For the enjoyment of the *jīva* (at the grosser level), earlier (refer verse 18), it was stated that out of the original material that is produced in the form of the *tanmātra-s* or nascent five great elemens, the *sūkṣma śarīra* is created. Now the third aspect of the *tamoguṇa* and the process of grossification it undergoes to create the *sthūla śarīra* (the gross body) and the gross objects of enjoyment, is dealt with.

Punaḥ bhogya bhogāyatana janmane : Two things are created namely, bhogya vastu - objects of enjoyment and the house (*āyatanaṁ*) for the enjoyment to take place. How is this done?

Bhagavān viyadādikaṁ pratyekaṁ pañcī karoti : By the will of the Lord, all the five great elements undergo a process of gossification (*pañcīkaraṇa*).

For example, taking one of the five elements, namely water, the definition of water in *vedānta śāstra* is 'that because of which taste is possible'. The '*rasa*' aspect is the *tanmātra* of water. It cannot be seen. Therefore, the grossification is that process by which the unseen *tanmātra-s* of the five great elements are brought to our cognition as objects of knowledge.

How this grossification takes place is explained in the next verse...

द्विधा विधाय चैकैकं चतुर्धा प्रथमं पुनः ।
स्वस्वेतरद्वितीयांशैर्योजनात्पञ्च पञ्च ते ।।२७।।

Dvidhā vidhāya caikaikaṁ caturdhā prathamaṁ punaḥ
Svasve tara dvitīyāṁ śaiḥ yojanāt pañca pañca te (27)

एकैकम् - each of the five elements;च - and; द्विधा - in two parts; विधाय - having divided; पुनः- thereafter; प्रथमम् - one of these halves of each element separately; चतुर्धा - in four equal parts (having divided); स्व - its own half; स्वेतर - other than itself; द्वितीय अंशैः- the divided four from the other half; योजनात् - having united; ते - these (each) element; पञ्च पञ्च - have become grossified.

Each of the element having halved, and retaining the first part as it is, the second half gets further divided into four equal parts (each 1/8). Then the first half of each element unites with the 1/8 of the each of the other four remaining elements to become grossifed. (27)

Dvidhā vidhāya ca eka, ekaṁ punaḥ prathamaṁ caturdhā : Each great element gets divided into two; the second half again gets divided into four parts (each being 1/8)

Svasvetara dvitīyāṁśaiḥ yojanāt pañca pañca te : The first half (which did not undergo any further division) of one element, then takes 1/8 th of the each of other four great elemens (making a total of half) and together becomes 'grossified' space, air, water etc., as the case may be. Thus, the five great elements become *pañcīkṛta* or attain grossification.

This grossification is only with reference to the *tamoguṇa.* The *sattva* and *rajo guṇa-s* do not undergo any grossification.

Now, after this grossification of the five great elements has been accomplished, the next step is to create the objects of

enjoyment and the 'house' or location (called the body) where the instruments of enjoyment are to lodged. How this is done is explained in the next verse...

तैरण्डस्तत्र भुवनं भोग्यभोगाश्रयोद्भवः।
हिरण्यगर्भः स्थूलेऽस्मिन्देहे वैश्वानरो भवेत् ।।२८।।

Tairaṇḍa statra bhuvanaṁ bhogya bhogā śrayod bhavaḥ
Hiraṇya garbhaḥ sthūle' smin dehe vaiśvā naro bhavet (28)

तैः- by these five grossified elements; अण्डः- the *Brahmāṇḍa*; तत्र - in this *Brahmāṇḍa*; भुवनम् - the fourteen worlds; भोग्य - the objects of experience; भोगाश्रयः- the gross body; उद्भवः- are created; हिरण्यगर्भः- the *Hiraṇyagarbhaḥ*; अस्मिन् स्थूले - in this gross; देहे - body; वैश्वानरः- *vaiśvānaraḥ*; भवेत् - attains.

From these five grossified elements are born the *Brahmāṇḍa* along with the worlds, objects of experience and the gross bodies. The *Hiraṇyagarbha* attains the status of *vaiśvānaraḥ* being identified with the total gross bodies. (28)

Taiḥ aṇḍaḥ : From these five great gossified elements, the *Brahmāṇḍa* is created. There are 14 *bhuvana*-s or worlds in the *Brahmāṇḍa* in two tiers of seven each.

In this *Brahmāṇḍa,* two types of things are created : *Bhogya bhogāśrayaḥ udbhavaḥ* : One, the objects of enjoyment (*bhogya vastu*), and the shelter or gross body in which the instruments of perception can function.

Asmin sthūle dehe Hiraṇyagarbhaḥ vaiśvānaraḥ bhavet : The *Hiraṇyagarbha* (*Īśvara* identified with the total *sūkṣma śarīra*) now identifies himself with the *sthūla śarīra* (total gross body). This includes the world of experience and also the houses where the different *jīva*-s are located to taste the experiences. *Hiraṇyagarbha* who is thus identified with the total gross body is called *vaiśvānaraḥ.*

This is the further fall of *Īśvara* down to the total gross body level.

Now what happens to the *jīva* (at the individual gross body level?) ...

तैजसा विश्वतां याता देवतिर्यङ्नरादयः ।
ते पराग्दर्शिनः प्रत्यक्तत्त्वबोधविवर्जिताः ।।२९।।

Taijasā viśvatāṁ yātā deva tiryaṅ narā dayaḥ
Te parāg darśi naḥ pratyak tattva bodha vivar jitāḥ (29)

तैजसाः- the *taijasā*; विश्वताम् - known as *viśva*; याता - attains, देव - Gods; तिर्यङ् - the animals; नरादयः- human beings etc.; ते - they; पराग्दर्शिनः- extrovert; प्रत्यक् तत्त्वबोध - the knowledge of one's essential nature; विवर्जिताः- devoid of.

The *taijasā* is further fallen to the state of *viśva* while identified with individual gross body, such as God, animals, human bodies etc.. They by nature, are extrovert and devoid of the knowledge of their essential nature. (29)

Taijasā deva tiryaṅ nara ādayaḥ viśvatāṁ yātā : It was seen earlier (vide verse 24) that when *prājña* becomes identified with the individual *liṅga śarīra*, he is called *taijasā.* When the *taijasā* becomes identified with the different individual gross bodies such as the *deva*-s, animals, human beings etc., it is called *viśva.*

Thus *Īśvara* is one, because he has no differentiation although differences exist, the *jīva*-s on the other hand, become many individual bodies who come to be called *viśva.* What is the quality of the *viśva*?

Te parāk darśinaḥ pratyak tattva bodha vivarjitāḥ : By their nature, the *jīva*-s are extrovert and have no knowledge about their own essential nature as they are too preoccupied with the gross body, the sense organs, the objects of the world and the interactions with the objects of the world.

There is no possibility of *pratyak bodha* of *cidānanda svarūpa jñānaṁ* in this situation. (K.U.II-IV-1).

Pratyak bodha is that state of self-knowledge, where there is no suffering because of one's own absence as an ego, or of being inert, or being unhappy. It is that which is ever present in both joy and misery, in knowledge and ignorance, in birth and in death. It is independent, belonging to nothing.

When we do not know our essential nature, we are *jīva*; when we come to know our essential nature, we are not only not *jīva*, but there is no one called *jīva*. Everything is *Paramātmā* and His glory.

What is the life story of this *jīva* who has so externalised his vision that he is unable to see the *pratyak-bodha* within himself?

कुर्वते कर्म भोगाय कर्म कर्तुं च भुञ्जते ।
नद्यां कीटा इवावर्तादावर्तांतरमाशु ते ।।
व्रजन्तो जन्मनो जन्म लभन्ते नैव निर्वृत्तिम् ।।३०।।

Kurvate karma bhogāya karma kartuṁ ca bhuñjate
Nadyāṁ kīṭā ivāvartād āvartāṁ tara māśu te
Vrajanto janmano janma labhante naiva nirvṛttim (30)

भोगाय - (the *jīva*) for gaining experience; कर्म - acting; कुर्वते - performs; कर्म - acting; कर्तुम् - doing; च - and; भुञ्जते - experiences; नद्यां - in the river; कीटा - insect; इव - like; आवर्तात् - one whirlpool; आवर्तांतरम् - to another whirlpool; आशु - fast; व्रजन्तः- keep moving; ते - these *jīva*; जन्मनः- from one birth; जन्म - to next birth; निर्वृत्तिम् - liberation; न एव - do not; लभन्ते - get.

The *jīva* engages himself in action for getting enjoyments and does actions again for enjoyment. They soon after, get lost in the rebirth from one birth to another, like the insect fallen into the river is swept from one whirlpool to another, and do not attain liberation. (30)

Bhogāya karma kurvate karma kartuṁ ca bhuñjate : The *jīva* performs actions for the sake of enjoyment, then because of the *karma*, one suffers again and again (and so the cycle goes on. *Punarapi jananaṁ, punarapi maraṇaṁ….*). *Nadyāṁ kīṭa iva, āvartāt āvartāntaraṁ āśu vrajanto* : Their fate is like an insect that has fallen into the river and is swept into one whirlpool after another.

Janmanā janma labhante na eva nirvṛttiṁ : In this way, the *jīva* migrates from one life to another in an endless cycle of birth and death. There is no redemption.

Then what is the way out of this misery?

सत्कर्मपरिपाकात्ते करुणानिधिनोद्धृताः ।
प्राप्य तीरतरुच्छायां विश्राम्यन्ति यथासुखम् ।।३१।।

Sat karma pari pākātte karuṇā nidhinod dhṛtāḥ
Prāpya tīra taru cchāyāṁ viśrā myanti yathā sukham (31)

ते - these insects; सत्कर्म - the meritorious deeds; परिपाकात् - on maturation; करुणा निधिना - by some man of oceanous compassion; उद्धृता - being lifted and saved; तीर तरुः छायाम् - in the shade of a tree on the bank (of the river); प्राप्य - having placed; यथा सुखम् - in great joy; विश्राम्यन्ति - relaxes.

(As) these insects, on account of ripening of their earlier noble deeds, is lifted away by a compassionate person and having got under the shadow of a tree on the bank of the river, relax at ease; (so is the case of the seeker coming in contact with a teacher). (31)

This verse conveys a warning to the spiritual seeker to guard himself from falling prey to spiritual arrogance. It is well to remember that every little step in one's spiritual path is by the Lord's Grace and not by one's effort alone.

Sat karma paripākāt : By the grace of the Lord, and when some *puṇya karma* (good deeds) done somewhere ripens and is ready for fructification, at the right moment;

Karuṇā nidhinā uddhṛtāḥ : some compassionate person happens to notice that the poor insect is struggling to get out of its misery and takes pity on it, and therefore,

Prāpya tīra taru chāyāṁ viśrāmyanti yathā sukhaṁ : he lifts that insect out of the water current and throws it under the shade of a tree on the river bank. And now that poor insect gets relief from its suffering and is happy.

What is the cause for that *viśrānti*? That compassionate man chanced to be there at that moment, not by request but by a strange coincidence called--- the Lord's Grace. So also, everything in life, good or bad happens without apparent logic or reason. When a saint or a sage comes into the life of a spiritual seeker, there is no logic for it.

When we go beyond cause and effect, the Lord alone remains. When His Grace prevails, only then do things happen in one's life. Once this knowledge is firmly rooted, then there is *viśrānti* and a sense of total relaxation and comfort with whatever happens in life.

Humility and surrender alone help in spiritual unfoldment. Three qualities are essential in a spiritual seeker and indeed rare to find together: *manuṣyatvaṁ* - the ability to live like a human being-nobly, *mumukṣatvaṁ* - the sense of urgency to go beyond the limitations; and for this *mumukṣatvaṁ* to be fulfilled, *Mahāpuruṣa samśrayaḥ* : the ability to surrender at the feet of Saints and Sages. (ref.: V.C. 3);

When by the Lord's Grace, the seeker realizes the importance of Saints and Sages in his spiritual progress, he approaches the teacher for guidance. This is stated in the next verse...

उपदेशमवाप्यैवमाचार्यात्तत्त्वदर्शिनः ।
पञ्चकोशविवेकेन लभन्ते निर्वृत्तिं पराम् ।।३२।।

Upadeśa mavā pyaivam ācāryāt tattva darśinaḥ
Pañca kośa vivekena labhante nir vṛttiṁ parām (32)

एवम् - in the same way; तत्त्वदर्शिनः- from the knower of the Truth; आचार्यात् - teacher; उपदेशम् - instructions; अवाप्य - having received; पञ्चकोश - the five sheaths; विवेकेन - by discrimination; पराम् - supreme; निर्वृत्तिम् - emancipation or liberation; लभन्ते - attain.

Having got instructions from the *Ācārya* and a man of realization; by the process of discrimination of the five sheaths, one attains supreme liberation. (32)

Tattva darśinaḥ ācāryāt upadeśaṁ avāpya : The spiritual student by the grace of the Lord, approaches the teacher for receiving *upadeśaṁ* (upa - near *deśa* - place, that which takes us nearest to ourselves is *upadeśa*; that which takes us away from ourselves is called *apadeśa*). To whom does he go for *upadeśa*? He goes first to the *Ācārya* and then to a *siddha puruṣa*, one who has realized the Self.

Thus there are two clear stages in the spiritual path. The first stage is where the student is full of questions and wants to "understand". To such a student, the teacher is the *Ācārya* who helps the student in studying the scriptural statements and arguments only to reach that point of understanding where it is clear that the Truth cannot be grasped by intellectual ability! (*nāyamātmā medhaya labhya*)

Now the student is ready to drop the intellect and go beyond the area of *Ācārya* to the realm of the *Tattvadarśinaḥ* (a *Brahmaniṣṭaḥ*). With the *upadeśa* of the *Ācārya*, the seeker can put in his own effort and reach only up to a particular limit. Then by the Lord's Grace, a realized *Siddha puruṣa* comes into his life.

Pañcakośa vivekena : The Ācārya's upadeśa of "*Tattvamasi*" *mahāvākya* was through the process of analysis and discrimination of the five *kośa-s* or sheaths. When the student has intellectually understood the nature of these *kośa-s*, to transcend them can be achieved only through the one who has realized; and when Gods's Grace brings him in contact with such a *siddha puruṣa* or *Tattva darśinaḥ*.

Labhante nivṛttiṁ parām : Thereafter, by a mere glance or a simple statement, the student is able to achieve that *aparokṣa anubhūti* which releases him from all limitations, gives him supreme bliss, most effortlessly.

What are the *pañcakośa-s* and what does *pañcakośa viveka* signify, is taken up in the next few verses...

अन्नं प्राणो मनो बुद्धिरानन्दश्चेति पञ्च ते ।
कोशास्तैरावृतः स्वात्मा विस्मृत्या संसृतिं व्रजेत् ।।३३।।

Annaṁ prāṇo mano buddhir ānandaśceti pañca te
Kośā stairā vṛtaḥ svātmā vismṛtyā saṁsṛtiṁ vrajet (33)

अन्नम् - Gross body; प्राणः- vital air; मनः- mental; बुद्धिः- intellectual; आनन्दः- bliss, च - and; इति - thus; ते - these; पञ्च - five; कोशाः- are sheaths; तैः- by these; आवृतः- covered; स्व आत्मा - the self; स्व विस्मृत्या - due to forgetting his essential nature; संसृतिम् - repeated migration from one life to another; व्रजेत् - attains.

The food, vital air, mind, intellect and bliss sheaths are the five sheaths, covered by them, the *Ātmā* forgets its own essential nature, and is subjected to cycle of birth and death. (33)

Annaṁ prāṇaḥ manaḥ buddhiḥ ānandaḥ ca iti te pañca kośaḥ : The five *kośa*-s or sheaths are: the *anna-maya*, *prāṇa-maya*, *mano-maya*, *buddhi* or *vijñāna-maya* and *ānanda-maya*.

Why are they called *kośa-s*? *Taiḥ āvṛtaḥ ātmā* : Because the pure *Sat-cit-ānanda svarūpaṁ ātmā* is, as if, covered by them.

This 'covering' has a very special meaning in this context. In normal usage, the covering is larger than that which is covered. Here, the object covered is bigger than the covering. As for example- the presence of the body 'covers' the space because of which the body's presence is possible.

Similarly, the five *kośa-s* are 'covering' the *Ātmā,* in the sense that it is because of the *Ātmā* that they exist and get value and importance. The *kośa-s* get their existence because of the *Ātma tattva.*

After the coverings have taken charge of the *Ātmā,* the *Ātmā* gets identified with them, leading to *jīvātmabhāva. Sva vismṛtya* : and then ones's own essential nature is forgotten. *Saṁsmṛtiṁ vrajet* : thereafter, the whole story of birth and death begins.

The release from this vicious cycle can come only if the *jīva* sheds its identification with the *kośa-s* by rejecting them, by a process of understanding their nature.

स्यात्पञ्चीकृतभूतोत्थो देहः स्थूलोऽन्नसंज्ञकः ।
लिङ्गे तु राजसैः प्राणैः प्राणः कर्मेन्द्रियैः सह ।।३४।।

Syāt pañcī kṛta bhūtottho dehaḥ sthūlo'nnasaṁ jñakaḥ
Liṅge tu rājasaiḥ prāṇaiḥ prāṇaḥ karmendriyaiḥ saha (34)

पञ्चीकृत - grossified; भूतोत्थोः- born of; स्थूलः देहः- the gross body; अन्नसंज्ञकः- called as the food sheath; स्यात् - is; लिङ्गे - in the subtle body; तु - indeed; राजसैः- made from rajo *guṇa*; प्राणैः- along with five vital airs; कर्मेन्द्रियैः- the organs of action; सह - all together; प्राणः- is the vital air sheath.

The gross body made up of the grossified elements is called the *anna-maya kośa* (food sheath). The *prāṇamaya kośa* is the *rajo guṇa* aspect of subtle body consisting of the *karmendriya* and the five *prāṇa-s* (34)

Pañcīkṛta bhūtthaḥ sthūla dehaḥ anna saṁjñkaḥ syāt : The *anna-maya kośa* consists of the gross body which is born out of the grossified five great elements.

Prāṇaḥ : The *prāṇa-maya kośa* is made out of, *Liṅge tu rājasaiḥ prāṇaiḥ prāṇaḥ karmendriyaiḥ,* the *rajo guṇa* aspect of the *liṅga śarīra* namely the five *karmendriya*-s and the five *prāṇa-s.*

The *mano-maya* and *vijñāna-maya kośa-s* are...

सात्त्विकैर्धीन्द्रियैः साकं विमर्शात्मा मनोमयः ।
तैरेव साकं विज्ञान मयो धीर्निश्चयात्मिका ।।३५।।

Sāttvi kair dhī indriyaiḥ sākaṁ vimar śātmā mano mayaḥ
Taireva sākaṁ vijñāna mayo dhīr niścayātmikā (35)

सात्त्विकैः- born from *sattva guṇa*; **धीन्द्रियैः**- the sense organs; **साकम्** - together; **विमर्शात्मा** - of the nature of doubt and agitations; **मनोमयः**- is mental sheath; **धीः**- the intellect; **तैः एव साकम्** - alongwith these sense organs; **निश्चयात्मिका** - of the nature of decision; **विज्ञानमयः**- is intellectual sheath.

The doubting mind alongwith the effects of *sattva guṇa* viz., *jñānendriyaḥ* is *mano-maya kośaḥ,* while the decisive intellect alongwith these sense organs is called *vijñāna-maya kośaḥ.* (35)

Vimarśātmā sāttvikaiḥ dhīḥ indriyaiḥ sākaṁ manomayaḥ : The mind that is always doubting, thinking, confused along with the five *jñānendriya-s* which are the effects of the sattva *guṇa* of the *liṅga śarīra,* constitutes the *mano-maya kośa.*

Niścayātmika dhīḥ taiḥ eva sākaṁ vijñānamayaḥ : That intellect which is of the nature of decisiveness along with the same *jñānendriya-s*, is called the *vijñāna-maya kośa* or intellectual sheath.

In this way, the seventeen elements of subtle body are divided to constitute the *prāṇa, mano and vijñāna-maya kośa-s.*

कारणे सत्त्वमानन्दमयो मोदादिवृत्तिभिः।
तत्तत्कोशैस्तु तादात्म्यादात्मा तत्तन्मयो भवेत् ।।३६।।

Kāraṇe sattvamānanda mayo modādi vṛttibhiḥ
Tattat kośaistu tādāt myād ātmā tat tanmayo bhavet (36)

कारणे - in the causal body; सत्त्वं - the knowledge aspect; मोदादिवृत्तिभिः- along with the thoughts of joy etc.; आनन्दमयः- is the bliss sheath; आत्मा - the self; तत्तत्कोशैः - with these sheaths; तादात्म्यात् - by identification; तत्तन्मयः- one with that sheath; भवेत् - becomes; तु - however, the Self is other than these sheaths.

The causal body associated with the different degrees of joy such as *moda*, *priya*, *pramoda* etc.. is the *ānanda-maya kośaḥ.* The *Ātmā* identified with individual *kośaḥ* assumes to have become *anna-maya kośaḥ* etc.. (36)

Kāraṇe modādi vṛttibhiḥ : In the *kāraṇa śarīra* which is *malīna sattva* associated with the *tamo guṇa* predominantly, along with the different types of *vṛtti-s* like *priya*, *moda* and *pramoda* (seeking, attaining and enjoying) cause different degrees of happiness. These degrees of happiness, in the form of thoughts constitute the *ānanda-maya-kośa.*

Ātma tattat kośaiḥ tadātmyāt tat tanmayo bhavet : The *Ātmā* then gets identified with each of the five *kośa-s* and acquires those respective qualities; e.g. identification with the *anna-maya kośa* results in thoughts of 'I am old or young, man, woman, etc..' Identification with *Prāṇa-maya kośa* leads to statements like 'I am thirsty or I am hungry' and so on.

Thus identification of the Pure Self with the five *kośa*-s gives rise to five types of expressions in which one or the other *kośa* predominates. They are all, however, expressions of the same *Ātmā.*

Now how does the seeker separate the *Ātmā* from the clutches of the five *kośa-s*?

अन्वयव्यतिरेकाभ्यां पञ्चकोशविवेकतः ।
स्वात्मानं तत उद्धृत्य परं ब्रह्म प्रपद्यते ।।३७।।

Anvaya vyati rekā bhyāṁ pañcakośa vivekataḥ
Svāt mānaṁ tata uddhṛtya paraṁ brahma prapa dyate (37)

अन्वयव्यतिरेकाभ्यां - By the technique of inclusion and analysis; पञ्च कोशः- the five sheath; विवेकतः- by discrimination; स्व आत्मानं- one's essential self; ततः- from these sheaths; उद्धृत्य - lifting above these; परम् ब्रह्म - the Supreme *Brahman*; प्रपद्यते - is attained by the seeker.

By the process of discrimination of five sheaths through the technique of *anvaya-vyatireka*, thus having transcended oneself above them, one attains the status of Supreme *Brahman* (37)

Anvaya vyatirekābhyāṁ svātmānaṁ tataḥ uddhṛtya paraṁ brahma prapadyate : By the technique of *anvaya* (presence) and *vyatireka* (absence) applied in conducting the *pañca kośa viveka* (discrimination), thus after having separated the Pure Self from the covering of the five sheaths, one attains the *Brahmatva bhāva.*

When, one discovers by *pañcakośa viveka,* that 'I' is someone other than the '*pañcakośa*', the next step is to discover that this 'I' is of the nature of *Brahman.* Spiritual unfoldment is thus a process of unlearning, of emptying. Once we get out of the clutches of the *pañcakośa*-s in this way, then one realizes one's true identification with the *Para Brahman.*

What is the meaning of *anvaya-vyatireka*? How does it help in separating the *Ātmā* from the *pañca kośa*-s?

अभाने स्थूलदेहस्य स्वप्ने यद्भानमात्मनः ।
सोऽन्वयो व्यतिरेकस्तद्भानेऽन्यानवभासनम् ।।३८।।

Abhāne sthūla dehasya svapne yadbhāna mātmanaḥ
So'nvayo vyatirekas tad bhāne'nyā nava bhāsanam (38)

स्वप्ने - in the dream; स्थूलदेहस्य - of the gross body; अभाने - being not aware of; आत्मनः- of the Pure Self; यत् भानं - that conscious aspect; सः- that; अन्वयः- is *anvayaḥ* i.e., inclusion; तद्भाने - although expressing as consciousness in dream state; अन्यानवभासनम् - not being aware of gross body; व्यतिरेकः- is exclusion.

In the dream state, there is no identification with the gross body, but there is illumination of dream by the *Ātmā.* This presence of the *Ātmā* is *anvaya.* Although, the *Ātman* is present, but does not identify with the gross body; hence it is called *vyatireka* (absence) of gross body in *Ātmā.* (38)

Svapne sthūla dehasya abhāne : In the dream state (*svapna avasthā*), the gross body is not identified with it, therefore is not available. This is *vyatireka* (absence) of gross body. *Yat ātmanaḥ bhānaṁ saḥ anvayaḥ* : But there is a presence which is illuminating the dream experience. That presence, the Truth or the *Ātmā* which is illuminating the dream state is called *Anvaya.*

Tad bhāne anyān avabhāsanaṁ vyatirekaḥ : The other aspect i.e., the absence of the gross body in the dream state is called *vyatireka* of the gross body in the *Ātmā.*

Similarly,

लिङ्गाभाने सुषुप्तौ स्यादात्मनो भानमन्वयः ।
व्यतिरेकस्तु तद्भाने लिङ्गस्याभानमुच्यते ।।३९।।

Liṅgā bhāne suṣuptau syād ātmano bhāna manvayaḥ
Vyati rekastu tadbhāne liṅgasyā bhāna mucyate (39)

सुषुप्तौ - in deep sleep; लिङ्ग अभाने - being unaware of the subtle body; आत्मनः- of the self; भानम् - is awareness; अन्वयः - inclusion of the Self; स्यात् - is; तद्भाने - although there is awareness of Self; तु - indeed; लिङ्गस्य अभानम् - there is no awareness of subtle body; व्यतिरेकः- the exclusion of subtle body; स्यात् - is; उच्यते - is called.

In the deep sleep state, although there is no identification with the subtle body, the presence of *Ātmā* is called *Anvaya*. However, although *Ātman* is present in the deep sleep, but the subtle body is not included in its cognition, it is called as *vyatireka* of subtle body. (39)

Liṅga abhāne ātmanaḥ suṣuptau bhānaṁ anvayaḥ : In the *suṣupti avasthā* i.e., in the deep sleep state, the subtle body or *liṅga śarīra* is discarded from identification. It is not available. This is called *vyatireka* or absence of the subtle body in the deep sleep state.

But this absence which is the content of the deep sleep state, is illuminated by the presence of the *Ātmā.* This presence is called *anvaya.*

Vyatirekaḥ tu tad bhāne liṅgasya abhānaṁ : The absence of the *liṅga śarīra* although *suṣupti* is illumined, is called *vyatireka* of the subtle body in the deep sleep state in *Ātmā.*

Why has the concept of *liṅga śarīra* been brought in while dealing with the *pañca kośa viveka* is now explained...

तद्विवेकाद्विविक्तास्युः कोशाः प्राणमनोधियः ।
ते हि तत्र गुणावस्थाभेदमात्रात्पृथक्कृताः ।।४०।।

Tad vivekād viviktā syuḥ kośāḥ prāṇa mano dhiyaḥ
Te hi tatra guṇā vasthā bheda mātrāt pṛthak kṛtāḥ (40)

तत् - of the subtle body; विवेकात् - discrimination; प्राणः- the vital air sheath; मनः- the mental sheath; धियः कोशाः- the intellectual sheath; विविक्ताः- discriminated; स्युः- happens; ते - they; हि - indeed; तत्र - in the subtle body; गुणावस्था - the predominance of *guṇa-s*; भेद मात्रात् - on account of difference; पृथक् कृताः- already explained separately.

By the discrimination of the subtle body - the vital air, mind and intellect sheaths are included together; because they are separated on the basis of the proportion of the three *guṇa-s.* (40)

Tatra guṇa avasthā bheda mātrāt prāṇaḥ manaḥ dhīyaḥ kośaḥ pṛthak kṛtāḥ : Because of the association of the three *guṇa-s* - *sattva*, *rajas*, *tamas*; the *liṅga śarīra* is divided into the three *kośa-s*: *prāṇa*, *mano* and *vijñānamaya.*

Tad vivekāt viviktā syuḥ : Therefore, the *anvaya*-vyatireka with reference to the *liṅga śarīra* included the *anvaya-vyatireka* of the three *kośa-s.*

Having separated the *Ātmā* from the gross body and the subtle body; now the causal body or *kāraṇa śarīra* is taken up for discrimination...

सुषुप्त्यभाने भानन्तु समाधावात्मानोऽन्वयः।
व्यतिरेकस्त्वात्मभाने सुषुप्त्यनवभासनम् ।।४१।।

Suṣuptya bhāne bhānantu samādhā vātmāno'nvayaḥ
Vyati rekas tvātma bhāne suṣuptya nava bhāsanam (41)

समाधौ - in *Samādhi*; सुषुप्ति अभाने - there is awareness of causal body; तु - but; आत्मानः- of the self; भानम् - awareness; अन्वयः- that is anvaya i.e., inclusion of *Ātmā*; आत्मभाने - although there is awareness of *Ātmā*; सुषुप्ति अनवभासनम् - no awareness of causal body; तु - certainly; व्यतिरेकः- is exclusion of ignorance of causal body.

In *Samādhi*, the deep sleep state is absent, however, the *Ātman* is present to illumine the *samādhi.* This is called *anvaya* of *Ātmā* in *samādhi.*

However, the deep sleep state is not included in the *Ātmā*. This is called *vyatireka* of deep sleep state. (41)

Suṣupti abhāne samādhau ātmanaḥ bhānaṁ anvayaḥ : In the fourth state or *samādhi avasthā*, the *suṣupti avasthā* is absent. But the *Ātma tattva* is present. This presence of the *Ātmā* in the *samādhi* state is called *anvaya*.

Ātmā bhāne suṣupti anavabhāsanaṁ vyatireka : Although the *Ātmā* is present, the *suṣupti avasthā* is absent in the *samādhi*. This is called *vyatireka* of *suṣupti* in *Ātmā*.

In this way, by the *anvaya-vyatireka* method, one is able to separate the *Ātmā* from the four states of *jāgrat, svapna, suṣupti and samādhi.*

Now the teacher cites *Kaṭhopaniṣad* to support this technique...

यथा मुञ्जादिषीकैवमात्मा युक्त्या समुद्धृतः।
शरीरत्रितयाद्धीरैः परं ब्रह्मैव जायते ।।४२।।

Yathā muñjā diṣī kaivam ātmā yuktyā samud dhṛtaḥ
Śarīra tritayād dhīraiḥ paraṁ brahmaiva jāyate (42)

यथा - as; मुञ्जात् - from the *muñjā* grass; इषीका - the core; युक्त्या - with proper method (is separated); एवम् - in the same way; आत्मा - the *Ātman*, शरीर त्रितयात् - from the three bodies; धीरैः- by the wise seeker; समुद्धृतः- having lifted above; परम् ब्रह्म एव - the nature of Supreme *Brahman*; जायते - becomes.

Just as the core of the *muñjā* grass is separated from the leafy portion, the *Ātmā* is separated from the three bodies by a wise person, through proper technique, to attain the Supreme *Brahmānubhūti*. (42)

Yathā muñjādi iṣīka : Just as the leafy portion is separated from the rib of the *muñjā* grass carefully and without causing any damage,

Śarīra triyāt Ātma yuktyā samuddhṛtaḥ : so also, having separated the *Ātmā* with proper understanding and correct technique from the three bodies, viz., gross, subtle and causal body

Dhīraḥ paraṁ brahma eva jāyate : the *dhīraḥ puruṣa*, one who has realized his essential nature, is not daunted by anything that happens in life. He attains *Brahmatva*, that is, he attains the knowledge that "I am essentially of the nature of *Brahman*". This is not knowledge that is told by, or to someone, but it "happens".

By comparing the *pañcakośa viveka* to the preparation of *muñjā* grass for *karma kāṇḍa*, two points are made :

a) the importance of a systematic approach and;
b) that discrimination should be based on knowledge.

The deeper the study of scriptures and reflection on the Truth, the weaker the attachment to the five *kośa-s*. The priorities are clearer in one's life and one is more confident to tread the spiritual path. Otherwise one's whole life will be wasted away into nothingness.

This clarity of thought, determination of priorities, strength of action and an unwavering focus on the true goal of one's life, mark the man of wisdom - the *dhīra puruṣa*. It is he who is able to transcend the four *avasthā-s* and attain *Para-brahmatva*.

In *śloka* 32, reference was made to the *upadeśa* which the seeker receives from the *Ācārya*. This *upadeśa* is of the *Mahāvākya* "*Tat tvaṁ asi*". This *upadeśa* begins from verse 43...

परापरात्मनोरेवं युक्त्या संभावितैकता ।
तत्त्वमस्यादिवाक्यैस्सा भागत्यागेन लक्ष्यते ।।४३।।

Parā parāt mano revaṁ yuktyā saṁbhā vitai katā
Tattva masyā divākyais sā bhāga tyāgena lakṣyate (43)

एवम् - in this manner; पर अपरात्मनोः- of the supreme and the lower self i.e., *Īśvara* and *jīvātmā;* एकता - oneness; युक्त्या - by proper logic and thinking; संभाविता - is established; सा - this oneness; भागत्यागेन - by the process of partial retention and partial rejection method; लक्ष्यते - is being indicated.

In this way, the oneness of the *jīvātmā* and the *Paramātmā* is logically established by the *Tat-Tvaṁ-Asi mahāvākya* by the technique of *bhāga-tyāga,* is being indicated. (43)

Evaṁ parāpara ātmanoḥ ekatā yuktyā saṁbhāvitā : In this way, the oneness or identity of the two *Ātmā-s,* the apara and para, the *jīva* and *Paramātmā* is declared conclusively by logical deduction.

Sat tat tvaṁ asi ādi vākyai bhāga tyāgena lakṣyate : This identity is established by *Mahāvākya-s* such as "*Tat tvaṁ asi*" by the process of rejecting all those attributes which do not belong to the *Ātmā.* (Rejecting irrelevant part and retaining appropriate part is *bhāga-tyāga*).

The meaning of each word in the "*Tat Tvaṁ Asi*" *Mahāvākya* is now explained...

जगतो यदुपादानं मायामादाय तामसीम् ।
निमित्तं शुद्धसत्त्वां तामुच्यते ब्रह्म तद्गिरा ।।४४।।

Jagato yadu pādānaṁ māyā mādāya tāmasīm
Nimittaṁ śuddha sattvāṁ tāmucyate brahma tadgirā (44)

यत् ब्रह्म - That *Brahman*; तामसीम् मायाम् - to the *tamo guṇa* aspect of *māyā*, आदाय - with the help of; जगतः- of the world of insentient and sentient things and beings; उपादानम् - material cause; शुद्धसत्त्वाम् ताम् - to pure *sāttvic māyā* (having taken support); निमित्तम् - the efficient cause i.e., the creator of the world; (तद्) ब्रह्म - that *Brahman*; तद् - is the meaning of the word '*tat*'; गिरा - in *Tat tvaṁ asi mahāvākya.*

The *Brahman* in association with the *tamo guṇi māyā* is the material cause of the world; and is the efficient cause in association with *sattva guṇi māyā*, is meant by the word '*tat*' in the *Tat tvaṁ asi mahāvākya.* (44)

Tat girā ucyate : By the word '*Tat*' is meant,

a) *Yat brahma Tāmasīm māyām ādāya jagataḥ upādānam* : That *Brahman*, which is the material cause of this gross world when associated with the *tamo guṇa* aspect of *māyā* (vide *śloka* 27); and

b) *Tām śuddha sattvāṁ nimittaṁ* : That same *Brahman*, which is the efficient cause of the world when associated with *sattva-guṇi māyā* and becomes the creator or *Īśvara* (refer verse 16 ante).

In this way, the word '*tat*' means the non–dual, efficient and material cause of the world (*abhinna, nimitta, upādāna kāraṇa tat vastu*)

The meaning of the word '*Tvaṁ*' is indicated in *śloka* 45...

यदामलिनसत्त्वां तां कामकर्मादिदूषिताम् ।
आदत्ते तत्परं ब्रह्म त्वं पदेन तदोच्यते ।।४५।।

Yadā malina sattvāṁ tāṁ kāma karmādi dūṣitām
Ādatte tatparaṁ brahma tvaṁ padena tadocyate (45)

तत् - That; परम् ब्रह्म - the supreme *Brahman*; यदा - when; मलिन सत्त्वाम् - the impure *sattva pradhāna* (i.e., *sattva* with *rajo* and *tamo guṇi māyā*); काम कर्मादि दूषिताम् - that has the impurities of desire, action etc.; ताम् - to that *māyā* or *avidyā*; आदत्ते - conditioned by; तदा - in such condition; त्वम् पदेन - by the word of *tvaṁ*; उच्यते - is referred.

When the *Paraṁ Brahma* is associated with the *māyā* that is contaminated by (the effects of *rajo guṇa*) desire, action etc., it is referred by the word "*tvaṁ*" in the *mahāvākya, Tat tvaṁ asi.* (45)

Yadā malina sattvāṁ (māyā) ādatte: When this *Para Brahma* takes the help of *malina sattvāṁ* (i.e., *sattva guṇa* associated with *rajo guṇa*).

Tām kāma karma ādi dūṣitām : *Kāma karma* falls within the purview of the *rajo guṇa.* When that *māyā*, which has less of *sattva* and more of *rajo guṇa*, and conditions the *Para Brahma*,

Tat paraṁ brahma tvaṁ padena ucyate : Such a conditioned *Para Brahma* is called "*Tvaṁ*" in *"Tat Tvaṁ Asi" mahāvākya*, by the word '*Tvaṁ*'

Now the significance of the *asi-pada* is explained in the most beautifully logical manner...

त्रितयीमपि तां मुक्त्वा परस्परविरोधिनीम् ।
अखण्डं सच्चिदानन्दं महावाक्येन लक्ष्यते ।।४६।।

Tritayī mapi tāṁ muktvā paras paraviro dhinīm
Akhaṇḍaṁ saccidā nandaṁ mahā vākyena lakṣyate (46)

त्रितयीम् - of the three (*sattva, rajo* and *tamo guṇa*) types of *māyā*, अपि - fully; परस्पर विरोधिनीम् - of opposite nature; ताम् - to that *māyā*, मुक्त्वा - having rejected; अखण्डम् - non-dual; सच्चिदानन्दम् – to the *Brahman* that is of the nature of Existence, Knowledge and Bliss; महा वाक्येन - by the *"Tat Tvaṁ Asi" mahāvākya*; लक्ष्यते - is indicated.

When the *Brahman* is freed from the limitations of mutually opposing three types of *māyā* (*by Tat tvaṁ asi mahāvākya viveka*); the identity between them is of being undivided non-dual *Saccidānanda* is established by the '*Asi*' word of the *mahāvākya.* (46)

Tritayīm api tāṁ paraspara virodhinīm muktvā : When the *Para Brahman* is liberated from the clutches of the three types of *māyā* namely, the *tāmasi, śuddha sattva* and *malina sattva*, which are opposed to each other, because *sattva guṇi māyā* is *jñāna pradhāna* (*jñānaṁ* is dominant), *rajo-guṇi māyā* is *kriya* or *karma pradhāna* and *tamo-guṇi māyā* is *dravya* (or matter) *pradhāna.* Thus their natures are mutually opposed.

When the *Para Brahman* is thus separated, what remains? *Akhaṇḍaṁ Saccidānandaṁ mahā vākyena lakṣyate* : When the three types of *māyā* are rejected, what is left behind is the third *pada* in the *mahāvākya* - *Asi*, the *Asitva*, oneness,being-ness. This being-ness is *akhaṇḍaṁ* with no splintering (*khaṇḍaṁ*). *Cara* and *Acara* that constitute the world of names and forms are *khaṇḍa*; separate from each other. But that which is the support and substratum for these separate existences, but itself remains unbroken one, that is *akhaṇḍa maṇḍalākāraṁ.*

Thus, when the conditioning of *Tat* and *Tvaṁ* is rejected, the oneness, the *Asi,* which is of the nature of *akhaṇḍaṁ*, of *Sat*, *Cit* and *Ānandaṁ* remains.

How does the removal of the conditioning establish the oneness, is discussed in the 47th sloka...

सोऽयमित्यादिवाक्येषु विरोधात्तदिदन्तयोः ।
त्यागेन भागयोरेक आश्रयो लक्ष्यते यथा ।।४७।।

So'ya mityā divākyeṣu virodhāt tadi dantayoḥ
Tyāgena bhāgayo reka āśrayo lakṣyate yathā (47)

सः अयम् - 'he is this'; इत्यादि - etc.; वाक्येषु - in the sentences; तद् इदन्तयोः - of the 'that-ness' and 'this-ness'; विरोधात् - being opposed in meaning; भागयोः- of the opposite parts from that-ness and this-ness; त्यागेन - by rejecting; एकः- one; आश्रयः- support for the opposites; यथा - as; लक्ष्यते - is indicated.

In the sentence like, "This is that *Devadatta*", the opposing 'this' and 'that'are rejected while their support - *Devadatta*, is indicated by arriving at the substratum (47).

Yathā saḥ ayam ādi vākyeṣu : In the standard phrase used in *Vedāntic* discussions viz., "This is that *Devadatta*", 'this' and 'that' both refer to the same person which apparently appears to be contradictory. A closer examination will show, however, that the intention is to reject the conditioning or *bheda* of time (that *kāla* and this *kāla*), of space (that *deśa* and this *deśa*), of *vastu* (that *vastu* and this *vastu*) and of *paristhiti* (that condition and this condition), and to establish that 'that' and 'this' refer to the same person (*āśrayaḥ*).

Tad idantayoḥ virodhāt tyāgena : When the seeming differences or conditionings, of *tat* and *idaṁ* – that place, that object, that time and this place, this object, this time, are rejected...

Bhāgayoḥ ekaḥ āśrayaḥ lakṣyate : Then that part which is the common factor, in 'this' and 'that', namely *Devadatta* is evident as the one substratum.

In the same way, in the *Tat Tvaṁ Asi mahāvākya*, 'Tat' is with reference to the material and efficient cause of this world; and '*Tvaṁ*' is the conditioning of the *malina sattva*. When the conditionings of Tat and *Tvaṁ* are rejected, one discovers that *Tat* and *Tvaṁ*, both are nothing but the *akhaṇḍa Sat-Cit-Ānanda*.

The example of *Devadatta* is now applied to the *mahāvākya*...

मायाऽविद्ये विहायैवमुपाधी परजीवयोः।
अखण्डं सच्चिदानन्दं परब्रह्मैव लक्ष्यते ।।४८।।

Māya'vidye vihā yaivam upādhī para jīvayoḥ
Akhaṇḍaṁ saccidānandaṁ para brahmaiva lakṣyate (48)

एवम् - in the same way; पर जीवयोः- of the *Paramātmā and jīvātmā*, उपाधी - conditionings; माया अविद्ये - *māyā* and *avidyā*; विहाय - having rejected; अखण्डं - the one without parts; सच्चिदानन्दम् - existence, knowledge, bliss; परम् ब्रह्म - the supreme *Brahman*, एव - indeed; लक्ष्यते – is indicated.

In the same way, when the conditionings of *jīva* and *Īśvara*, namely *avidyā* and *māyā* are rejected, the substratum which is non-dual, infinite conscious existence --- the *Para Brahma* indeed is indicated. (48).

Evam māyā avidye upādhi para jīvayoḥ vihāya akhaṇḍam saccidānandam param brahma eva lakṣyate : In this way, when the *māyā* and *avidyā* --- the conditionings of *Paramātmā* and *jīvātmā* are rejected or denied, the *akhaṇḍa Sat-Cit-Ānandam* which is of the nature of *Para Brahma* (*satyaṁ jñānaṁ anantaṁ Brahma*), this nature of *Para Brahma* is indicated.

Therefore, the *jīvātmā* can never become *Īśvara* and vice versa, because the two exist only in relation to each other. The *jīvātmā*, after due *sādhanā* discards both, his own limitations as well as those of *Īśvaratva*, and comes to discover as being the substratum, the *Para Brahma Paramātmā.*

Now a peculiar doubt is raised as to whether the *Para Brahman* is *Savikalpa* or *Nirvikalpa* i.e., with or without modification...

सविकल्पस्य लक्ष्यत्वे लक्ष्यस्य स्यादवस्तुता ।
निर्विकल्पस्य लक्ष्यत्वं न दृष्टं न च सम्भवि ।।४९।।

Savi kalpasya lakṣyatve lakṣyasya syāda vastutā
Nirvi kalpasya lakṣyatvaṁ na dṛṣṭaṁ na ca sambhavi (49)

सविकल्पस्य - of the *Brahman* with modifications; लक्ष्यत्वे - if this is meant by indication; लक्ष्यस्य - those modifications; अवस्तुता स्यात् - the *Brahman* will become non-reality; निर्विकल्पस्य - of that, that does not have any modifications; लक्ष्यत्वम् - indicativeness; न - not; दृष्टम् - is seen; न च - nor; सम्भवि - is ever possible.

The indication of *Brahman* with modifications by the *mahāvākya* is not possible, the modifications being ever changing, nor we can imagine to investigate the *Brahman* which is neither seen nor thought of. (49)

A doubt is now raised : "By the *'Tat Tvaṁ Asi' mahāvākya*, the *Para Brahman* was indiated as *akhaṇḍaṁ* and *sat-cit-ānandaṁ*. Now is this *Brahman Savikalpa* or *nirvikalpa*?"

Savikalpasya lakṣyatve lakṣyasya avastutā syāt : If we say that the *Tat-tvaṁ-asi mahāvākya* refers to the *savikalpa Brahman*, with its modifications, these modifications (by their very definition) will keep changing. And that which is constantly changing cannot be indicated as a permanent thing. It therefore, seems unlikely that the *mahāvākya* can be referring to the *Savikalpa Brahman*.

On the other hand, *Nirvikalpasya lakṣyatvaṁ na dṛṣṭaṁ na ca sambhavi* : If we say that the *Mahāvākya* refers to the *nirvikalpa Brahman* i.e., that which is not associated with any modifications, then such a *Brahman* cannot be perceived or conceived because there is no frame of reference. It cannot become the object of knowledge or the point of investigation.

The teacher replies to this doubt in a sarcastic vein...

विकल्पो निर्विकल्पस्य सविकल्पस्य वा भवेत् ।
आद्ये व्याहतिरन्यत्रानवस्थाऽऽत्माश्रयादयः।।५०।।

Vikalpo nirvi kalpasya savikalpasya vā bhavet
Ādye vyāhati ranyatrā navasthā''tmā śrayā dayaḥ (50)

निर्विकल्पस्य - of the modificationless; सविकल्पस्य - of that which is with modifications; वा - or, like this; विकल्पः- the modifications; भवेत् - is; आद्ये - in the first preposition; व्याहतिः- the fallacy of contradiction; अन्यत्र - in later preposition; अनवस्था - infinite regress; आत्मा आश्रय आदयः- the fallacy of resting on oneself etc..

Are we talking about modifications of the *Brahman*, which is without modification or with modification? If it is about the former, it is self-cancelled; in latter case, the fallacies like mutual dependence, self dependence etc., will result. (50)

The teacher replies to this doubt in this and the following verse:

Vikalpa nirvikalpasya savikalpsya vā. Ādye vyāhati : How can nirvikalpa be indicated as *savikalpa* by the *Tat-tvaṁ-asi mahāvākya*? This is a fallacious statement. This is called *vyāhati doṣa*, an impossible doubt like in the classical example, 'I do not have a tongue'. To say such a statement, one should have a tongue; and if one did not have the tongue, such a statement could not have been said! This is a repetitious statement because '*Savikalpa*' itself means 'with modifications'.

Anyatra anavasthā ātmāśraya ādayaḥ : This falls under the category of *anāvastha doṣa* i.e., fallacy of mutual dependence. *Brahman* is beyond the limitations of all kinds. The use of *savikalpa* etc., will lead to other fallacies like self-dependence, circular logic, or infinite regress etc.. Therefore, this doubt has no basis; it is only the result of confusion in the usage of words.

This is elaborated further in the next verse...

इदं गुणक्रियाजातिद्रव्यसम्बन्धवस्तुषु ।
समं तेन स्वरूपस्य सर्वमेतदितीष्यताम् ।।५१।।

Idaṁ guṇakriyā jāti dravya sambandha vastuṣu
Samaṁ tena svarūpasya sarva meta ditīṣyatām (51)

इदम् - these fallacies indicated in the last verse; गुण - quality; जाति - class; क्रिया - action; द्रव्य - object; सम्बन्ध - relationship; वस्तुषु - in the things; समम् - is similar; तेन - therefore; एतत् - this quality etc.; सर्वम - all; स्वरूपस्य - is belonging to the thing and therefore imagined; इति - this; ईष्यताम् - should be known.

These fallacies are of similar nature as we can see with reference to attribute, action, type, object, relationship with the object. Therefore, the same should be understood with reference to the *Brahman* also. (51).

Idaṁ guṇā kriyā jāti dravya sambandha vastuṣu : These types of *doṣa-s* are of similar nature with reference to relationship between the objects and their attributes like quality, action and type. These words cannot be associated with any object. Should we say that the attribute is attributeless for that which is already with attributes? Should we say that the action is in the actionless or one with action? In these examples, in the former case, it is self contradiction fallacy; while the fallacy like self-dependence etc., in the latter alternative.

Tena svarūpasya etat sarvaṁ iti īṣyatām : In the same way, the usage of words like *savikalpa* and *nirvikalpa* is of no relevance with reference to the *Brahman*.

The conclusion from above discussion is...

विकल्पतदभावाभ्यामसंस्पृष्टात्मवस्तुनि ।
विकल्पितत्त्वलक्ष्यत्वसम्बन्धाद्यास्तु कल्पिताः ।।५२।।

Vikalpa tada bhāvā bhyām asaṁ spṛṣṭāt ma vastuni
Vikalpi tattva lakṣyatva sambandhā dyāstu kalpitāḥ (52)

विकल्प तद् अभावाभ्याम् - By the modifications and the absence of modifications; असंस्पृष्ट - untouched; आत्मवस्तुनि - in the *Ātman*; विकल्पितत्त्व - modification-ness; लक्ष्यत्व - indicativeness; सम्बन्धाद्याः- the relation-ness etc., तु - only; कल्पिताः- are imagined.

The presence or absence of the modifications do not touch the Pure Self. The relationship of association with modifications, indication of the *Brahman*, the relative existence of *jīva, Īśvara*, are all superimposed on the *Para Brahman* (52).

Vikalpa tad abhāvābhyām ātma vastuni asaṁspṛṣṭā : The absence of *vikalpa* is called *nirvikalpattva.* These modifications have nothing to do with the *Ātmā.*

Vikalpitattva lakṣyattva sambandha ādi tu kalpitāḥ : They are only imagined. When the waves are described as modifications of the ocean, it does not mean that something is added to the ocean or that when the waves are absent, something is lost from the ocean. The waves 'appear' as modifications but ocean undergoes no modification. The wave-ness is essentially ocean-ness, it is only *kalpitamātra* i.e., the name and form of wave-ness are imagined.

Thus the *Tat-tvam-asi lakṣyārtha* does not give any importance either to the *samaṣṭi Īśvaratva* or *vyaṣṭi jīvatva,* but indicates that *jīvatva bhāva* and *Īśvaratva bhāva* are imagined or superimposed on the substratum of *Parabrahman* because of ignorance. *Jīvatva* and *Īśvaratva* being of relative existence, have no meaning in theAbsolute *Akhaṇḍa, Sat-cit-ānanda-Brahman.*

The thought that commenced in verse 43 is now concluded...

इत्थं वाक्यैस्तदर्थानु सन्धानं श्रवणं भवेत् ।
युक्त्या सम्भावितत्त्वानु संधानं मननन्तु तत् ।।५३।।

Ittharh vākyais tadar thānu sandhā narh śravaṇarh bhavet
Yuktyā sambhā vitat tvānu sarhdhānarh mana nantu tat (53)

इत्थम् - in this manner; वाक्यैः- by enquiry in *Tat tvarh asi mahāvākya*, तद् अर्थ अनुसन्धानम् - the contemplation of the indicative meaning (i.e., identity between individuality and totality); श्रवणम् - listening; भवेत - is called; युक्त्या - by proper logic; सम्भावि - the conviction about the possibility of what is heard; तत्त्व अनुसंधानम् - thus continuous contemplation on this meaning of the Truth; तत् - that; तु - indeed; मननम् - is called reflection.

In this way, the investigation on the meaning of the *mahāvākya* is called *śravanarh* (i.e., listening). The *mananam* (reflection) is reflection on what is heard by the technique of logic according to scriptures (53).

Ittharh vākyaiḥ tad artha anusarhdhānarh śravaṇarh bhavet: By this *Tat tvarh asi mahāvākya upadeśa*, in this manner, the total analysis with sound understanding of what is meant by *tat*, *tvarh* and *asi*, whether *Brahman* is *Savikalpa* or *nirvikalpa*, or whether these are only superimpositions etc., and the identity between *tat* and *tvarh*, (ref. verses 43-52) constitutes the *śravaṇarh* of the *mahāvākya*,

Yuktyā sambhāvitattva anusarhdhānarh : The enquiry and contemplation on the basis of logic and in accordance with the scriptures (ref. verses 3 to 41) is called *mananam* or reflection.

Now, *nididhyāsanarh* is explained...

ताभ्यां निर्विचिकित्सेऽर्थे चेतसः स्थापितस्य यत्।
एकतानत्वमेतद्धि निदिध्यासनमुच्यते ।।५४।।

Tābhyāṁ nirvicikitse'rthe cetasaḥ sthāpi tasya yat
Eka tānatva metaddhi nidi dhyāsana mucyate (54)

ताभ्यां - by these two, listening and reflection; निर्विचिकित्से अर्थे - when the doubtless meaning of the *mahāvākya* takes place; स्थापितस्य - of the established; चेतसः- mind; यत् - that; एकतानत्व - single pointed thought flow; एतद् निदिध्यासनम् - meditation; उच्यते - is called.

The *nididhyāsana* is the single pointed-ness of the stabilised mind by the process of *śravaṇaṁ* and *mananam* (54)

Tābhyāṁ nirvicikitse arthe : By these two, *śravaṇaṁ* (listening) and *mananam* (reflection), when the meaning is grasped without a single doubt and doubtless knowledge is created or gained,

Yat cetasaḥ sthāpitasya ekatānatva : thereafter, the mind (*cetas*) is fully established in this meaning of the *mahāvākya*, namely, that which is *akhaṇḍa, sat-cit-ānanda*, that *Brahman* I am. This knowledge is without a breach even for a second (*ekatānatva*). Such an application of the mind to the thought that "I am that *sat-cit-ānanda*".

Etat hi nididhyāsanaṁ ucyate : This is called *nididhyāsanaṁ* i.e., contemplation.

From the above it follows that, without proper and systematic study, understanding of every aspect and removal of doubts, meditation is not possible. Without proper *śravaṇaṁ* and sufficient *mananam*, *ekatānatva* cannot be achieved. When the mind is fully fixed on the Truth alone, only the *Paramātma tattva* is reminded in every experience, good or bad, pleasant or otherwise.

Tulasidas compares this *ekatānatva* to the lusty person who has only *kāma vāsana* wherever he goes and whatever he sees, or to the covetous person who thinks about everything only in terms of money.

When such a one-pointed perception develops through *nididhyāsanaṁ*, then *sārvātmyabhāva* results. i.e., That great vision where *Paramātmā* alone is in and through every expression.

When *nididhyāsanaṁ* is practiced for some time, it leads to *Samādhi.* What is the meaning of *Samādhi* is indicated in verse 55...

ध्यातृध्याने परित्यज्य क्रमाद्ध्येयैकगोचरम् ।
निवातदीपवच्चित्तं समाधिरभिधीयते ।।५५।।

Dhyātṛ dhyāne pari tyajya kramād dhyeyaika gocaram
Nivāta dīpa vaccittaṁ samādhi rabhi dhīyate (55)

ध्यातृ ध्याने - the meditator and the meditation; क्रमात् - respectively; परित्यज्य - have renounced; ध्येय एक गोचरम् - going to the object of meditation alone; चित्तम् - to mind; समाधिः- *samādhi*; अभिधीयते - is called; निवातदीपवत् - like a lamp kept in a place protected from wind.

When the meditator and process of meditation is dropped (on the strength of practice of *nididhyāsana*), in stages, the mind gets fully absorbed in the *dhyeya* alone, this state is called *Samādhi*, when the mind is steady like a flame in a breezeless spot. (55)

In *nididhyāsana*, the meditator makes an effort to meditate on the object of meditation which is the *Paramātmā*, through the process of meditation called *dhyāna*. Thus the *dhyātṛ*, the *dhyāna* and *dhyeya* difference or *bheda* is maintained.

In *Samādhi abhyāsa*, as *nididhyāsana* or contemplation becomes mature, in that maturity; *Dhyātṛ dhyāne parityajya kramād dhyeyaika gocaraṁ* : one by one, step by step, the *bheda* is dropped. First, the *dhyātṛ*, the meditator is rejected i.e., the *kartṛtva abhimāna* that I am doing meditation is rejected. With long and sustained *abhyāsa*, when the *dhyātṛ bhāva* is dropped, automatically, the process of *dhyāna* also gets dropped, because if there is no meditator, then who will do the *dhyāna*?

So when the meditator and the process of meditation are rejected, one by one (*kramāt*), then only, the one *Paramātmā*, the *dhyeya*, the object of meditation remains. That cetas will become single pointed in which the mind will totally and absolutely be absorbed (*ekatva*).

The *Muṇḍakopaniṣad* conveys a similar thought in comparing the *praṇava* or *oṁkāra* to the bow, the *jīvātmā* who is doing meditation to the arrow and the *dhyeya vastu* or *lakṣya* is the *Parabrahman* (M.U.; II-2.4). Only when all efforts born out of individuality (*apramattena*) and doubt ceases, only then one enters the area of *Samādhi*.

Having overcome *kartṛtva abhimāna* at the gross body level, the *bhoktṛtva abhimāna* at the subtle body level; the last *abhimāna* would be at the causal body level, the *dhyātṛtva abhimāna*, the *prājña*. Once this is also rejected, then the mind is totally absorbed in the *Sat-cit-ānanda Brahman*. That state of absorption is compared to -

Nivāt dīpavat cittaṁ : A flame which is kept in a place where there is no wind, is steady with no flicker. So also, is the mind fixed steadily on the *Brahman*.

Samādhi abhidhīyate. This is called *Samādhi*.

The question now raised is, "If the mind is totally absorbed in *samādhi*, then how does one know that it is *samādhi* and not just deep sleep state? This doubt is answered in the next verse...

वृत्तयस्तु तदानीमज्ञाता अप्यात्मगोचराः।
स्मरणादनुमीयन्ते व्युत्थितस्य समुत्थितात् ।।५६।।

Vṛtta yastu tadānīm ajñātā apyātma gocarāḥ
Smaraṇā danu mīyante vyutthi tasya samut thitāt (56)

आत्मगोचराः - those going to self; वृत्तयः- thoughts; तु - indeed; तदानीम् - during *samādhi*, अज्ञाता - are unknown; अपि - although; व्युत्थितस्य समुत्थितात् - he who got up from the *samādhi;* स्मरणात् - by the memory of the knowledge; अनुमीयन्ते - can be inferred.

In *Samādhi,* although the thoughts going to the Self are not known, however, they are remembered by the one who has come out of the *Samādhi*, by his memory. (56)

Tadānīm ātmagocarā vṛttayaḥ ajnātā api : In the *Samādhi,* there is no *vṛtti jñānaṁ. Vṛtti jñānaṁ* is knowledge of some thing as object of knowledge. But when I say "I know myself", 'I' is not the object of my knowledge, because I am the knower and I am also the known. This is subjective knowledge. Thus in *nirvikalpa Samādhi*, thoughts are totally absent, because all thoughts are turned towards the Pure Self.

Vyutthitasya samutthitāt smaraṇāt anumīyante : This is inferred when the individual discards the state of *Samādhi* and enters the waking state; he recalls his experience when his thoughts were totally submerged in the Pure Self, that is, when the object of knowledge was *Paramātmā* and nothing else.

Now another subtle question is raised: In *Nirvikalpa Samādhi*, there is no effort, because there is no one to make the effort. Such being the case, how are the thoughts continuously pointed towards the *ātma tattva*? How is the state of *nirvikalpa Samādhi* sustained over a length of time?

This is explained in verse 57...

वृत्तिनामनुवृत्तिस्तु प्रयत्नात्प्रथमादपि ।
अदृष्टासकृदभ्याससंस्कारसचिवाद्भवेत् ।।५७।।

Vṛtti nāma nuvṛttistu prayat nāt pratha mādapi
Adṛṣṭā sakṛda bhyāsa saṁskāra sacivād bhavet (57)

वृत्तिनाम् - of the thoughts that are directed towards the self; अनुवृत्तिः- the continuous flow of these thoughts; तु - indeed; प्रथमात् - initially before *samādhi*; अपि - though; प्रयत्नात् - by conscious efforts; अदृष्टा - the unknown meritorious results of earlier acts; असकृत् - repeated; अभ्यास - practice; संस्कार - impressions; सचिवात् - with the help of; भवेत् - starts happening effortlessly.

The constant flow of thoughts during *nirvikalpa samādhi* towards *Paramātmā* is possible firstly, due to the earlier efforts put during *savikalpa samādhi* and secondly, due to deep impressions gathered as a result of earlier good deeds and practice put together. (57)

The constant flow of thoughts towards *Paramātmā*, our own essential nature, in the *nirvikalpa samādhi* is possible because of two reasons :

First; *Prathamāt prayatnāt api* : in the earlier stages of *sādhanā*, he has been constantly putting forward efforts, rejecting all extraneous thoughts. This is called *savikalpa samādhi*, where the *sākṣi bhāva* is awakened and no importance is given to the presence of the thoughts or to their content or theme. By the strength of this *abhyāsa*, the seeker develops the skill of tuning the mind in the desired direction effortlessly and maintain it in this state of single pointedness.

Second; *Adṛṣṭā asakṛt abhyāsa saṁskāra sacivāt* : whatever *sādhanā* had been done in the previous life, has a cumulative effect, if not in this embodiment, the journey will continue towards its completion (ref. also to B.G.; VI)

Thus, *nirvikalpa samādhi* is not an instant miracle but the result of continuous efforts over several births, the momentum building up from one birth to another till it reaches its fulfilment.

The teacher now cites the *Bhagavad Gītā* to support the above statement...

यथा दीपो निवातस्थ इत्यादिभिरनेकधा ।
भगवानिममेवार्थमर्जुनाय न्यरूपयत् ।।५८।।

Yathā dīpo nivāta stha ityādibhi ranekadhā
Bhagavā nima mevā rtham arjunāya nyarū payat (58)

यथा - as; निवातस्थः- placed in breezeless spot; दीपः- lamp; इत्यादिभिः- by words like these; भगवान् - *Bhagavān Kṛṣṇa*; अनेकधा - in many ways; इमम् - this type; एव - alone; अर्थम् - meaning; अर्जुनाय - to Arjuna; न्यरूपयत् - explained.

Bhagavān Kṛṣṇa explained Arjuna similar meaning by word like; 'as the lamp kept in a breezeless spot" etc.. (58)

Bhagavān imam eva artham arjunāya yathā dīpo nivātastha ityādibhiḥ anekadhā nyarūpayat : This idea has been told by *Bhagavān Kṛṣṇa* to Arjuna in several ways, that when the seeker who is in *nirvikalpa samādhi*, a *yogi*, fixes his mind without any *vikalpa* on the goal of *Brahma tattva*, the state of his mind is like a lamp kept in a secluded place where there is no breeze.

After having studied sufficiently in depth (*śravaṇaṁ*), followed by the reflection (*mananam*) and then contemplation (*nididhidhyāsana*), when such doubtless knowledge is gained, the seeker starts *abhyāsa* of *nirvikalpa samādhi*.

In this *samādhi* state, the mind is weaned away from unnecessary engagement about worldy affairs. He is able to be quiet and serene, effortlessly. To face quiet-ness, one requires strength.

When this is practiced for a length of time, the seeker spends most of the time by himself, only listening to the silence. The knowing-ness is withdrawn into being-ness.

He tries to maintain this *nirvikalpa samādhi avasthā* 'as long as possible'. This *samādhi,* being also a state of the mind, it supports both the quiet-ness and the concept of time. This *nirvikalpa samādhi* is a very essential stage in spiritual evolution.

When this *abhyāsa* is continued for a long time, what are the results and benefits? This is stated in the next verse...

अनादाविह संसारे सञ्चिताः कर्मकोटयः।
अनेन विलयं यान्ति शुद्धो धर्मो विवर्धते ।।५९।।

Anādā viha saṁsāre sañcitāḥ karma koṭayaḥ
Anena vilayaṁ yānti śuddho dharmo vivar dhate (59)

अनादौ - Beginning-less; इह - in this; संसारे - world; सञ्चिताः- accumulated; कर्म कोटयः- crores of *karma*; अनेन - by this *nirvikalpa samādhi abhyāsa*; विलयम् - get totally dissolved; यान्ति - attains; शुद्धः- pure; धर्मः- inner instrument and qualifications; विवर्धते - gross.

By the long practise of *nirvikalpa samādhi*, the accumulated impression from many many lives in this beginning-less *saṁsāra,* get attenuated and absorbed and the *antaḥkaraṇa* becomes purified. (59)

Iha saṁsāre anādau karma koṭayaḥ sañcitaḥ anena vilayaṁ yānti : In this world, from time immemorial, we have been accumulating the result of past actions in the form of likes, dislikes, bad and good thoughts etc.. These thoughts constitute the *vāsanā-s* of repeated births. They rise like volcanic eruptions to plague the seeker while on the seat of meditation.

When however, by the *abhyāsa* of *nirvikalpa samādhi,* one is able to observe these thoughts as witness and surrender all the thoughts and the contents of these thoughts at the feet of the Lord, by slow degrees, the pressure of one's own past, of habitual living gets attenuated, and one gains the 'hobby' of living where every moment is a joyful experience. The *vāsanā-s* inherited from the past lives get washed away without having to experience them through the gross body.

Then *śuddho dharmo vivardhate* : *Dharma* means *antaḥkaraṇa*. The *antaḥkaraṇa* becomes purified, the mind no more entertains *rāga-dveṣa*. As *Bhagavān Kṛṣṇa* says (chapter V-23), the thoughts in the mind are not the problem but when one is carried away and tossed around by them, one gets influenced by *kāma, krodha* etc.. With pure *antaḥkaraṇa*, the person becomes self-withdrawn. Such a mind is fully turned-within seeking its own source, always listening to the silence.

In this way, *samādhi abhyāsa* simultaneously purifies the *antaḥkaraṇa* of all subtle impurities, and manifiestation of the Pure Self becomes possible.

What is purification of the heart is indicated in the 60th sloka...

धर्ममेघमिमं प्राहुस्समाधिं योगवित्तमाः ।
वर्षत्येष यतो धर्मामृतधारास्सहस्त्रशः ॥६०॥

Dharma megha mimaṁ prāhus samādhiṁ yoga vittamāḥ
Varṣa tyeṣa yato dharmā mṛta dhārā ssaha sraśaḥ (60)

योगवित्तमाः - the knowers of *yoga* of self realization; **इमम्** - this; **समाधिम्** - *samādhi*; **धर्ममेघम्** - *dharma megha*; **प्राहुः**:- call; **यतः**:- because; **एषः**:- this *samādhi*; **धर्म अमृत धारा** - the shower of nectar flow; **सहस्त्रशः**:- in thousands of ways; **वर्षति** - showers.

The men of wisdom call this *samādhi* as *dharma megha samādhi*. Because it showers the nectar of the self bliss in a million ways. (60)

Yoga vittamāḥ imaṁ dharma megha samādhiṁ prāhuḥ : Those who are established in this supreme knowledge call this *samādhi* as *'dharma megha samādhi'* (*samādhi* like a cloud of rain);

eṣa dharmā mṛta dhārā sahasraśaḥ varṣati, because in this *abhyāsa* of *samādhi*, the manifestation of the Pure Self is like countless showers of bliss.

The major aspects manifested by the Pure Self as a result of *dharma megha samādhi* are :

(a) manifestation of *Sat* where the fear of death is no more present;

(b) manifestation of *Cit* where there is no doubt about anything;

(c) manifestation of *Ānanda* where there is no more dependence for the discovery of bliss.

This *abhyāsa* of *samādhi* helps in two ways :

(i) the purification of the heart wherein the *sañcita karma* of millions of earlier lives are washed away; and

(ii) the manifestation of the Pure Self become easier, being self evident.

This thought continues at different levels...

अमुना वासनाजाले निश्शेषं प्रविलापिते ।
समूलोन्मूलिते पुण्यपापाख्ये कर्मसञ्चये ।।६१।।

Amunā vāsanā jāle niśśeṣaṁ pravi lāpite
Samūlon mūlite puṇya pāpākhye karma sañcaye (61)

अमुना - by this *dharma megha samādhi*; वासना जाले - the snare of limitations i.e., I-ness, my-ness etc.; निःशेषं - totally; प्रविलापिते - destroyed; पुण्य पाप आख्ये - called as the merit and sin; कर्म - fruits of action; सञ्चये - hoards; समूल उन्मूलिते - is uprooted in seed and roots.

When by the practice of this *samādhi abhyāsa,* the share of *vāsanā-s* is extremely thinned, the accumulated *karma* like merit and sin are uprooted in bud and root – (continued in next verse). (61)

The doership (*ahaṁtā*), the ownership (*mamatā*) and the product trio, together constitue *vāsanā jāla*; a collection of all impurities in the form of limitations, *paricchinnatā* and *parokṣatā.*

Niśśeṣam pravilapite : By the *Samādhi abhyāsa*, the *kartṛtva abhimāna*, the sense of doership, associated with every action is reduced to the lowest level possible.

Puṇya pāpākhye karma sañcaye samūla unmūlite : All the impurities are completely uprooted, the merit and sins of accumulated actions are removed and the individuality is no more evident from that point of manifestation.

Continuing further on the outcome of *samādhi abhyāsa...*

वाक्यमप्रतिबद्धं सत् प्राक्परोक्षावभासिते ।
करामलकवद्बोधमपरोक्षं प्रसूयते ।।६२।।

Vākya maprati baddhaṁ sat prāk parokṣā vabhāsite
Karā malaka vad bodham aparokṣaṁ prasūyate (62)

वाक्यम् - the *'Tat tvaṁ asi' mahāvākya-s;* अप्रतिबद्धम् - without any obstacles; सत् - the Truth; प्राक् - earlier; परोक्ष - indirectly; अवभासिते - known; कर अमलकवत् - like a fruit in the palm; अपरोक्षम् - immediate and direct; बोधम् - realization; प्रसूयते - delivers.

The earlier obstacles in understanding the meaning of *mahāvākya* being overcome, the indirect knowledge being gained, the direct immediate self-knowledge takes place as distinctly as a fruit of *Amala* on one's own palm. (62)

Vākyam aprati-baddhaṁ sat prāk parokṣā avabhāsite : The earlier obstacles in the understanding of the meaning of the *mahāvākya* being removed, the earlier *parokṣa jñāna* leads further. (By the study of the *mahāvākya,* only *parokṣa jñāna* takes place; there is no touch of direct experience).

However, this first step is essential for futher development.

Although the *Paramātma tattva* is abundantly present, it is not evident to us because of the lack of sharp and subtle intellect to perceive it. It is only *samādhi abhyāsa* that gives us such an instrument, a *sūkṣma* and *agrayā* (single pointed) *buddhi* (intellect) (K.U.III.12)

It is only a total and exclusive involvement and *abhyāsa* in the search for the Truth that makes the instrument qualified.

Thereafter, *Kara amalaka-vat aparokṣam bodhaṁ prasūyate,* (once this doubtless *parokṣa jñānaṁ* has been gained), the direct knowledge about one's own essential nature becomes as evident and self-revealing as the *amalaka* fruit on the palm of one's hand.

This *parokṣa* and *aparokṣa jñānaṁ* aided by *samādhi abhyāsa* leads to two results, one is stated in verse 63 and the other in verse 64.

परोक्षं ब्रह्मविज्ञानं शाब्दं देशिकपूर्वकम् ।
बुद्धिपूर्वकृतं पापं कृत्स्नं दहति वह्निवत् ।।६३।।

Parokṣaṁ brahma vijñānaṁ śābdaṁ deśika pūrvakam
Buddhi pūrva kṛtaṁ pāpaṁ kṛtsnaṁ dahati vahnivat (63)

देशिकपूर्वकम् - From the teacher; शाब्दम् - the instructions on *mahāvākya*; परोक्षम् - indirect; ब्रह्मविज्ञानम् - the knowledge of *Brahman*; बुद्धिपूर्वकृतम् - intentionally committed; कृत्स्नम् पापम् - all the sins; वह्निवत् - like fire; दहति - burns.

The indirect knowledge of *Brahman* gained by the study with the *ācārya* (teacher) burns completely the sins and merits committed intentionally, like the fire (burns the fuel). (63)

Deśika pūrvakam śābdaṁ parokṣaṁ Brahma vijñānaṁ : The *parokṣa jñānaṁ* gained by approaching the *Guru* and studying the scriptures and contemplating on the *Tat tvaṁ asi mahāvākya* is only word knowledge with no *anubhava* or direct experience. However, the student is very clear about his understanding about the subject. And what does this understanding lead to?

Buddhi pūrva kṛtaṁ kṛtsnam pāpaṁ vahnivat dahati : All the omissions and erroneous commissions one has committed in the past and that are haunting him, are burnt up as by a fire. Unless one is able to drop a curtain on the past, it is impossible to go forward and qualify for *amrta-anubhava*. Only when the *apara vidyā* is discarded, is there scope for *parā vidyā* or the supreme knowledge to dawn (M.U. 1.1.5)

This Supreme Knowledge which is attained by keeping the goal all the time and fully in our vision, without getting lost in the by-lanes of pseudo-knowledge, it is like a fire which burns up all the past *buddhi, kṛta, pāpaṁ* etc.. (B.G. 4.37). This is the effect of *parokṣa jñānaṁ.*

What does *aparokṣa jñānaṁ* give us?

अपरोक्षात्मविज्ञानं शाब्दं देशिकपूर्वकम् ।
संसारकारणाज्ञानतमसश्चण्डभास्कर : ।।६४।।

Aparo kṣātma vijñānaṁ śābdaṁ deśika pūrva kam
Saṁsāra kāraṇā jñāna tamasaś caṇḍa bhāskaraḥ (64)

देशिकपूर्वकम् - From the teacher; शाब्दम् - the instructions on the *mahāvākya*; अपरोक्ष - direct and immediate; आत्मविज्ञानम् - knowledge of self; संसार कारण - the cause of the world of plurality; अज्ञान तमसः- the darkness of ignorance; चण्ड भास्करः- is like the high noon sun.

The direct self knowledge gained by studying at the feet of the *ācārya* is like the high noon-sun for the ignorance – the cause of this world of repeated transmigration. (64).

Deśika-pūrvakam śābdam aparokṣam ātma vijñānam : When the student has thus studied and gained *parokṣa jñānaṁ* under the guidance of a teacher, thereafter, he is further guided by a *Brahmaniṣṭha Puruṣa.* Then *aparokṣa jñānaṁ* takes place. He attains direct experience (*anubhūti*).

The *parokṣa jñānaṁ* was able to destroy the *puṇya* and *pāpa* while *saṁsāra kāraṇa ajñāna tamasaḥ caṇḍa bhāskaraḥ* : the *aparokṣa jñānaṁ* destroys (burns up) the root cause of this *saṁsāra* of repeated births and deaths, namely the individuality born out of *tamas* or ignorance. Just as the sun of high-noon is so bright that there is no possibility of darkness, the *aparokṣa jñānaṁ* takes care of the ignorance because of which one constantly considers oneself to be an individual conditioned by the *pañca-kośa-s.* In this way, *Tattva viveka* takes place.

The 65th sloka gives the *phala śruti...*

इत्थं तत्त्वविवेकं विधाय विधिवन्मनस्समाधाय ।
विगलित संसृतिबन्धः प्राप्नोति परं पदं नरो न चिरात् ।।६५।।

Itthaṁ tattva vivekaṁ vidhāya vidhi vanmanas samādhāya
Vigalita saṁsṛti bandhaḥ prāpnoti paraṁ padaṁ naro na cirāt (65)

नरः- The student of this chapter; इत्थम् - in this manner; तत्त्वविवेकम् - the discrimination of the Truth from the conditionings; विधाय - carries out; विधिवत् - by proper technique; मनः- mind; समाधाय - having stabilized; संसृति बन्धः- the bondage of rebirth; विगलित - having liberated; परम् पदम् - the supereme state; न चिरात् - immediately; प्राप्नोति - attains.

In this way, when a seeker carries out the *Tattva viveka* as explained in the chapter, stabilizing the mind and dissolving the cause of repeated transmigration, he attains the supreme state of bliss instantaneously. (65)

Naraḥ itthaṁ tattva vivekaṁ vidhāya : In this way, when a student carries out *Tattva viveka* (the discrimination of the essential principle) as delineated in this chaper,

Vidhivat manaḥ samādhaya, by stabilizing the mind as per the *śāstra vicāra.*

Samsṛti bandhaḥ vigalita : the bondage of *saṁsmṛti* - the cause for constant transmigration from one life to another is totally destroyed.

Paraṁ padaṁ na cirāt prāpnoti; then, he attains the Supreme Bliss instantaneously.

In this way, this first chapter of *Pañcadaśī* called *Tattva viveka prakaraṇaṁ*, provides full guidance to the spiritual seeker for study, reflection and contemplation.

OM TAT SAT

Summary

Verse No.	Subject matter covered
1	Salutations to *Guru*
2	Subject matter is for qualified student as defined here.
3 - 7	Discrimination of Consciousness from waking, dream, deep sleep, objects and their experiences and the identity of *Sat* and *Cit*.
8 - 10	*Ānanda* aspect of Consciousness which is one's own Self
11	An objection is raised about Self being Blissful.
12	Objection replied and obstacle in Knowledge pointed.
13 - 14	Cause of obstacles viz. ignorance.
15	Nature of ignorance and its operation
16 - 17	Definition of *jīva* and *Īśvara*.
18 - 23	Effect of ignorance or causal body and nature of subtle body.
24 - 25	*Taijasa, Hiraṇyagarbha, Vyaṣṭi and samaṣṭi.*
26 - 28	Effect of *Tamoguṇa* and creation of gross world and the different gross bodies.

29 - 31 *Karma cakra* for *jīva-s*

32 - 37 Way out of the *Karma cakra*, enquiry, instructions and discrimination.

38 - 42 Process of discrimination by *anvaya* and *vyatireka*.

43 - 48 *'Tat-tvaṁ-asi' mahāvākya upadeśaḥ*

49 - 52 A doubt about *Brahman* to be with or without modification.

53 - 55 *Śravaṇam (listening), mananam (reflection) nididhyāsanam (contemplation) and Samādhi.*

56 - 60 Further elaboration about *Samādhi.*

61- 64 Effect of practice of *Samādhi*

65 *Phala śruti* i.e., the final emancipation as a result of *Tattva viveka*.

* * *

2

२५

Chapter II

PAÑCA - BHŪTA VIVEKA PRAKARAṆA

Or

DISCRIMINATION OF THE FIVE GREAT ELEMENTS

The main purpose of this book is to help the seeker develop a faculty of discrimination by which the seeker is able to separate out the Substratum from the super-imposed. This was achieved by differentiating the Pure Self from the conditionings through which the Self is functioning, in the first chapter. The present chapter aims at discovering the Substratum, namely the Non-Dual Existence from objective aspect of the experience. In every experience, we have the experiencer, the experience and the experienced. This chapter focusses the attention of the student on the discrimination of Pure Existence from the super-imposed namely, the five great elements which are the objective aspects of the experience.

सदद्वैतं श्रुतं यत्तत्पञ्चभूत विवेकतः ।
बोद्धुं शक्यं ततो भूतपञ्चकं प्रविविच्यते ।।१।।

Sad-advaitaṁ śrutaṁ yat-tat-pañca-bhūta vivekataḥ
Boddhuṁ śakyaṁ tato bhūta-pañcakaṁ pravi vicyate (1)

यत् - That which (is referred as the cause of the world); सत् - Existence अद्वैतम् - one without a second; श्रुतम् - heard (in the *upaniṣad*); तत् - that; पञ्च भूत विवेकतः- by the discrimination of the five elements; बोद्धुम् शक्यम् - can be ascertained; ततः- therefore; भूत पञ्चकम् - the five elements; प्रविविच्यते - are being enquired.

That which is referred as the non-dual *brahman* in the *Upaniṣad-s* can be ascertained by the discrimination of the five elements. Hence, the enquiry about them is made. (1)

The elements are enumerated...

शब्दस्पर्शौ रूपरसौ गन्धो भूतगुणा इमे ।
एकद्वित्रिचतुःपञ्चगुणाः व्योमादिषु क्रमात् ।।२।।

Śabda-sparśau rūpa-rasau gandho bhūta-guṇā ime
Eka-dvi-tri-catuḥ pañca guṇāḥ vyomādiṣu kramāt (2)

शब्दः- Sound; स्पर्शः- touch; रूप - form; रसः- taste; गन्धः- smell; इमे - these; भूत गुणाः- are the qualities of the elements; व्योम आदिषु - in the space etc.; क्रमात् - in the same order; एक - one; द्वि - two; त्रि - three; चतुः- four; पञ्च - five; गुणाः- qualities.

The five elements viz., *space, air, fire, water* and *earth* have *sound, touch, form, taste* and *smell* as their respective qualities. The elements have one, two, three, four and five qualities repectively (i.e., the space has only one quality of sound, the air has sound and touch, the fire has three qualities viz., sound, touch and form, while the water has in addition to these the fourth quality of taste and the earth has the fifth additional quality of smell). (2)

The presence of these qualities are shown in the following verses...

प्रतिध्वनिर्वियच्छब्दो वायौ बीसीति शब्दनम् ।
अनुष्णाशीतसंस्पर्शः वह्नौ भुगुभुगुध्वनिः ।।३।।

Pratidhvanir viyacchabdo vāyau bīsīti śabdanam
Anuṣṇā-śīta saṁsparśaḥ vahnau bhugu-bhugu-dhvaniḥ (3)

प्रति ध्वनिः- sound of echo; वियत् शब्दः- sound is the quality of space; वायौ - in the air; बीसीति - rustling sound; शब्दनम् - is the sound of air; अनुष्णाशीत संस्पर्शः- the quality of touch that is neither hot nor cold (is seen in the air); वह्नौ - in the fire; भुगु भुगु ध्वनिः - crackling sound.

The presence of echo in the space is the quality of 'sound' in the space. The rustling sound is the quality of 'sound' in the air. The air has its quality of touch that is neither hot nor cold (thus air has two qualities). The crackling sound is the quality of 'sound' seen in the fire. (3)

उष्णस्पर्शः प्रभारूपं जले बुलुबुलुध्वनिः ।
शीतस्पर्शः शुक्लरूपं रसो माधुर्यमीरितः ।।४।।

Uṣṇa-sparśaḥ prabhā-rūpaṁ jale bulu-bulu-dhvaniḥ
Śīta-sparśaḥ śukla-rūpaṁ raso mādhuryam-īritaḥ (4)

उष्णः स्पर्शः- (in the fire) the warmth is the touch; प्रभारूपम् - brightness is the colour aspect and form; जले - in the water; बुलु बुलु ध्वनिः- the rippling sound (is heard); शुक्लरूपम् - whiteness is the colour; रसः- taste; माधुर्यम् - sweetness; ईरितम् - is said.

The fire is warm to touch. It has brightness as its colour and form. The water makes rippling sound, has cooler touch and white colour. Sweetness is the quality of water. (4)

The earth has all the five qualities...

भूमौ कडकडाशब्दः काठिन्यं स्पर्श इष्यते ।
नीलादिकं चित्ररूपं मधुराम्लादिको रसः ।।५।।

Bhūmau kaḍkaḍā-śabdaḥ kāṭhinyaṁ sparśa iṣyate
Nīlādikaṁ citra-rūpaṁ madhurāmlādiko rasaḥ (5)

भूमौ - in the earth; कडकडा - rattling; शब्द - sound; काठिन्यम् - hardness; स्पर्शः- touch; इष्यते - said to be; नील आदिकम् - blue etc.; चित्ररूपम् - different colours; मधुर आम्ल आदिकः- sweet, sour etc.; रसः- taste.

The earth has a rattling sound, hard touch, colourful forms and tastes such as sweet, sour etc.. (5)

The quality of smell in the earth is explained now...

सुरभीतरगंधौ द्वौ गुणाः सम्यग्विवेचिताः ।
श्रोत्रं त्वक्चक्षुषी जिह्वा घ्राणं चेन्द्रियपञ्चकम् ।।६।।

Surabhī tara gaṅdhau dvau guṇāḥ samyag vivecitāḥ
Śrotraṁ tvak-cakṣuṣī jivhā ghrāṇaṁ cendriya pañcakam (6)

सुरभीतर गंधौ द्वौ - both pleasant and unpleasant smells; गुणाः - are qualities of earth; सम्यग् विवेचिताः- (thus) we have enquired and discriminated (about the qualities of the elements); श्रोत्रम् - ear; त्वक् - skin; चक्षुषी - eyes; जिह्वा - tongue; घ्राण - nose; च - and; इन्द्रिय पञ्चकम् - are the five senses.

(The earth has) both pleasant and unpleasant smells as its quality. Thus far, we have enquired and discriminated about the elements and their qualities. The five senses viz., ear, skin, eyes, tongue and nose are formed from the five elements starting with space etc., respectively. (6)

The structural locations, their functions etc., are...

कर्णादिगोलकस्थं तच्छब्दादिग्राहकं क्रमात् ।
सौक्ष्म्यात्कार्यानुमेयं तत् प्रायो धावेद्बहिर्मुखम् ।।७।।

Karṇādi golakasthaṁ tacchabdādi grāhakaṁ kramāt
Saukṣmyāt-kāryānumeyaṁ tat prāyo dhāved-bahir-mukham (7)

कर्ण आदि गोलक स्थम् - in the locus of ear etc.; तत् - that शब्दादि - sound etc.; ग्राहकम् - function; क्रमात् - respectively; सौक्ष्म्यात् - being subtle; कार्य अनुमेयम् - inferred from the effects; प्रायो - naturally; धावेत् - run; बहिःमुखम् - outgoing.

The senses viz., hearing, touching, seeing, tasting and smelling are located in the ears, skin, eyes, tongue and nose respectively and function in their respective fields of sound etc.. The senses being subtle are inferred from their effects. These senses naturally run in the outer world of sounds etc.. (7)

The senses are made of the ungrossified nascent elements and are therefore, not directly perceptible. They can be inferred only by observing the functioning of these senses in an individual.

The senses are also able to function in the fields of sounds etc., which are internal in our body...

कदाचित्पिहिते कर्णे श्रूयते शब्द आन्तरः ।
प्राणवायौ जाठराग्नौ जलपानेऽन्नभक्षणे ।।८।।

Kadācit-pihite karṇe śrūyate śabda āntaraḥ
Prāṇa vāyau jāṭharāgnau jalapāne-'nna-bhakṣaṇe (8)

कदाचित् - sometimes; पिहिते कर्णे - when the ears are closed; प्राणवायौ - during respirations; जाठराग्नौ - sound in the stomach; जलपाने - while drinking water; अन्न भक्षणे - while eating food; आन्तर - inner; शब्दः- sound; श्रूयते - is heard.

Sometimes, when the ears are plugged, one hears the inner sounds of respiration, stomach etc., while drinking water and eating food... (this thought is completed in the next *śloka*). (8)

व्यज्यन्ते ह्यान्तराः स्पर्शा मीलने चान्तरं तमः ।
उद्गारे रसगन्धौ चेत्यक्षाणामान्तरग्रहः ।।९।।

Vyajyante hyāntarāḥ sparśā mīlane cāntaraṁ tamaḥ
Udgāre rasagandhau cetyakṣāṇāmāntaragrahaḥ (9)

व्यज्यन्ते - are experienced; हि - indeed; अन्तराः- inner; स्पर्शाः- touches; मीलने - when the eyes are closed; च - and; तमः - darkness is perceived; उद्गारे - while belching; रस गन्धौ - the taste and smell; च - and; इति - thus; अक्षाणाम् - of the senses; आन्तरग्रहः - inner perceptions.

While drinking water and eating food, the inner touches of the cold or hot etc., are felt. Similarly, on the closure of the eyes, the darkness is experienced. In belching, one has the experience of the taste and the smell. Thus, the senses function in the inner objects of sound etc.. (9)

In the next two verses, the two organs of action, their fields etc., are discussed...

पञ्चोक्त्यादानगमनविसर्गानन्दकाः क्रियाः
कृषिवाणिज्यसेवाद्याः पञ्चस्वन्तर्भवन्ति हि ।।१०।।

Pañcokty-ādāna-gamana visarg-ānandakāḥ kriyāḥ
Kṛṣi-vāṇijya-sevādyāḥ pañcasvantar bhavanti hi (10)

उक्ति - speech; आदान - holding; गमन - locomotion; विसर्ग - excretion; आनन्दकाः- sex pleasure; पञ्च - five; क्रिया - actions; कृषि - agriculture; वाणिज्य - commerce; सेवा - service; आद्याः- etc.; पञ्चसु - in the five; अन्तः भवन्ति - are included; हि - indeed.

The five actions of speech, holding, movement, excretion and sex pleasure are the five types of actions. All other actions in relation to agriculture, commerce, service etc., are included in these five types. (10)

वाक्पाणिपादपायूपस्थैरक्षैस्तत्क्रियाजनिः ।
मुखादिगोलकेष्वास्ते तत्कर्मेन्द्रियपञ्चकम् ।।११।।

Vāk-pāṇi-pāda-pāyūpasthair akṣais tat kriyājaniḥ
Mukhādi-golakeṣv āste tat karmendriya pañcakam (11)

वाक् पाणि पाद पायूपस्थैः- By the organs of speech, hand, legs, reproduction and excretion; अक्षैः तत् क्रिया जनिः- the actions referred in the above verse are carried out respectively; तत् कर्म इन्द्रिय पञ्चकम् - that set of five organs of action; मुख आदि गोलकेषु - in the organs like mouth etc.; आस्ते - are located.

The five organs of action viz., speech, hands, legs, reproduction and excretion are located in the mouth, hand etc., and perform the actions referred above respectively. (11)

Now, the teacher explains about the mind, its field etc...

मनो दशेन्द्रियाध्यक्षं हृत्पद्मे गोलके स्थितम् ।
तच्चान्तःकरणं बाह्येष्वस्वातन्त्र्याद्विनेन्द्रियैः ।।१२।।

Mano daśendriyā dhyakṣaṁ hṛt-padme golake sthitam
Taccāntaḥ karaṇaṁ bāhyeṣva svātantryāt vinen-driyaiḥ (12)

मनो दश इन्द्रिय अध्यक्षम् - the mind presides over the ten organs; हृत् पद्म गोलके स्थितम् - (and it is) located in the lotus of the heart; तत् - that; च - and; अन्तःकरणम् - inner instrument; इन्द्रियैः विना - without these ten organs; बाह्येषु - (to function in the) outer objects; अस्वातन्त्र्यात् - is not independent.

The mind presides over the ten organs. Located in the heart, without the help of these organs, it is not independent to contact the external objects. (12)

How the mind presides over the organs and the qualitative differences in the mind are...

अक्षेष्वर्थार्पितेष्वेतद्गुणदोषविचारकम् ।
सत्त्वं रजस्तमश्चास्य गुणा विक्रियते हि तैः ।।१३।।

Akṣeṣvarthār-pite ṣvetad guṇa doṣa vicārakam
Sattvaṁ rajas tamaś-cāsya guṇā vikriyate hi taiḥ (13)

अक्षेषु अर्थ अर्पितेषु - when the senses contact their respective objects; **एतत्** - this; **गुण दोष विचारकम्** - thinks about the good and the bad qualities of the object; **सत्त्व रजः तमः च अस्य गुणाः** - *Sattva*, *rajas* and *tamas* are its qualities (*guṇa*-s); **हि तैः विक्रियते** - by these *guṇa-s,* it suffers the modifications.

When the senses come in contact with their objects, it is this mind that classifies these objects as good or bad, with the help of the three *guṇa-s* viz., *Sattva*, *rajas* and *tamas*. (13)

The senses are mere instruments of perception. This is nature's phenomenon. The labelling of these objects is the function of the mind. Although the mind is made up of the *Sattva guṇa* of all the five elements, it does have influence of the these three *guṇa-s.*

What are the modifications on account of these three *guṇa-s?...*

वैराग्यं क्षान्तिरौदार्यमित्याद्यास्सत्त्वसम्भवाः ।
कामक्रोधौ लोभयत्नौवित्याद्याः रजसोत्थिताः ।।१४।।

Vairāgyaṁ kṣāntir-audāryam ityādyās-sattva-sambhavāḥ
Kāma-krodhau lobha-yatnau vityādyāḥ rajaso-tthitāḥ (14)

वैराग्यम् - desireless-ness; क्षान्तिः - forgiveness; औदार्यम् - large-heartedness; आद्याः - etc.; सत्त्व सम्भवाः- are born of *sattva guṇa;* कामः- desire; क्रोधः- anger; लोभः- greed; यत्नः- efforts; इति आद्याः- etc.; रजसः उत्थिताः- are born of *rajo guṇa.*

The interaction of the mind with the *sattva guṇa* leads to noble qualities like, desirelesness, forgiveness, large-heartedness etc.. The *rajo guṇa* manifests in mind as, desire, anger, greed, efforts, etc.. (14)

The effects of *tamo guṇa* and the consequences of these effects in the life of an individual are...

आलस्यं भ्रान्तितन्द्राद्या विकारास्तमसोत्थिताः ।
सात्त्विकैः पुण्यनिष्पत्तिः पापोत्पत्तिश्च राजसैः ।।१५।।

Ālasyaṁ bhrānti tandrādyā vikārās tamasot thitāḥ
Sāttvikaiḥ puṇya niṣpattiḥ pāpot pattiś ca rājasaiḥ (15)

आलस्यम् - laziness; भ्रान्तिः- delusion; तन्द्रा - sleep; विकाराः- modifications; तमसः उत्थिताः- are born of *tamo guṇa*; सात्त्विकैः- by the *sāttvik* modifications; पुण्य निष्पत्तिः- merit is earned; पाप उत्पत्तिः च राजसैः- by the *rajo guṇa* modifications, sin is earned.

Laziness,delusion, sleep, etc. are the modifications born of *tamo guṇa.* The *sāttvik* modifications of the mind leads to merit, and that of *rajo guṇa,* to sin. (15)

What about the *tamo guṇa* modifications?...

तामसैर्नोभयं किन्तु वृथायुःक्षपणं भवेत् ।
अत्राहंप्रत्ययी कर्तेत्येवं लोके व्यवस्थितिः ।।१६।।

Tāmasair-nobhayaṁ kintu vṛthāyuḥ kṣapaṇaṁ bhavet
Atrāhaṁ pratyayī karteti evaṁ loke vyavasthitiḥ (16)

तामसैः- by the *tamas* modifications; उभयम् न - both (merit & sin) are not earned; किन्तु - however; वृथा - in vain; आयुः - life; क्षपणम् भवेत् - is wasted; अत्र - here with respect to sin etc.; अहम् प्रत्ययी - the sense of doership; कर्ता - is the doer; इति एवम् - in this way; लोके व्यवस्थितिः - is seen in the worldly things.

The *tamo guṇa* modifications produce neither merit nor sin. But the life is wasted without any purpose. Here, with regard to the creation of sin etc., the sense of doership is the agent called ego. In the world, it is seen that the doer suffers the results. (16)

In the following *śloka,* the teacher concludes that the objects and the senses that perceive are both the effects of the five great elements...

स्पष्टशब्दादियुक्तेषु भौतिकत्वमतिस्फुटम् ।
अक्षादावपि तच्छास्त्रयुक्तिभ्यामवधार्यताम् ।।१७।।

Spaṣṭa śabdādi yukteṣu bhauti katva mati sphuṭam
Akṣā dāvapi tat śāstra yuktibhyām avadhāryatām (17)

स्पष्ट शब्दादि युक्तेषु - in the gross objects like sound etc.; भौतिकत्वम् - being effects of elements; अति स्फुटम् - is distinctly clear; अक्षादौ - in the senses; अपि - also; तत् - that; शास्त्र - scriptures; युक्तिभ्याम् - by the logic; अवधार्यताम् - be understood.

It is, thus far, concluded that the gross objects like sound etc., are the effects of the five elements. With the help of the logic in line with the scriptures, it can be understood that the senses are also the effects of the elements. (17)

Upto this point the teacher has discussed the five elements along with their effects. Hereafter, the scriptural statement, *'Sadeva somya idam agra āsit'*, meaning - "O! Somya, dear student, before this (world), *Sat* (Existence) alone was." is discussed.

In the following *śloka,* the teacher first describes the meaning of the term *'idam'* i.e., this world...

एकादशेन्द्रियैर्युक्त्या शास्त्रेणाप्यवगम्यते ।
यावत्किंचिद्भवेदेतदिदंशब्दोदितं जगत् ।।१८।।

Ekādaśen driyair yuktyā śāstreṇā pyava gamyate
Yāvat kiṁcit bhave detat idaṁ śabdo ditaṁ jagat (18)

एकादश इन्द्रियैः- with the help of the ten organs and the mind; युक्त्या - by the logic; शास्त्रेण - by the scriptures; अपि - also; यावत् - whatever; किञ्चित् - even the insignificant; एतत् - this; जगत् - world; अवगम्यते - is understood; इदम् - *'idam'* (this); शब्दोदितम् - included; भवेत् - to be.

Whatever is perceived by the senses and the mind, and also that which is described in the scriptures, even the most insignificant, is to be understood as included in the word *'idam'* i.e., the world. (18)

The authority for the above statement is quoted...

इदं सर्वं पुरा सृष्टेरेकमेवाद्वितीयकम् ।
सदेवासीन्नामरूपे नास्तामित्यारुणेर्वचः ।।१९।।

Idaṁ sarvaṁ purā sṛṣṭer-ekam-evā-dvitīyakam
Sad-ev-āsīn-nāma-rūpe nāstām-ity-āruṇer-vacaḥ (19)

सृष्टेः पुरा - before creation; इदम् सर्वम् - all this; एकम् - one; एव - only; अद्वितीयकम् - without a second; सत् - *Sat* (Existence); एव - alone; आसीत् - was; नामरूपे - names and forms; न आस्ताम् - were not; इति - thus; आरुणेः वचः - is the statement of *Āruṇi.*

Before the creation of all 'this', was 'one existence without a second'. There was neither name nor form, is the statement of *Āruṇi.* (from the C.U. 6.2). (19)

The teacher now explains the meaning of *'ekam eva advitīyakam'* i.e., one Pure existence without a second, by first explaining the possible types of differences through some examples...

वृक्षस्य स्वगतो भेदः पत्रपुष्पफलादिभिः ।
वृक्षान्तरात्सजातीयो विजातीयश्शिलादितः ।।२०।।

Vṛkṣasya svagato bhedaḥ patra puṣpa phalādi-bhiḥ
Vṛkṣān tarāt sajātīyo vijātīyaś-śilāditaḥ (20)

वृक्षस्य - of a tree; पत्र पुष्प फलादिभिः - by leaves, flowers and fruits; स्वगतः भेदः- the differeces within an object; वृक्ष अन्तरात् - on account of different tree species; सजातीयः- difference among the ojects of the same kind; शिलादितः-(between tree and) stone; विजातीयः (भेदः भवति) - (is the difference) among kinds.

The difference on account of the leaves, flowers and fruits of the same tree is called the difference within the same object. The difference on account of different trees is the difference among the species of the same kind. The difference on account of the Stone and Tree is the difference among the different kinds. (20).

Having observed the three types of differences in this world (in the *'idam'*) one may expect to know the status of the 'Existence' with reference to these differences...

तथा सद्वस्तुनो भेदत्रयं प्राप्तं निवार्यते ।
ऐक्यावधारणद्वैतप्रतिषेधैस्त्रिभिः क्रमात् ।।२१।।

Tathā sad-vastuno bheda trayaṁ prāptaṁ nivāryate
Aikyā vadhāraṇa dvaita prati ṣedhai stribhiḥ kramāt (21)

तथा - similarly (like the differences in *'idam'* i.e., not-self); सद् वस्तुनः- in the absolute Existence; प्राप्तम् - possible; भेद त्रयम् - three types of differences; ऐक्य अवधारण - for establishing oneness; द्वैत प्रतिषेधैः- for the negation of the duality; त्रिभिः- by the three; क्रमात् - respectively; निवार्यते - is being negated.

The possibility of presence of three types of differences in the Absolute Existence is being negated and the oneness of the Existence is being established by the three logics in the following *śloka-s.* (21)

Some *Asad-vādin-s* believe that the non-existence of the world is the reality. To answer this...

सतो नावयवाश्शंक्यास्तदंशस्यानिरूपणात् ।
नामरूपे न तस्यांशौ तयोरद्याप्यनुद्भवात् ।।२२।।

Sato nāva yavāś śaṅkyās tadaṁśasyā nirūpaṇāt
Nāmarūpe na tasyāṁśau tayo radyā pyanud bhavāt (22)

सतः- of the Absolute; अवयवाः- parts; न शंक्या - should not be suspected; तद अंशस्य - part of the Absolute; अनिरूपणात् - cannot be described; नाम रूपे - names and form; तस्य - of the Absloute; अंशौ - parts; न - not; अद्यः - prior; तयोः अपि - of the names and forms; अनुद्भवात् - were not existing (before creation).

Parts of the Absolute should not be suspected. Because they cannot be explained to exist in the Absolute. The names and forms are not parts of the Absolute because they did not exist before creation. (22)

Why is there an absence of names and forms before creation?...

नामरूपोद्भवस्यैव सृष्टित्वात्सृष्टितः पुरा ।
न तयोरुद्भवस्तस्मान्निरंशं सद्यथा वियत् ।।२३।।

Nāmarūpo dbhava syaiva sṛṣṭi tvāt sṛṣṭitaḥ purā
Na tayo rudbhavas tasmāt niraṁśaṁ sad yathā viyat (23)

नाम रूप उद्भवस्य एव - the appearence of names and forms is; सृष्टित्वात् - being the creation; सृष्टितः पुरा - before creation; तयोः- their; उद्भवः न - were not present; तस्मात् - therefore; सत् - *Sat* (Absolute); निरंशम् - without parts; यथा - as; वियत् - space.

The apperance of the names and forms is itself creation, as they were totally absent before creation. Therefore, the *Sat* i.e., Absolute is without parts. (23)

This confirms the absence of the difference within one i.e., absence of *svagata bheda*......, What about *sajātīya bheda*?.....

सदन्तरं सजातीयं न वैलक्षण्यवर्जनात् ।
नामरूपोपाधिभेदं विना नैव सतो भिदा ।।२४।।

Sadantaraṁ sajātīyaṁ na vailakṣaṇya varjanāt
Nāma rūpo pādhi bhedaṁ vinā naiva sato bhidā (24)

सजातीय - of the similar kind; सद् अन्तरम् - other than *Sat*; न - is not; वैलक्षण्य वर्जनात् - due to absence of different kinds of *Sat* (Absolute); नामरूपोपाधि - the conditioning of names and forms; विना - without; भेदम् - difference; सतः- of the *Sat*; भिदा - difference; न एव - is not.

There cannot be other kind of *Sat*, for the other kind would be *Asat* - i.e., non-existence. Without the conditionings of names and forms, there cannot be any difference, and it would be that of the conditionings and not of *Sat*. (24).

Thus having proved the absence of difference on account of difference of the same kind (*sajātīya bheda*), the third type of difference is analysed...

विजातीयमसत्तत्तु न खल्वस्तीति गम्यते ।
नास्यातः प्रतियोगित्वं विजातीयाद्भिदा कुतः ।।२५।।

Vijātīya masattattu na khalva stīti gamyate
Nāsyātaḥ prati yogitvaṁ vijātīyāt bhidā kutaḥ (25)

विजातीयम् असत् - the different kinds would be *asat* - non existent; तत्तु न अस्ति - but it cannot exist; इति - thus; खलु - indeed; गम्यते - is known; अतः- therefore; अस्य - of this (non-existence); प्रतियोगित्वम् - opposition; न - not; विजातीयात् - of the different kind; भिदा - the difference; कुतः - could be.

The different kind of *Sat* would be *Asat* i.e., non-existence. The non-existence cannot be considered to exist to oppose the existence. Therefore, there cannot be difference on account of different kinds. (25).

Thus, all the three kinds of differences are totally absent in the *Sat*. To remove any kind of further doubt regarding this, the teacher examines the view of the *asat vādin-s* i.e., the one who believes in non-existence...

एकमेवाद्वितीयं सत्सिद्धमत्र तु केचन ।
विह्वला असदेवेदं पुरासीदित्यवर्णयन् ।।२६।।

Ekamevā dvitīyaṁ sat siddha matra tu kecana
Vihvalā asadevedaṁ purā sīditya varṇayan (26)

एकम् - one; एव अद्वितीयम् - without a second, thus; सत् सिद्धम् - is concluded; अत्र तु - however; केचन विह्वलाः - some confused ones; पुरा आसीत् - was before; इदम् - this world; असदेव - was non-existent; इति - thus; अवर्णयन् - they describe.

Thus far, the *Sat* is concluded to be one without a second. However, some still confused people (*asat vādin-s mādhyamika*) say that the nature of the world before creation was non-existence. (26)

The reason for such an impossible confusion is....

मग्नस्याब्धौ यथाक्षाणि विह्वलानि तथास्य धीः ।
अखण्डैकरसं श्रुत्वा निष्प्रचारा बिभेत्यतः ।।२७।।

Magnasy-ābdhau yathā-kṣāṇi vihvalāni tathāsya dhīḥ
Akhaṇḍaikarasaṁ śrutvā niṣpracārā bibhetyataḥ (27)

अब्धौ - in the ocean; मग्नस्य - submerged; अक्षाणि - senses; यथा - as; विह्वलानि - become confused i.e., are uncomfortable; तथा - similarly; अस्य - of the *asat vādin*; धीः- understanding; अखण्डैक रसम् श्रुत्वा - having heard of the non-dual absolute nature of the *Brahman*; निष्प्रचारा - is stunned; अतः - therefore; बिभेति - is afraid.

Just as the senses of a person submerged in the ocean become confused and non-functional, so also the understanding of the *asat vādin* gets confused having heard of the Absolute non-dual nature of the *Brahman*. Therefore, such a one is afraid. (27)

A reference to this effect is quoted *from Gauḍapādācārya...*

गौडाचार्या निर्विकल्पे समाधावन्ययोगिनाम् ।
साकारब्रह्मनिष्ठानामत्यन्तं भयमूचिरे ।।२८।।

Gauḍācārya nirvikalpe samādhāvanyayoginām
Sākārabrahmaniṣṭhānāmatyantaṁ bhayamūcire (28)

गौडाचार्या - *Gauḍapādācāryā*; निर्विकल्पे समाधौ - with regard to the thoughtless state of consciousness; साकार - with form; ब्रह्म निष्ठानाम् - believers of the consciousness with form; अन्य योगिनाम् - the other *yogi*-s; अत्यन्तम् - excessive; भयम् - fear; ऊचिरे - is said.

The *Ācārya Gauḍapāda* declares a great fear for the other types of *yogi*-s believing in the consciousness with form, with regard to the state of consciousness without thoughts. (28)

Quotation from *Gauḍapādācārya* is...

अस्पर्शयोगो नामैष दुर्दर्शस्सर्वयोगिभिः ।
योगिनो बिभ्यति ह्यस्मादभये भयदर्शिनः ।।२९।।

Asparśa yogo nāmaiṣa durdarśas-sarva-yogibhiḥ
Yogino bibhyati hy-asmād-abhaye bhaya darśinaḥ (29)

अस्पर्श योगो नाम - the oneness with the non-dual *Brahman*; **एषः** - this; **सर्व योगिभिः** - by all the *yogi*-s perceiving duality in *Brahman*; **दुर्दर्शः** - very difficult to conceive; **हि** - indeed; **योगिनः** - the *yogi*-s; **अभये** - in the fearless; **भय दर्शिनः** - the seer of fear; **अस्मात्** - from this (very thought of oneness with non-dual *Brahman*); **बिभ्यति** - are afraid.

The *yogi*-s established in the thought of duality in the *Brahman*, are afraid of the very thought of conceiving the oneness with the non-dual *Brahman*. Indeed, they see fear in the fearless! (29)

Similar view is accepted by *Śaṅkarācārya*...

भगवत्पूज्यपादाश्च शुष्कतर्कं पटूनमून् ।
आहुर्माध्यमिकान्भ्रान्तानचिन्त्येऽस्मिन् सदात्मनि ।।३०।।

Bhagavat pūjya pādāśca śuṣka tarka paṭūnamūn
Āhur mādhyamikān bhrāntān acintye'smin sadātmani (30)

भगवत् पूज्य पादाः- highly respected *Bhagavān Śaṅkarācārya*; **च** - and; **शुष्क तर्क पटूनमून्** - to the dry logic expert; **माध्यमिकान्** - the *mādhyamikā-s*; **अचिन्त्ये** - this unthinkable; **सदात्मनि** - self-existent; **भ्रान्तान्** - confused; **आहुः**- are called.

The most respected *Bhagavān Śaṅkarācārya* also declares these expert dry logicians (going contrary to Vedic thought) to be fully confused with regard to the Absolute, self-existing and unthinkable *Brahman*. (30)

The original quotation is given...

अनादृत्य श्रुतिं मौर्ख्यादिमे बौद्धास्तमस्विनः ।
आपेदिरे निरात्मत्वमनुमानैकचक्षुषः ।।३१।।

Anādṛtya śrutiṁ maurkhyād-ime bauddhās-tamasvinaḥ
Āpedire nirāt matvam anumānaika cakṣuṣaḥ (31)

अनादृत्य - disregarding; श्रुति - Veda-s; मौर्ख्यात् - foolishly; इमे - these; बौद्धाः- *Bauddha*-s; तमस्विनः- overpowered by *tamo guṇa*; आपेदिरे - understood; निरात्म त्वम् - non-existence; अनुमान एक चक्षुषः- believers of inferential knowledge as the highest.

These *Bauddha-s* overpowered by ignorance disregarding the Veda-s, taking refuge in the inferential knowledge to be the supreme, have attained an understanding of non-existence to be Existence. (31)

The error and the fallacy of 'nothingness' (*Asatvād*) is ...

शून्यमासीदितिब्रूषे सद्योगं वा सदात्मताम् ।
शून्यस्य न तु तद्युक्तमुभयं व्याहतत्वतः ।।३२।।

Śūnyam-āsīd iti brūṣe sadyogaṁ vā sadātmatām
Śūnyasya na tu tadyuktam ubhayaṁ vyāha-tatvataḥ (32)

शून्यम् आसीत् - nothing was; इति - thus; ब्रूषे - you said; सद् योगम् - with reference to *Sat* (Existence); वा - or; सदात्मताम् - the nothing is considered as Existence; तत् उभयम् - both these; शून्यस्य - of the nothingness; व्याहतत्वतः - being contradictory; न - not; तु - indeed; युक्तम् - correct.

When you (Buddhists) say that nothing existed, you have associated the nothing with existence or if you mean that nothing is of the nature of existence; both ways the nothing is denied. (32)

The denial of 'nothingness' is illustrated through an example....

न युक्तस्तमसा सूर्यो नापि चासौ तमोमयः ।
सच्छून्ययोर्विरोधित्वाच्छून्यमासीत्कथं वद ।।३३।।

Na yuktas-tamasā sūryo nāpi cāsau tamomayaḥ
Sac-chūnyayor-virodhi tvāt śūnyam āsīt-kathaṁ vada (33)

सूर्यः- Sun; तमसा - with darkness; न - not; युक्तः- is associated; न - not; अपि - also; च - and; असौ - this Sun; तमोमयः- of the nature of darkness; सत् शून्ययोः- of the 'existence' and 'nothing'; विरोधित्वात् - being opposed to each other; शून्यम् - nothing; आसीत् - was; कथं वद - can you say.

The Sun cannot be asociated with darkness nor can it be said to be of the nature of darkness. (similarly) The Existence and nothing being of opposite nature, how can you say nothing was? (33)

One may think that the presence of elements like space etc., is also contradicting the non-dual nature of the *Bṛahman*...

वियदादेर्नामरूपे मायया सुविकल्पिते ।
शून्यस्य नामरूपे च तथा चेज्जीव्यतां चिरम् ।।३४।।

Viyadāder nāmarūpe māyayā suvikalpite
Śūnyasya nāmarūpe ca tathā cet jīvyatāṁ ciram (34)

वियदादेः- of the space etc.; नाम रूपे - name and form; मायया - by the *māyā*; सुविकल्पिते - are imagined in *Brahman*; शून्यस्य - of the 'nothing'; नाम रूपे - name and form; च - also; तथा - similarly; चेत् - if; जीव्यताम् चिरम् - may you live long.

The names and forms of the elements like space etc., are imagined by *māyā* on the Non-dual *Brahman*. If you also say that the name and form of the 'nothing' is also superimposed on the 'Non-dual' *Brahman*, may you live long (i.e., you agree with our non-dual *Brahman*). (34)

If the name and form of the elements are superimposed on 'Existence', we may consider that the name and form of the *Sat* are also imagined?...

सतोऽपि नामरूपे द्वे कल्पिते चेत्तदा वद ।
कुत्रेति निरधिष्ठानो न भ्रमः क्वचिदीक्ष्यते ।।३५।।

Sato'pi nāma rūpe dve kalpite cet tadā vada
Kutreti niradhiṣ ṭhāno na bhramaḥ kvacit īkṣyate (35)

सतः- of the 'Existence'; अपि - also; नामरूपे - name and form; द्वे - both; कल्पिते - imagined; चेत् - if said so; तदा - then; वद - explain; कुत्रेति - where is; निरधिष्ठानो - without substratum; न - no; भ्रमः- illusion; क्वचित् ईक्ष्यते - can hardly be considered.

If the attributes of name and form of the Existence are also considered as imagined (like that of space etc..) then how can you explain? The answer is, can an illusion be considered by any one, without the substratum? i.e., it cannot be considered. (35)

Note:

(i) The name and form of Existence cannot be considered to be superimposed on Existence. In other words, the substratum and the superimposed are one

(ii) That nothing cannot be the substratum of Existence and the latter cannot be an illusion that can appear on the Nothing. Because, an illusion needs a substratum to appear.

(iii) Nor can the Existence be considered as a superimposition on the world which itself is the effect of delusion. Therefore, in the absence of any possible substratum, the names and the forms of the Existence cannot be imagined. In other words, the names and forms of the space etc. are illusion, but not that of Existence. Knowledge of the rope as rope is not an illusion. But calling the rope as snake is, illusion. Therefore, in this example, the name rope is not an illusion but calling the rope as 'snake' is an illusion

Let there be no misunderstanding regarding the duality in Non-dual Existence on account of names etc...

सदासीदिति शब्दार्थभेदे वैगुण्यमापतेत् ।
अभेदे पुनरुक्तिस्स्यान्मैवं लोके तथेक्षणात् ।।३६।।

Sadāsī diti śabdārtha bhede vai guṇya māpatet
Abhede punaruktiḥ syāt maivaṁ loke tathekṣaṇāt (36)

सत् आसीत् इति - 'Existence' was, thus; शब्दार्थ भेदे - if there is difference in the meaning of 'Existence' and 'was'; वैगुण्यम् - the possibility of duality; आपतेत् - arises; अभेदे - if there is no difference between the two; पुनरुक्तिः स्यात् - the error of repetition occurs; मा एवम् - do not think in this way; लोके - in the world, we always talk like this; तथेक्षणात् - is observed.

'The Existence was', in this sentence, if we take the meaning of 'Existence' and 'was' as separate, then the possibility of duality comes up. If we understand that these two words have the same meaning, then the error of repetition takes place. Don't think to arrive at wrong conclusions. For, we see such ways of expression in the world. (36)

In the normal way of taking, we come across many more words with the same meaning in use, as shown in the following *śloka*...

कर्तव्यं कुरुते वाक्यं ब्रूते धार्यस्य धारणम् ।
इत्यादिवासनाविष्टं प्रत्यासीत्सदितीरणम् ।।३७।।

Kartavyaṁ kurute vākyaṁ brūte dhāryasya dhāraṇam
Ityādi vāsanā viṣṭaṁ pratyā sītsadi tīraṇam (37)

कर्तव्यम् कुरुते - action is done; वाक्यम् ब्रूते - speech is spoken; धार्यस्य धारणम् - the burden is borne; इत्यादि - etc; वासनाविष्टम् - those who are accustomed to use the words in anticipation; प्रति - for them; आसीत् सत् - 'Existence was'; इतीरणम् - is spoken.

We use the terms like 'the worthy action is done', 'the speech was spoken', 'the burden is borne', etc.. Those who are accustomed to use the terms in anticipation of the event, for them, 'The Existence was' is spoken. (37)

In the Vedic statement 'before the creation etc..' one may think the existence of time. This will lead to the possibility of duality in non-dual *Brahman* with reference to time.

To avoid such a doubt...

कालाभावे पुरेत्युक्तिः कालवासनया युतम् ।
शिष्यं प्रत्येव तेनात्र द्वितीयं न हि शंक्यते ।।३८।।

Kālābhāve pure tyuktiḥ kāla vāsanayā yutam
Śiṣyaṁ pratyeva tenātra dvitīyaṁ na hi śaṁkyate (38)

काल अभावे - although there is no 'time'; पुरा - before; इति उक्तिः- thus having said; काल वासनया युतम् - accustomed to the understanding with reference to time; शिष्यम् प्रति एवम् - for such a student alone; तेन अत्र - by such a statement in this case; द्वितीयम् - the duality; न हि शंक्यते - should not be suspected.

Although there is nothing like 'time' (in the statement before creation), the time is mentioned because the student is accustomed to understand with reference to time alone. Because of this, one should not suspect the reference of duality in the Vedic statement (before creation...) (38)

Thus the posibility of duality with reference to time is not established...

चोद्यं वा परिहारो वा क्रियतां द्वैतभाषया ।
अद्वैतभाषया चोद्यं नास्ति नापि तदुत्तरम् ।।३९।।

Codyaṁ vā parihāro vā kriyatāṁ dvaita bhāṣayā
Advaita bhāṣayā codyaṁ nāsti nāpi taduttaram (39)

चोद्यम् वा परिहारो वा - the question and its answer; द्वैत भाषया - in the language of duality; क्रियताम् - may be possibly done; अद्वैत भाषया - in the language of non-duality; चोम् नास्ति - there is no question; न अपि तद उत्तरम् - nor there is an answer to it.

From the view of the language of duality, there is a possibility of question and its answer. From the Absolute non-dual stand point, neither question nor an answer is ever possible. (39)

From the Absolute stand point, there is no duality. This is quoted from the scriptures...

तदा स्तिमितगम्भीरं न तेजो न तमस्ततम् ।
अनाख्यमनभिव्यक्तं सत्किञ्चिदवशिष्यते ।।४०।।

Tadā stimita gambhīraṁ na tejo na tamastatam
Anākhya manabhi vyaktaṁ sat kiñcit avaśiṣyate (40)

तदा - then (before creation) or an attainment of non-dual being; स्तिमित गम्भीरम् - absolute deep silence; न तेजो - neither light; न तमस्ततम् - nor there is darkness; अनाख्यम् - without name; अनभिव्यक्तम् - beyond the grasp of speech; सत् किञ्चित् - only 'Existence'; अवशिष्यते - remains.

Before creation or after the end of duality, there is neither light nor darkness. What remains is Absolute Existence without any name or description. (40)

In the above descriptions, the reference of time as a possible point of creating duality is raised to establish non-dual *Brahman* and not for discussing the time.

Now a doubt is raised with reference to the creation and space. One is able to understand the destruction of all other elements but.... **how can we understand that the space is unreal as it cannot be destroyed?...**

ननु भूम्यादिकं मा भूत्परमाण्वन्तनाशतः ।
कथं ते वियतोऽसत्त्वं बुद्धिमारोहतीति चेत् ।।४१।।

Nanu bhūmyā dikaṁ mā bhūt paramāṇ vanta nāśataḥ
Kathaṁ te viyato'Sattvaṁ buddhimā rohatīti cet (41)

ननु - a doubt is raised; भूमि आदिकम् - the elements like earth etc.; मा भूत् - may not be '*Sat*'; परमाण्वन्त नाशतः - being able to be destroyed upto sub-atomic level; वियत् - of the space; असत्त्वम् - non-existence; ते बुद्धिम् - your understanding; कथम् - how; आरोहति - taken place; इति चेत् - if we raise a doubt like this.

If we say that the earth and other elements can be understood to be non-existent, as they are destroyed up to a sub-atomic level, how can you accept the understanding that the space is non-existent? (41)

The above doubt is cleared...

अत्यन्तं निर्जगद्व्योम यथा ते बुद्धिमाश्रितम् ।
तथैव सन्निराकाशं कुतो नाश्रयते मतिम् ।।४२।।

Atyantaṁ nirjagad vyoma yathā te buddhi māśritam
Tathaiva sannirākāśaṁ kuto nāśrayate matim (42)

यथा - as; अत्यन्तम् - absolutley; निः जगत् - worldless; व्योम - space; ते बुद्धिम् - your intellect; आश्रितम् - can grasp; तथा एव - similarly; निराकाशम् - spaceless; सत् - 'existence'; मतिम् - intellect; कुतः- why; न आश्रयते - should not grasp.

If one is able to grasp the space without the reference to the world, why is one unable to grasp the 'Existence' without space, i.e., it is possible to understand the Existence. (42)

The view of the '*Nayyāyikā-s*' is refuted on this topic...

निर्जगद्व्योम दृष्टं चेत्प्रकाशतमसी विना ।
क्व दृष्टं किञ्च ते पक्षे न प्रत्यक्षं वियत्खलु ।।४३।।

Nirjagad vyoma dṛṣṭaṁ cet prakāśa tamasī vinā
Kva dṛṣṭaṁ kiñca te pakṣe na pratyakṣaṁ viyat khalu (43)

निः जगत् - worldless; व्योम - space; दृष्टम् - seen; चेत् - if; प्रकाश तमसी - light and darkness; विना - without; क्व - where; दृष्टम् - seen; किम् - moreover; च - and; ते पक्षे - in your philosophy; वियत् - space; खलु - indeed; न प्रत्यक्षम् - not directly perceptible.

If one argues that he has seen the space without the world and its contents, and in the absence of light and darkness, where did you see the world? And moreover, according to your (*Nayyāyikā-s*) opinion, the space is not an object of perception.(43)

From above logic, yet another doubt comes up. As the non-existent space can be seen, so also the 'Existence' that is perceived is also non-existent.

To remove such wrong thinking...

सद्वस्तु शुद्धन्त्वस्माभिर्निश्चित्तैरनुभूयते ।
तूष्णीं स्थितौ न शून्यत्वं शून्यबुद्धेश्च वर्जनात् ।।४४।।

Sadvastu śuddhan tvasmābhiḥ niścittair anubhūyate
Tūṣṇīṁ sthitau na śūnyatvaṁ śūnya buddheśca varjanāt (44)

शुद्धम् - pure; सत् वस्तु - the 'Existence'; तु - indeed; निश्चितैः- certainly; अस्माभिः- by us; अनुभूयते - is experienced; तूष्णीम् स्थितौ - in the absence; शून्यत्वम् - the nothingness; न - not; शून्यबुद्धेः- perception of nothingness; च - and; वर्जनात् - in the absence of a perceiver.

The Absolute Existence, (without the reference of the world) is certainly experienced by us (even) in the absence of mental thoughts etc.. We do not experience our absence, because there is no thought to experience in the nothingness. (44)

What is meant here is that, for the perception of anything other than our Self, thought process is essential. But for knowing one's Self, no thoughts are required nor are they possible.

How?...

सद्बुद्धिरपि चेन्नास्ति माऽस्त्वस्य स्वप्रभत्वतः ।
निर्मनस्कत्वसाक्षित्वात्सन्मात्रं सुगमं नृणाम् ।।४५।।

Sad buddhi rapi cennāsti mā'stvasya sva prabhat vataḥ
Nirmanaskatva sākṣi tvāt san mātraṁ sugamaṁ nṛṇām (45)

सद् बुद्धि - the thought perception; अपि न अस्ति - if not seen; चेत् - if; मा अस्तु - let it not be; अस्य - of the 'Existence'; स्वप्रभत्वतः- Self illumined; निर्मनस्कत्व - thoughtlessness; साक्षित्वात् - being witness, सत् मात्रम् - the pure existence; नृणाम् - for the people; सुगमम् - easy.

If you object that the Existence cannot be perceived by thought, we say, let it be so. Because the Existence being self illumined and being the witness of the thoughtlessness, the Pure Existence is easily grasped by man (in the absence of any mentations). (45)

The same-ness of the witness and the Existence is indicated in the absence of the thoughts and the world respectively...

मनोजृम्भणराहित्ये यथा साक्षी निराकुलः ।
मायाजृम्भणतः पूर्वं सत्तथैव निराकुलम् ।।४६।।

Mano jṛmbhaṇa rāhitye yathā sākṣī nirākulaḥ
Māyā jṛmbhaṇataḥ pūrvaṁ sattathaiva nirākulam (46)

मनो जृम्भण राहित्ये - in the absence of mentations; यथा - as; साक्षी - witness; निराकुलः- uninfluenced; माया जृम्भणतः पूर्वम् - before the wake of *māyā*; सत् - 'Existence'; तथा एव - similarly; निराकुलः - without modification.

As the witness is uninfluenced in the absence of mentations, so also , the Existence is without any modification before the wake of *māyā*. (46)

The concept of *māyā* is introduced in the *Vedānta* for the easier perception of the Truth, the characteristics of which are...

निस्तत्वा कार्यगम्यास्य शक्तिर्मायाऽग्निशक्तिवत् ।
न हि शक्तिः क्वचित्कैश्चिद्बुध्यते कार्यतः पुरा ।।४७।।

Nistatvā kārya gamyāsya śaktir māya'gni śaktivat
Na hi śaktiḥ kvacit kaiścit budhyate kāryataḥ purā (47)

निस्तत्वा - non-existent and illusory; कार्यगम्या - inferred from the effects; अस्य शक्तिः माया - power of the Existence called *māyā*; अग्नि शक्तिवत् - like the power of fire; शक्तिः - power; कैश्चित् - by any one; क्वचित् - any where; कार्यतः पुरा - before effect; न हि बुध्यते - is not known.

The non-existent illusory power of the Existence called *māyā* and inferred from the effects it produces is like, the burning power of fire. The power of any one or any thing cannot be known before its effects. (47)

The nature of this *māyā* is discussed...

न सद्वस्तु सतः शक्तिर्नहि वह्नेः स्वशक्तिता ।
सद्विलक्षणतायां तु शक्तेः किं तत्त्वमुच्यताम् ।।४८।।

Na sadvastu Sataḥ śaktiḥ na hi vahneḥ svaśaktitā
Sadvilakṣaṇa tāyāṁ tu śakteḥ kiṁ tattva mucyatām (48)

सद् वस्तु - the Existence; सतः शक्तिः न - is not of the nature of its power, the *māyā*; हि वह्नेः स्वशक्तिता न - as fire is not of the nature of its power; सत् विलक्षणतायाम् - if the power of *māyā* is different from the Existence; तु - indeed; शक्तेः- of the power; किम् तत्त्वम् - what is its nature?; उच्यताम् - please say.

The Existence is not of the nature of *māyā*, as fire is not its burning power. In that case, if the power of *māyā* is different than the existence, what is its nature? (48)

From the above it is implied that the *māyā* is not of the nature of Existence. Do we mean that its nature is non-existence like the horn of a hare? Or do we mean that it is of the nature of the snake on the rope i.e., an illusion?

That is being discussed...

शून्यत्वमिति चेच्छून्यं मायाकार्यमितीरितम् ।
न शून्यं नापि सद्यादृक्तादृक्त्वमिहेष्यताम् ।।४९।।

Śūnyatva miti cet śūnyaṁ māyā kārya mitīritam
Na śūnyaṁ nāpi sadyādṛk tādṛktva miheṣyatām (49)

शून्यत्वम् - the *māyā* is absolutely non-existent like son of a barren woman; इति चेत् - if we say so; शून्यं माया कार्यम् ईरितम् - the nothingness is the effect of *māyā*, so we said earlier (in the 34th *śloka*); शून्यं न अपि सत् - therefore the *māyā* is neither non-existent nor existent; यादृक् तादृक्त्वम् - in this way (indescribable) is the nature of *māyā*; इह इष्यताम् - is accepted in (*Vedānta*).

If we say that *māyā* is absolutely non-existent (like the son of a barren woman), it cannot be so for, we have already said in the earlier *śloka* 34, that the nothingness is the effect of *māyā* (therefore the *māyā* cannot be called as non-existent). Therefore, the *māyā* is said to be of the nature of that which cannot be called as existing nor can it be called as non-existing. This indescribable nature of *māyā* is accepted in *Vedānta*. (49)

The teacher quotes *Nāsadīya Sūkta* of *Ṛg* Veda 10.129.1...

नाऽसदासीन्नो सदासीत्तदानीं किंत्वभूत्तमः ।
सद्योगात्तमसः सत्त्वं न स्वतस्तन्निषेधनात् ।।५०।।

Nā'sadā sinno sadāsit tadānim kim tvabhūttamaḥ
Sadyogā ttamasaḥ sattvam na svatasta nniṣe dhanāt (50)

तदानीम् न असत् आसीत् न सत् - that time (i.e., before creation), neither there was 'nothing' nor was there 'Existence'; किन्तु - but; तमः अभूत् - darkness was (i.e. *māyā*); सत् योगात् - in association with existence; तमसः सत्त्वम् - there was existence of darkness; न स्वतः - not of its own; तत् निषेधनात् - the *māyā* did not have its own independent existence (so is said by the *śruti*).

The *'Nāsadīya Sūkta'* tells us that there was neither nothing nor anything before creation. But there was darkness (i.e. *māyā*). This *māyā* had its existence only on account of its association with the Existence, and not of its own, because the *śruti* quoted above denies its existence (50)

To conclude the non-validity of duality in Absolute Existence on account of *māyā*, the teacher says...

अत एव द्वितीयत्वं शून्यवन्न हि गण्यते ।
न लोके चैत्रतच्छक्त्योर्जीवितं लिख्यते पृथक् ।।५१।।

Ata eva dvitīyatvam śūnya vanna hi gaṇyate
Na loke caitra tat śaktyor jīvitam likhyate pṛthak (51)

अत एव - therefore; शून्यवत् - like the 'nothing'; द्वितीयत्वम् - duality; न गण्यते - is not accepted; हि लोके - in the world; चैत्र - spring; तत् शक्त्योः- the manifestation of its powers; जीवितम् - life; पृथक् - separately; न लिख्यते - is not written.

Therefore, with reference to *māyā*, there cannot be duality in the Absolute Existence, as nothingness is opposed to somethingness. It is seen in the world that the spring and its powers are not described separately while referring to spring. (51)

The possibility of duality due to māyā is negated.

Due to one's inability to perceive the non-existence of *māyā* as an independent entity, a doubt is raised further...

शक्त्याधिक्ये जीवितं चेद्वर्धते तत्र वृद्धिकृत् ।
न शक्तिः किंतु तत्कार्यं युद्धकृष्यादिकं तथा ।।५२।।

Śaktyā dhikye jīvitaṁ cet vardhate tatra vṛddhi kṛt
Na śaktiḥ kiṁ tu tat kāryaṁ yuddha kṛṣyā dikaṁ tathā (52)

शक्ति आधिक्ये - by the increase in power; वर्धते - the life grows or is prolonged; चेत् - if argued; तत्र - in this; वृद्धिकृत् - the prolongator of life; न शक्तिः - the power is not; किन्तु - but; तत् कार्यम् - its effects; युद्ध - war; कृषि आदिकम् - agriculture etc.; तथा - similarly.

If one argues that with the increase in power, the life is prolonged, it is not so. The prolongation of life is not due to the power but its effect, as is seen in the case of the power of war, agriculture etc., are not reponsible for the life style but their effects. (52)

Thus the duality due to *māyā* is negated. However, one still can object that the effects of *māyā* are creating the duality in '*Sat*'...

This is answered...

सर्वथा शक्तिमात्रस्य न पृथग्गणना क्वचित् ।
शक्तिकार्यं तु नैवास्ति द्वितीयं शङ्क्यते कथम् ।।५३।।

Sarvathā śakti mātrasya na pṛthak gaṇanā kvacit
Śakti kāryaṁ tu naivāsti dvitīyaṁ śaṅkyate katham (53)

क्वचित् - any where; शक्तिमात्रस्य - of the power alone; पृथक् - separate; गणना - accounted; सर्वथा न - is never made; शक्तिकार्यम् - the effect of *māyā* power; तु न एव अस्ति - was not there (before creation); द्वितीयम् - duality; कथम् - how; शङ्क्यते - is doubted to be?

Anywhere the power is not counted separately (without its effects). More so, before the creation, there was no effect of *māyā* i.e., the world. Therefore, how can there be a possibility of duality on account of the world (i.e., the effect of *māyā*)? (53)

Thus far, the teacher has removed the possibility of duality on account of *māyā* and its effect - the world - in Absolute Existence.

The *māyā* and its operation is now discussed...

न कृत्स्नब्रह्मावृत्तिः सा शक्तिः किंत्वेकदेशभाक् ।
घटशक्तिर्यथा भूमौ स्निग्धमृद्येव वर्तते ।।५४।।

Na kṛtsna brahmā vṛttiḥ sā śaktiḥ kiṁ tveka deśa bhāk
Ghaṭa śaktir yathā bhūmau snigdha mṛdyeva vartate (54)

न - not; कृत्स्न ब्रह्म आवृत्तिः- pervading the *Brahman* totally; सा - that; शक्ति - *māyā*; किन्तु - but; एक देश भाक् - localised in a part; यथा - as; घट शक्तिः- power of turning into pot; भूमौ - in the earth; स्निग्ध मृदि - in soft wet mud; एव - alone; वर्तते - exists.

The *māyā śakti* does not occupy the whole of *Brahman*, but is localised in a part of the *Brahman* as the power to get modified into a pot which exists in smooth and wet earth only (not in the total earth). (54)

The teacher quotes the *Puruṣa Sūktam* as authority for this...

पादोऽस्य सर्वा भूतानि त्रिपादस्ति स्वयंप्रभः ।
इत्येकदेशवृत्तित्वं मायया वदति श्रुतिः ।।५५।।

Pādo'sya sarvā bhūtāni tripādasti svayaṁ prabhaḥ
Ityeka deśa vṛttitvaṁ māyayā vadati śrutiḥ (55)

सर्वा भूतानि - all the things and beings; अस्य - of the *Brahman*; पादः- are in a quarter; त्रिपाद् अस्ति - the remaining three quarters are; स्वयं प्रभः- in their original self effulgence; श्रुतिः- scripture; मायया - of the *māyā*; इति एक देश वृत्तित्वम् - localised pervasiveness; वदति - says.

The *Puruṣa Sūktam* declares that the things and beings are in a quarter of the *Brahman* and the three quarters of it remains in its effulgent glory. Thus the scripture also talks about the localised existence of *māyā* in *Brahman*. (55)

The Bhagavad *Gītā* also supports this view:

विष्टभ्याहमिदं कृत्स्नमेकांशेन स्थितो जगत् ।
इति कृष्णोऽर्जुनायाह जगतस्त्वेकदेशताम् ।।५६।।

Viṣta bhyāham idaṁ kṛtsnam ekāṁśena sthito jagat
Iti kṛṣṇo'rju nāyāha jagata stveka deśatām (56)

अहम् - I; इदम् कृत्स्नम् जगत् - this total world; एकांशेन - by a part; विष्टभ्यः - having supported; स्थितः- remain; इति - thus; कृष्णः- *Kṛṣṇa*; अर्जुनाय - to Arjuna; जगतः- of the world; तु - indeed; एक देशताम् - localised existence; आह - said.

I (Lord *Kṛṣṇa*), support the total world by a part of mine, and remain untouched, thus said Lord *Kṛṣṇa* to Arjuna, the localised presence of the world in Him. (56)

The *Brahman* is without *māyā* and any modification born out it. The scripture is quoted in this regard...

स भूमिं विश्वतो वृत्वाऽत्यतिष्ठदशाङ्गुलम् ।
विकारावर्ति चात्रास्ति श्रुतिसूत्रकृतोर्वचः ।।५७।।

Sa bhūmiṁ viśvato vṛtvā atyatiṣṭha daśāṅgulam
Vikārāvarti cātrāsti śruti sūtra kṛtor vacaḥ (57)

सः- He (the Lord); भूमिम् - to the world; विश्वतो वृत्वा - from all sides; हि - indeed; दशाङ्गुलम् - ten fingers; अत्यतिष्ठः - goes beyond; विकारावर्ति - without any modifications; च - and; अत्र - is here; अस्ति श्रुति सूत्र कृतोर्वचः- are the words of Veda *Vyāsa*, the composer of *Vedā-s* and Brahma *sūtra.*

Bhagavān Veda Vyāsa, the compiler of *Veda-s* and *Brahmasūtra-s*, also declare that the Lord (*Brahman*) is pervading the whole world, and exists beyond it by ten fingers (i.e., crosses the limit of the manifested world) and yet remains without any modifications. (57)

If the *Brahman* is without any parts, how come the scriptures declare that the *māyā* is in a part of the Absolute. Because, there cannot be a relative in the Absolute.

To answer to this objection...

निरंशेऽप्यंशमारोप्य कृत्स्नेंशे वेति पृच्छतः ।
तद्भाषयोत्तरं ब्रूते श्रुतिः श्रोतृहितैषिणी ।।५८।।

Niraṁśe'pyaṁśa māropya kṛtsneṁśe veti pṛcchataḥ
Tad bhāṣayo ttaraṁ brūte śrutiḥ śrotṛ hitaiṣiṇī (58)

निरंशे अपि - although without part; अंशम् आरोप्य - superimposing parts; कृत्स्ने - in the total; वा अंशे - or in a part; इति पृच्छतः - thus asking; तद् भाषया - in the same language; उत्तरम् - reply; ब्रूते - said; श्रुतिः- scripture; श्रोतृ हितैषिणी - the doer of good to the listener student.

Although without any parts, when one superimposes parts on the *Brahman* and thus asks, if the *māyā* is on the total *Brahman* or in the part thereof, the scripture, the well wisher of the student, speaks in the same language. (Thus the scriptures do not consider the presence of parts in the Absolute *Brahman*). (58)

The purpose for which the superimposition of *māyā* on *Brahman* is imagined is discussed along with a simile...

सत्तत्त्वमाश्रिता शक्तिः कल्पयेत्सति विक्रियाः ।
वर्णा भित्तिगता भित्तौ चित्रं नानाविधं तथा ।।५९।।

Sattattva māśritā śaktiḥ kalpayet sati vikriyāḥ
Varṇā bhitti gatā bhittau citraṁ nānā vidhaṁ tathā (59)

सत्तत्त्वम् आश्रिता - depending on the absolute Existence i.e.,*Sat*; शक्तिः - *māyā*; सति - in the *Sat*; विक्रियाः- modifications; कल्पयेत् - imagines/ superimposes; वर्णाः- colours; भित्ति गता - having coated the wall; भित्तौ - on the wall; चित्रम् - pictures; नाना विधम् - many types; यथा - as.

As the colour coatings supported by the wall create many types of figures on the wall, (which are illusory and in turn cover the wall itself), so also the *māyā* superimposed on the *Brahman* creates many types of figures and names (as an illusion and thereby covers the *Brahman* supporting the *māyā*). (59)

The multitude of creation is illusory, thus having proved, the teacher now explains the first modification superimposed on the *Sat*...

आद्यो विकार आकाशः सोऽवकाशस्वरूपवान् ।
आकाशोऽस्तीति सत्तत्त्वमाकाशेऽप्यनु गच्छति ।।६०।।

Ādyo vikāra ākāśaḥ so'va kāśa svarū pavān
Ākāśo'stīti Sattattvam ākāśe'pyanu gacchati (60)

आद्यः- first; विकारः- modification; आकाशः- space; सः- it; अवकाश स्वरूपवान् - being of the nature of emptiness; आकाशः- space; अस्ति - is; इति सत् तत्त्वम् - thus is presence of *'Sat'*; आकाशे - in the space; अपि - also; अनुगच्छति - is accompanied with.

The first modification imagined by *māyā* on *Sat* is Space. The ability to give room to everything is its nature. When we say that 'The space is', the *Sat* (Existence) is associated with the space. (60)

The purpose to establish that the space is the effect of *Sat*, is illustrated here as under...

एकस्वभावं सत्तत्त्वम् आकाशो द्विस्वभावकः ।
नावकाशः सति व्योम्नि स चैषोऽपि द्वयं स्थितम् ।।६१।।

Eka svabhāvaṁ sattatvam ākāśo dvi svabhāvakaḥ
Nāva kāśaḥ Sati vyomni sa caiṣo'pi dvayaṁ sthitam

सत् तत्त्वम् - the Pure Existence (*Sat*); एक स्वभावम् - has only one attribute; आकाशः- space; द्वि स्वभावकः- has two attributes; अवकाशः- emptiness; न - not; सति - in *Brahman*; व्योम्नि - in the space; स - the Existence is; च एष अपि - this (space) also; द्वयम् - both; स्थितम् - are;

The nature of *Brahman* is Existence only. There is no space in the *Brahman*. But in space, the Existence and the space are both present. (61)

The single aspect and the double aspect of the *Brahman* and space is given below...

यद्वा प्रतिध्वनिर्व्योम्नो गुणो नासौ सतीक्ष्यते ।
व्योम्नि द्वौ सद्ध्वनि तेन सदेकं द्विगुणं वियत् ।।६२।।

Yadvā prati dhvanir vyomno guṇo nāsau Satī kṣyate
Vyomni dvau sad dhvani tena sadekaṁ dviguṇaṁ viyat (62)

यद्वा - or; प्रतिध्वनिः- echo sound; व्योम्नः- of the space; गुणाः- quality; असौ - this; सति - in the *Sat*; न - not; ईक्ष्यते - seen; व्योम्नि - in the space; द्वौ - both; सत् ध्वनि - existence and sound; तेन - therefore; सत् - *Sat*; एकम् - one; वियत् - space; द्विगुणम् - with two attributes.

Yet another observation is that echo sound is the quality of space. This quality is not seen in the *Sat*. But in the space, both 'Existence and sound' are seen. Therefore, *Sat* is only Existence and the space is with two qualities. (62)

If the space is the effect of Existence (*Brahman*), then one should be able to perceive the Existence with space. But our perception is other way round i.e., we perceive 'space is'.

How come such a thing happens?...

या शक्तिः कल्पयेद्व्योम सा सद्व्योम्नोरभिन्नताम् ।
आपाद्य धर्मधर्मित्वं व्यत्ययेनावकल्पयेत् ।।६३।।

Yā śaktiḥ kalpayed vyoma sā sadvyomnora bhinnatām
Āpādya dharma dharmitvaṁ vyatya yenāva kalpayet (63)

या शक्तिः- that power (*māyā*); कल्पयेत् - superimposes; व्योम - space; सा - that; सद् व्योम्नोः- of the Existence and space; अभिन्नताम् - oneness; आपाद्य - having given rise to; धर्म - attribute; धर्मित्वम् - the substance; व्यत्ययेन - other way round, i.e., exchanging their positions; अवकल्पयेत् - erroneous perception.

The power (*māyā*) that superimposes space on the *Brahman* creates an illusion of exchange of positions of the substance and the attributes; and establishes oneness in them. In this way, giving rise to erroneous perception (63)

How this error of perception is seen in the world...

सतो व्योमत्वमापन्नं व्योम्नः सत्तां तु लौकिकाः ।
तार्किकाश्चावगच्छन्ति मायाया उचितं हि तत् ।।६४।।

Sato vyomatva māpannaṁ vyomnaḥ sattāṁ tu laukikāḥ
Tārkikā ścāva gacchanti māyayā ucitaṁ hi tat (64)

सतः- the *Sat*; व्योमत्वम् - spaceness; आपन्नम् - is attained; तु - indeed; लौकिकाः- worldly; तार्किकाः- logicians; च - and; सत्ताम् - of the existence; व्योम्नः- of the space; अवगच्छन्ति - understand; तत् - that perception; मायायाः- of the *māyā*; उचितम् - correct; हि - indeed.

The *Sat* has attained and appears as space, but the worldly (i.e., those who lack the spiritual way of perception) people and logicians understand that the Existence is the property of space. Such erroneous perception is expected of the effect of *māyā*. (64)

The trick of *māyā* in our regular life is also seen...

यद्यथा वर्तते तस्य तथात्वं भाति मानतः ।
अन्यथात्वं भ्रमेणेति न्यायोऽयं सार्वलौकिकः ।।६५।।

Yadyathā vartate tasya tathātvaṁ bhāti mānataḥ
Anyathātvaṁ bhrameṇeti nyāyo'yaṁ sārva laukikaḥ (65)

यत् - any object; यथा - as; वर्तते - is; तस्य - its; तथात्वम् - correct perception; मानतः- by proper means of knowledge; भाति - is gained; अन्यथात्वम् - of the opposite perception; भ्रमेण - because of delusion; इति - thus; अयं न्यायः- this logic; सार्वलौकिकः- is seen everywhere.

The correct perception of an object is gained by proper means of knowledge. The opposite perception is the result of delusion, and this is seen everywhere in the world. (65)

Having understood that the erroneous perception is the result of delusion and wrong means of knowledge, how to get rid of this wrong perception?...

एवं श्रुतिविचारात् प्राग्यथा यद्वस्तु भासते ।
विचारेण विपर्येति ततस्तच्चिन्त्यतां वियत् ।।६६।।

Evaṁ śruti vicārāt prāg yathā yadvastu bhāSate
Vicāreṇa viparyeti tatas taccintyatāṁ viyat (66)

एवम् - in this way; श्रुति - the statement of the scripture; विचारात् प्राक् -before enquiry; यद् वस्तु - the *Brahman*; यथा - as; भासते - grasped; तत् - that perception of *Brahman*; विचारेण - by proper enquiry; विपर्येति - understood in a different way; ततः- therefore; वियत् - space; चिन्त्यताम् - should be enquired.

In this way, when one enquires the meaning of the scriptural statement, the meaning grasped before enquiry, changes to correct perception of the object i.e., here space and *Brahman*.(66)

Therefore, one should enquire about the nature of the space...

भिन्ने वियत्सती शब्दभेदाद्बुद्धेश्च भेदतः ।
वाय्वादिष्वनुवृत्तं सन्नतु व्योमेति भेदधीः ।।६७।।

Bhinne viyatSatī śabda bhedād buddheśca bhedataḥ
Vayvādi ṣvanuvṛttaṁ Sat na tu vyometi bhedadhīḥ (67)

भिन्ने वियत्सती - the space and *Sat* are different; शब्द भेदात् - the word 'space' and the word 'exists' being different; बुद्धेः- of the understanding;च - and; भेदतः- is different; वायु आदिषु - in the air etc.; सत् - *Sat*; अनुवृत्तम् - is associated; व्योम - space; तु - indeed; न - not; इति - thus; भेद धीः- it is called as discrimination.

By the word 'space' and the word 'Existence', two different understandings take place in our knowledge; therefore, the space and Existence are different. The Existence is associated with other elements like air etc., but the space is not associated with them. This is called as discrimination between the element space and the Existence. (67)

This discrimination between the space and the Existence will lead to the understanding of the nature of the space as illusion and the substratum, Existence - remains as it is...

Continuing further...

सद्वस्त्वधिकवृत्तित्वाद्धर्मि व्योम्नस्तु धर्मता ।
धिया सतः पृथक्कारे ब्रूहि व्योम किमात्मकं ।।६८।।

Sadvas tvadhika vṛttitvāt dharmi vyomnastu dharmatā
Dhiyā Sataḥ pṛthakkāre brūhi vyoma kimātmakaṁ (68)

सद् वस्तु - existence; अधिक वृत्तित्वात् - being more pervasive;धर्मि - substratum; व्योम्नः- of the space; तु धर्मता - indeed superimposition of quality; धिया सतः - by proper discrimination of *'Sat'*; पृथक् कारे - having separated; व्योम - space; किम् आत्मकम् - what is its nature; ब्रूहि - tell.

The Existence being associated with all the elements is more pervasive and is the substratum for the superimposition of space. When one separates the existence from the space by proper discrimination (as indicated in the above *śloka*), what will be the nature of the space i.e., the space does not have its own independent existence and hence is an appearence on the Pure Existence. (68)

The conclusion of the last *śloka* is that the space cannot be described as existing, being an illusion. However, one can still argue that its existence is possible.

This fallacy is raised and cleared...

अवकाशात्मकं तच्चेदसत्तदिति चिन्त्यताम् ।
भिन्नं सतोऽसच्च नेति वक्षि चेद् व्याहतिस्तव ।।६९।।

Avakāśā tmakaṁ tat cet aSattaditi cintyatām
Bhinnaṁ Sato'sacca neti vakṣi ced vyāhati stava (69)

तत् - the space; अवकाश आत्मकम् - is of the nature of emptiness; चेत् - if said; तत् असत् - the space is an illusion being other than existence; इति - thus; चिन्त्यताम् - enquire and be firm on this thought; सतः भिन्नम् - the space is different than the existence (i.e. non-existence); असत् च न - and also not non-existent; इति - thus; वक्षि चेत् - if you assert then; व्याहतिस्तव - you are contradicting your own words.

If one argues that the space can be described as being of roomy nature and other than existence, then it will be non-existent.This is the right way of discrimination. If you insist that the space is other than the existence and also not not-existent, then you are contradicting your own thoughts and words. (69)

Yet another doubt is raised! If the space is non-existent being other than the existence, one should not be able to perceive, but our experience is that we know the space.

How can a non-existent thing be perceived?...

भातीति चेद्भातु नाम भूषणं मायिकस्य तत् ।
यदसद्भासमानं तन्मिथ्या स्वप्नगजादिवत् ।।७०।।

Bhātīti cet bhātu nāma bhūṣaṇaṁ māyikasya tat
Yadasad bhāsa mānaṁ tat mithyā svapna gajādi vat (70)

भाति इति चेत् - the space is perceived, hence it is not unreal; भातु नाम - may it be perceived; तत् - that; मायिकस्य भूषणम् - is the glory of an illusory object; यद् असत् - that non-existent; भासमानम् - yet being perceived; तत् मिथ्या - that is illusion; स्वप्न गजादिवत् - like the elephant in a dream.

If one argues that the space is perceived, hence it cannot be unreal, the answer is that let it be seen. It is a glory of illusion. The illusion is the perception of the non-existing thing, like the elephant in a dream seems to be real, but it is not! (70)

It is impossible to separate the substratum and the illusion on it. Then how can one discriminate between the space - the illusion and the Existence - the substratum?... The illusion and the substratum appear simultaneously.

How do we proceed in this regard?...

जातिव्यक्ती देहिदेहौ गुणद्रव्ये यथा पृथक् ।
वियत्सतोस्तथैवास्तु पार्थक्यं कोऽत्र विस्मयः ।।७१।।

Jāti vyaktī dehi dehau guṇa dravye yathā pṛthak
Viyat sato stathai vāstu pārthakyaṁ ko'tra vismayaḥ (71)

जाति व्यक्ती - the species and the specimen; देहि देहौ - the embodied and the body; गुण द्रव्ये - the quality and the substance; यथा - as; तथा - similarly; वियत् सतोः- of the space and the Existence; पार्थक्यम् - discrimination; एव अस्तु - be understood; अत्र - in this case; कः विस्मयः - why there is difficulty.

As the species and the specimen, the quality and the substance, and the embodied and the body, although being different are peceived simultaneously and yet discriminated without any difficulty, why there should be any difficulty in discriminating the space from the Existence? i.e., there is no difficulty. (71)

Although one may get the intellectual knowledge but one is not able to get into the conviction about this discrimination.

What is the cause for this and what is its remedy?...

बुद्धोऽपि भेदो नो चित्ते निरूढिं याति चेत्तदा ।
अनैकाग्र्यात्संशयाद्वा रूढ्यभावोऽस्य ते वद ।।७२।।

Buddho'pi bhedo no citte nirūḍhiṁ yāti cettadā
Anaikāgryāt saṁśayād vā rūḍhya bhāvo'sya te vada (72)

भेदः बुद्धः अपि - although the discrimination is intellectually grasped; चित्ते निरूढिं नो याति - one is not convinced in his understanding; चेत् तदा - if this is so; अस्य - of this discrimination; रूढ्यभाव - lack of conviction; ते अनैकाग्र्यात् - on account of inability to be single pointed; संशयाद् वा - or on account of doubt in the mind about the discrimination; वद् - explain.

Although one has intellectually understood the discrimination, why one is not able to have full conviction of this discrimination, if this is the question, then know that it is due to your inability to focus your mind single-pointedly or due to some doubt about the very discrimination. (72)

How are these obstacles removed?...

अप्रमत्तो भव ध्यानादाद्येऽन्यास्मिन् विवेचनम् ।
कुरु प्रमाणयुक्तिभ्यां ततो रूढतमो भवेत् ।।७३।।

Apramatto bhava dhyānāt ādye'nyāsmin vivecanam
Kuru pramāṇa yuktibhyāṁ tato rūḍha tamo bhavet (73)

आद्ये - in the case of the first obstacle (i.e. of non-single pointedness); ध्यानात् - by contemplation; अप्रमत्तः भव - be alert; अन्यास्मिन् - in case of other obstacle (the doubt about the very discrimination); प्रमाण युक्तिभ्याम् - by logic that is in line with the scriptures; विवेचनम् कुरु - discriminate; ततः- thereafter; रूढतमः- conviction; भवेत् - is firmly developed.

In case of the first obstacle of multipointedness of the mind, practice contemplation with alertness; and in the case of the second obstacle of doubt, discriminate with the help of the logic that is falling in line with the scriptures. (73)

The ultimate purpose achieved by the above exercise is ...

ध्यानान्मानाद्युक्तितोऽपि रूढे भेदे वियत्सतोः ।
न कदाचिद्वियत्सत्यं सद्वस्तु च्छिद्रवन्न च ।।७४।।

Dhyānāt mānāt yuktito'pi rūḍhe bhede viyat satoḥ
Na kadācit viyat satyaṁ sadvastu cchidra vanna ca (74)

ध्यानात् - by contemplation; मानात् - by the study of scriptures; युक्तितः- by logic in accordance with scriptures; अपि - even; रूढे भेदे - having developed the conviction in the discrimination; वियत् सतोः- of the space and *sat*; न कदाचित् वियत् सत्यम् - the space can never be real; सद् वस्तु च्छिद्रवत् न च - and the Existence can never be mistaken as non-existent.

When the discrimination between space and Existence is firm by the process of contemplation and study of the scriptures and having logically understood, one will never mistake the space to be real and the *Sat* to be empty non-existence! In other words, one will be fully convinced of the illusory nature of the space and will come to realise the *Sat* as Pure Existence and substratum of space. (74)

The result of the discrimination is ...

ज्ञस्य भाति सदा व्योम निस्तत्त्वोल्लेखपूर्ववत् ।
सद्वस्त्वपि विभात्यस्य निच्छिद्रत्वपुरस्सरम् ।।७५।।

Jñasya bhāti sadā vyoma nistattvo llekha pūrvavat
Sadvastvapi vibhā tyasya nicchidratva puraḥ saram (75)

ज्ञस्य - for the man of discrimination; व्योम - space; निस्तत्त्वोल्लेख पूर्ववत् - is understood as an illusion; सदा भाति - will be thereafter known; अस्य - for him; सद् वस्तु अपि - the Existence also; निच्छिद्रत्व पुरः सरम् - will not be known as 'nothing'; विभाति - be revealed.

Such a man of discrimination thereafter will always know the space as an illusion and the *Brahman* as real. (75)

A constant contemplation on the above Truth will lead to...

वासनायां प्रवृद्धायां वियत्सत्यत्ववादिनाम् ।
सन्मात्राबोधयुक्तं च दृष्ट्वा विस्मयते बुधः ।।७६।।

Vāsanāyāṁ pravṛddhāyāṁ viyat satyatva vādinam
Sanmātrā bodha yuktaṁ ca dṛṣṭvā vismayate budhaḥ (76)

वासनायां प्रवृद्धायाम् - when the understanding that the space is an illusion and the *Brahman* is the reality grows stronger; बुधः- a man of wisdom; वियत् सत्यत्व वादिनाम् - of the one who think that the space is the reality; सन्मात्र अबोध युक्तं च - and the one who is totally devoid of the knowledge of the reality; दृष्ट्वा - having seen; विस्मयते - is surprised.

When the understanding that the space is an illusion and the *Brahman* is the reality grows stronger, the wise man is surprised to see the ignorant ones who still believe that the space is the reality and has no knowledge of the Pure Existence. (76)

Thus having completed the process of discrimination of the space and the *Sat*, the teacher now advises the student to proceed in regard to other elements like air etc...

एवमाकाशमिथ्यात्वे सत्सत्यत्वे च वासिते ।
न्यायेनानेन वाय्वादेः सद्वस्तु प्रविविच्यताम् ।।७७।।

Evamā kāśa mithyātve Sat Sat yatve ca vāsite
Nyāye nānena vāyvādeḥ sadvastu pravi vicyatām (77)

एवम् - in this manner; आकाश मिथ्यात्वे - having understood the illusory nature of space; सत् सत्यत्वे च वासिते - and having known the reality of *Brahman* (behind the space); न्यायेन अनेन - by the same process of discrimination; वाय्वादेः- from the element air etc.; सद्वस्तु - the pure Existence; प्रविविच्यताम् - may be discriminated upon.

In this manner, having understood the space to be an illusion and the *Brahman* to be the reality behind the space, one should enquire and discriminate the *Sat*, from the other elements like air etc.. (77)

The sequence of the apperance of the illusion of air on the *Sat* is indicated...

सद्वस्तुन्येकदेशस्था माया तत्रैकदेशगम् ।
वियत्तत्राप्येकदेशगतो वायुः प्रकल्पितः ।।७८।।

Sadvastu nyeka deśasthā māyā tattraika deśagam
Viyat tatrāpyeka deśa gato vāyuḥ prakalpitaḥ (78)

सद् वस्तुनि - in the *Brahman*; एक देश स्था - in a part localised; माया - *māyā*; तत्र - in it; एक देशगम् - in a part; वियत् - space; तत्र अपि - there also; एक देश गतः- in a part; वायुः- air; प्रकल्पिता - is imagined.

The *māyā* is imagined in a part of the *Brahman*. In the *māyā* is localised the space. In a part of the space, air is imagined. (78)

For easier discrimination of the air from *Brahman*, now the attributes of air are shown...

शोषस्पर्शौ गतिर्वेगः वायुधर्मा इमे मताः ।
त्रयः स्वभावाः सन्मायाव्योम्नां ये तेऽपि वायुगाः ।।७९।।

Śoṣa sparśau gatir vegaḥ vāyu dharmā ime matāḥ
Trayaḥ svabhāvāḥ sanmāyā vyomnāṁ ye te'pi vāyugāḥ (79)

शोष स्पर्शौ - dehydration and touch; गतिः- movement; वेगः- speed; वायु धर्मा - are the attributes of air; इमे - these; मताः- known; त्रयः स्वभावाः- the three aspects; सत् माया व्योम्नाम् - of the *Sat*, *māyā* and the space; ये - those; ते - these; अपि - also; वायुगाः- are seen in air.

The capacity to dehydrate,touch, movement and speed are the qualities of air. In addition to these, the qualities of the three things called the *Sat*, the *māyā* and the space are also seen in the air. (79)

How the three aspects of *Sat*, *māyā* and space are seen in the air?...

वायुरस्तीति सद्भावः सतो वायौ पृथक्कृते ।
निस्तत्वरूपता मायास्वभावो व्योमगो ध्वनिः ।।८०।।

Vāyu rastīti sadbhāvaḥ Sato vāyau pṛthak kṛte
Nistatva rūpatā māyā svabhāvo vyomago dhvaniḥ (80)

वायुः अस्ति इति - the air is, thus; सत् भावः- the presence of *Sat*; सतो वायौ पृथक् कृते - when *Sat* is separated from air; निस्तत्वरूपता - (the air) is non-existent; माया स्वभावः- this *māyā's* attribute (associated in air); व्योमगः- of the space; ध्वनिः- sound.

When we say that 'the air is', it is because of the association of *Sat* with air. When the *Sat* is separated from the air, the air will be non-existent (yet it is), is the attribute of *māyā* found in air. The quality of space viz., the sound, is seen in the air. (80)

In an earlier statement (*śloka* no.67), it was said that the space is not associated with air etc.. Now we are told that the quality of the space is seen in air. How come?...

सतोऽनुवृत्तिः सर्वत्र व्योम्नो नेति पुरेरितम् ।
व्योमानुवृत्तिरधुना कथं न व्याहतं वचः ।।८१।।

Sato'nuvṛttiḥ sarvatra vyomno neti pure ritam
Vyomānu vṛtti radhunā kathaṁ na vyāhataṁ vacaḥ (81)

सतः अनुवृत्तिः सर्वत्र - the presence of *Sat* in all the elements; but; व्योम्नः न - not that of the space; इति पुरा ईरितम् - thus was said earlier (*śloka no. 67*); अधुना - now in this verse; व्योमानुवृत्तिः वचः - presence of space associated with air is said; कथं न व्याहतम् - is it not a contradiction?

In the earlier *śloka* (no. 67), it was said that the *Sat* is associated with all the elements but not the space. Now it is said that the space is said to be associated with the air. Is it not a contradiction? (81)

No, there is no contradiction of the earlier statement...

छिद्रानुवृत्तिर्नेतीति पूर्वोक्तिरधुना त्वियम् ।
शब्दानुवृत्तिरेवोक्ता वचसो व्याहतिः कुतः ।।८२।।

Chidrā nuvṛttir netīti pūrvokti radhunā tviyam
Śabdānu vṛtti revoktā vacaso vyāhatiḥ kutaḥ (82)

छिद्रानुवृत्तिः न इति - the emptiness of the space is not associated thus; इति - so; पूर्वोक्तिः - was said earlier; अधुना तु - but now; इयम् - this; शब्द अनुवृत्तिः- the quality of sound and its association; एव - alone; उक्ता - is said; वचसः- in the statement; व्याहति - contradiction; कुतः- where is.

There was a mention of absence of association of the emptiness of space with other elements earlier (in *śloka* 67). Now, in the above *śloka*, what is said is, the association of the quality of sound of the space with the air etc.. Therefore, where is the contradiction of our words? i.e., there is no such contradiction. (82)

A doubt is raised that, if the air is non-existent i.e., being other than Existence, why can't it be of the opposite nature of *māyā* i.e., *non-māyā* (meaning *Sat*), the *māya* being unmanifest and the air being manifest?

This is explained...

ननु सद्वस्तुपार्थक्यादसत्त्वं चेत्तदा कथम् ।
अव्यक्तमायावैषम्यादमायामयताऽपि नो ।।८३।।

Nanu sadvastu pārthakyāt asattvaṁ cettadā katham
Avyakta māyā vaiṣamyāt amāyā maya tā'pi no (83)

ननु - a doubt is raised; सद् वस्तु पार्थक्यात् - being other than Existence; असत्त्वं चेत् - non-existent is the nature of air; तदा - in the same way; अव्यक्त माया वैषम्यात् - being other than *māyā;* अमायामयता - non-illusory is the air; अपि - if we say; कथम् नो - why it will not be?

A doubt is raised - As the air, being other than Existence, it is said to be non-existent. Similarly, may we call the air to be non-illusory being other than *māyā* i.e., the latter being unmanifest and the air being manifest? (83)

This doubt is explained...

निस्तत्त्वरूपतैवात्र मायात्वस्य प्रयोजिका ।
सा शक्तिकार्ययोस्तुल्या व्यक्ताव्यक्तत्वभेदिनोः ।।८४।।

Nistattva rūpatai vātra māyātvasya prayojikā
Sā śakti kāryayo stulyā vyaktā vyaktatva bhedinoḥ (84)

निस्तत्त्वरूपता - being illusory; एव - alone; मायात्वस्य - of the *māyā*; अत्र - here; प्रयोजिका - is referred to be the essence; सा - that; व्यक्ता अव्यक्तत्व भेदिनोः - the differences of manifest and unmanifest; शक्ति कार्ययोः- the *māyā* and its effects; तुल्या - are same.

The essence of *māyā* is being 'illusory' and not being 'unmanifest'. The illusory aspect of *māyā* is common in the *māyā* and its effect i.e. air, in this case. The umanifest and manifest nature of *māyā* and the air is basically same i.e., illusory. (Thus the air is not 'real', being manifest). (84)

If the nature of both, the *māyā* and the air is illusory, why are they unmanifest and manifest i.e., different?...

सदसत्वविवेकस्य प्रस्तुतत्वात्स चिन्त्यताम् ।
असतोऽवान्तर भेद आस्तां तच्चिन्तयात्र किम् ।।८५।।

Sadasatva vivekasya prastu tatvāt sa cintya tām
ASato'vāntara bheda āstāṁ tat cinta yātra kim (85)

सदसत्व विवेकस्य - what we are discriminating is between the existence and non-existence; प्रस्तुतत्वात् - therefore; स - that; चिन्त्यताम् - reflect; असतः- of the non-existent; अवान्तरः- different; भेदः आस्ताम् - alternatives may be; तत् चिन्तया - thinking of that; अत्र - here; किम् - what is achieved.

In the present context, we are discriminating between the Existence and non-existence, and not the different alternatives of the illusion. Let there be different opinions about the illusion. What is the use of that discrimination about the differences in the illusion? (85)

(One may see a snake or a stick or a crack in the earth or a dried garland in place of the rope. The esential point is to know the rope and not to waste arguments in discriminating whether there is an illusion of snake or stick etc.. The different illusions are illusions after all. It does not matter what they are!).

To conclude the discussion on the above subject...

सद्वस्तु ब्रह्म शिष्टोंशो वायुर्मिथ्या यथा वियत् ।
वासयित्वा चिरं वायोर्मिथ्यात्वं मरुतं त्यजेत् ।।८६।।

Sadvastu brahma śiṣṭoṁśo vāyur mithyā yathā viyat
Vāsayitvā ciraṁ vāyor mithyātvaṁ marutaṁ tyajet (86)

सद् वस्तु ब्रह्म - the existence in the air is *Brahman*; शिष्टः अंशः वायुः - the remaining *vāyu*; मिथ्या - is an illusion; यथा - like that; वियत् - space;

वायोः मिथ्यात्वम् - the illusoriness of the air; चिरम् वासयित्वा - having contemplated upon for long; मरुतम् त्यजेत् - reject the air to be an illusion.

The existence part of the air is *Brahman* and the air part, is the illusion of air, as we have seen in the case of space earlier. Thus, having firmly decided the air to be an illusion, one should reject the air. (i.e., know the *Brahman*). (86)

Now the discrimination of the fire, the third element from that of *Brahman* is discussed...

चिन्तयेद्वह्निमप्येवं मरुतो न्यूनवर्तिनम् ।
ब्रह्माण्डावरणेष्वेषा न्यूनाधिकविचारणा ।।८७।।

Cintayet vahni mapyevaṁ maruto nyūna vartinam
Brahmāṇḍā varaṇe ṣveṣā nyūnā dhika vicāraṇā (87)

चिन्तयेत् - enquire and discriminate; एवम् - in the same way; वह्निम् अपि - the fire also; मरुतः- in comparison to air; न्यूनवर्तिनम् - being less pervasive; ब्रह्माण्ड आवरणेषु - about the covering of *Brahmāṇḍa*; एषा - this; न्यूनाधिक - relative expanse; विचारणा - consideration.

In the same way like that of the air, one may discriminate the fire which is less pervasive than the air. There is consideration about the relative expanse of the elements that are covering the *Brahmāṇḍā*. (87)

What is the relative expanse of the fire in comparison to air?...

वायोर्दशांशतो न्यूनो वह्निर्वायौ प्रकल्पितः ।
पुराणोक्तं तारतम्यं दशांशैर्भूतपञ्चके ।।८८।।

Vāyor daśāṁ śato nyūno vahnir vāyau prakalpitaḥ
Purāṇoktaṁ tāratamyaṁ daśāṁ śair bhūta pañcake (88)

वायोः दशांशतः- one tenth of the air; न्यूनः वह्निः- less is fire; वायौ - in the air; प्रकल्पितः- is imagined; भूत पञ्चके - in the five elements; दशांशैः- one tenth; तारतम्यम् - relativity; पुराणोक्तम् - is described in the *Purāṇa-s.*

The fire is imagined in the one tenth of the air. This relative composition of the five elements is described in the *Purāṇa-s.* (i.e., one tenth of space is air, one tenth of air is fire, one tenth of the fire is water, and one tenth of the water is earth). (88)

The nature of fire is...

वह्निरुष्णः प्रकाशात्मा पूर्वानुगतिरत्र च ।
अस्ति वह्निः स निस्तत्वः शब्दवान् स्पर्शवानपि ।।८९।।

Vahni ruṣṇaḥ prakāśātmā pūrvānu gati ratra ca
Asti vahniḥ sa nistatvaḥ śabdavān sparśa vānapi (89)

वह्निः उष्णः प्रकाशात्मा - the fire is of the nature of heat and light; अत्र - here; च - also; पूर्व अनुगति - the essence of the earlier ones (i.e., of existence, *māyā*, space and air); वह्निः अस्ति - fire is; स निस्तत्वः- it is an illusion; शब्दवान् - with sound; स्पर्शवान् - with touch; अपि - also.

The nature of the fire is heat and light. Here also, the qualities of the Existence, *māyā*, space and air are also seen. The fire exists, in this the existence is seen. Without the existence, the fire is an illusion; therefore, the quality of *māyā* is seen. It has sound, the quality of space, and also is hot to touch, the quality of air is seen (89)

These are the inherent qualities of fire mainly. Now the essential nature of the fire is shown...

सन्मायाव्योमवाय्वंशैर्युक्तस्याग्नेर्निजो गुणः ।
रूपं तत्र सतः सर्वमन्यद्बुद्ध्या विविच्यताम् ।।९०।।

Sanmāyā vyoma vāyvaṁśair yukta syāgner nijo guṇaḥ
Rūpaṁ tatra sataḥ sarvam anyad buddhyā vivicyatām (90)

सन् माया व्योम वाय्वंशैः युक्तस्य - of the fire associated with the qualities of *Sat*, *māyā*, space and air; अग्नेः निजः गुणः रूपम् - its own quality is colour and form; तत्र - in this case; सतः अन्यत् सर्वम् - all other than the *Sat Brahman*; बुद्ध्या - by proper enquiry; विविच्यताम् - be discriminated.

The fire is associated with the qualities inherited from the *Sat Brahman*, *māyā*, space and air. The fire has, 'colour and form' as its quality. In this case also, like in earlier cases, one should discriminate the *Sat Brahman* from the fire. (90)

The purpose of this discrimination is...

सतो विवेचिते वह्नौ मिथ्यात्वे सति वासिते ।
आपो दशांशतो न्यूनाः कल्पिता इति चिन्तयेत् ।।९१।।

Sato vivecite vahnau mithyātve sati vāsite
Āpo daśāṁśato nyūnāḥ kalpitā iti cintayet (91)

सतः वह्नौ विवेचिते - having discriminated the *Sat* from the fire; मिथ्यात्वे वासिते सति - thus having convinced of the illusion of the fire in the *Sat*; दशांशतः न्यूनाः- one tenth less; आपः- water; कल्पिता - be imagined; इति चिन्तयेत् - thus think.

The discrimination of the *Sat* from the fire and having been convinced of the illusory nature of the fire imagined in the *Sat Brahman*, one may imagine the water in the one tenth of the fire. (91)

The water is now described on the same lines as that of fire...

सन्त्यापोऽमूः शून्यतत्त्वाः सशब्दस्पर्शसंयुताः ।
रूपवत्योऽन्य धर्मानुवृत्त्या स्वीयो रसो गुणः ।।९२।।

Santyāpo'mūḥ śūnyatattvāḥ saśabda sparśa saṁyutāḥ
Rūpavatyo'nya dharmā nuvṛttyā svīyo raso guṇaḥ (92)

आपः सन्ति अमूः- this water is; शून्यतत्त्वाः- without Existence, it is an illusion; सशब्द स्पर्श - with sound and touch; संयुताः- associated with; रूपवत्यः- with form; अन्य धर्म अनुवृत्त्या - thus associated with the qualities of other earlier ones; स्वीयः गुणः- its own quality; रसः- taste.

This water is also an illusion associated with the inherited qualities of the *Sat* (Existence), *māyā* (illusion), space (sound), air (touch), fire (colour and form) and its own quality is taste. (92)

Now the discrimination of earth and *Sat* is being done...

सतो विवेचितास्वप्सु तन्मिथ्यात्वे च वासिते ।
भूमिर्दशांशतो न्यूना कल्पिताप्स्विति चिन्तयेत् ।।९३।।

Sato vivecitāsvapsu tanmithyātve ca vāsite
Bhūmir daśāṁśato nyūnā kalpitā psviti cintayet (93)

सतः अप्सु विवेचितासु - having discriminated the *Sat* from the water; च - and; तन्मिथ्यात्वे वासिते - having determined the illusion of water; दशांशतः- one tenth; अप्सु - in the water; कल्पिता - projected; इति - thus; न्यूनाः- less; भूमिः- earth; चिन्तयेत् - thus imagine.

Having arrived at the conclusion that the water is an illusion and discriminating the *Sat* from the water, one should imagine the earth is projected to be one tenth of the waters. (93)

To ascertain the illusion of the earth, the qualities of the earth are now being determined...

अस्ति भूस्तत्त्वशून्याऽस्यां शब्दस्पर्शौ सरूपकौ ।
रसश्च परतो गन्धो नैजः सत्ता विविच्यताम् ।।९४।।

Asti bhūstattva-śūnyā'syāṁ śabda-sparśau sarūpakau
Rasaśca parato gandho naijaḥ sattā vivicyatām (94)

भूः अस्ति - the earth is; तत्त्व शून्या - being an illusion; अस्याम् - of the earth; शब्द स्पर्शौ - sound, touch; सरूपकौ - with form; रसः च - and the taste; परतः- are inherited qualities; नैजः गन्धः- its own quality is smell; सत्ता - Pure Existence; विविच्यताम् - be discriminated out.

The earth exists, the existence is associated with it. Without the existence, it is an illusion (*māyā*). The other qualities inherited are sound, touch, form, taste - from the space, air, fire and the water respectively. The quality of the earth, of its own, is smell. The *Sat* may be discriminated from the earth. (94)

Now the illusion of *Brahmāṇḍa* is being discussed...

पृथक्कृतायां सत्तायां भूमिर्मिथ्याऽवशिष्यते ।
भूमेर्दशांशतो न्यूनं ब्रह्माण्डं भूमिमध्यगम् ।।९५।।

Pṛthakkṛtāyāṁ sattāyāṁ bhūmir mithyā 'vaśiṣyate
Bhūmer daśāṁśato nyūnaṁ brahmāṇḍaṁ bhūmi madhyagam (95)

सत्तायां पृथक् कृतायाम् - having discriminated the Existence; भूमिः- the earth; मिथ्या - illusion; अवशिष्यते - is concluded; भूमेः दशांशतः - one tenth of the earth; न्यूनम् - less; ब्रह्माण्डम् - the *Brahmāṇḍa*; भूमि मध्यगम् - in the core of earth.

Having discriminated the Existence from the earth, the latter is concluded to be an illusion. One tenth of the earth is the core of the earth called the *Brahmāṇḍa*. (95)

The contents of the *Brahmāṇḍa* are given...

ब्रह्माण्डमध्ये तिष्ठन्ति भुवनानि चतुर्दश ।
भुवनेषु वसन्त्येषु प्राणिदेहा यथायथम् ।।९६।।

Brahmāṇḍa madhye tiṣṭhanti bhuvanāni caturdaśa
Bhuvaneṣu vasantyeṣu prāṇidehā yathā yatham (96)

ब्रह्माण्ड मध्ये - in the *Brahmaṇḍa*; चतुर्दश - fourteen; भुवनानि - *lokā-s*; तिष्ठन्ति - are; एषु भुवनेषु - in these *lokā-s*; प्राणि देहाः- the bodies of the beings; यथा यथम् - are appropriately; वसन्ति - exist.

In the *Brahmāṇḍa*, there are fourteen areas (*lokā-s*) with the appropriate bodies of the beings. [These *loka-s* are: *Bhūḥ, Bhuvaḥ, Svaḥ, Mahaḥ, Janaḥ, Tapaḥ, Satyam* in the upper regions; and the *Atala, Vitala, Sutala, Talātala, Mahātala, Rasātala and Pātāla* in the lower half region]. (96)

The discrimination of the *Brahmāṇḍa* along with its contents from the Pure Existence will lead to...

ब्रह्माण्डलोकदेहेषु सद्वस्तुनि पृथक्कृते ।
असन्तोऽण्डादयो भान्तु तद्भानेऽपीह का क्षतिः ।।९७।।

Brahmāṇḍa loka deheṣu sadvastuni pṛthak kṛte
Asanto'ṇḍādayo bhāntu tadbhāne' pīha kā kṣatiḥ (97)

ब्रह्माण्ड लोक देहेषु - the *Brahmāṇḍa* along with its *lokā-s* and the bodies of the beings; सद् वस्तुनि - from the *Sat Brahman*; पृथक् कृते - having discriminated; अण्डादयः- the *Brahmāṇḍa* etc.; असन्त - will be known as non-existent; भान्तु - may it be so; तद्भाने - having known them; अपि - even; इह का क्षतिः- what is the loss.

Having discriminated the Pure *Sat* from the *Brahmāṇḍa* along with its contents of the *lokā-s* and the beings with their bodies, if they are known to be an illusion, what is the loss for us? (i.e., there is no loss or gain due to this discrimination). (97)

The final conclusion of the total analysis conducted so far is to be firm in this discrimination...

भूतभौतिकमायानामसत्त्वेऽत्यन्तवासिते ।
सद्वस्त्वद्वैतमित्येषा धीर्विपर्येति न क्वचित् ।।९८।।

Bhūta bhautika māyānām asattve 'tyanta vāsite
Sad vastva dvaita mityeṣā dhīr viparyeti na kvacit (98)

भूत - the five elements; भौतिक - their effects; मायानाम् - *māyā;* अत्यन्त - absolutely; असत्वे वासिते - having distinctly known to be an illusion; सद् वस्तु - the *Sat Brahman*; अद्वैतम् इति - is non-dual; एषा धीः- this understanding; विपर्येति - destroyed; न क्वचित् - never.

Once the understanding that the *māyā*, the five elements along with their effects are an illusion and the *Sat Brahman* is the Reality, is gained, this knowledge is never clouded and destroyed. (98)

How does a man of this knowledge function in the world, because for Him, everything is an illusion...

सदद्वैतात् पृथक् कृते द्वैते भूम्यादिरूपिणि ।
तत्तदर्थक्रिया लोके यथा दृष्टा तथैव सा ।।९९।।

Sadadvaitāt pṛthak kṛte dvaite bhūmyā dirūpiṇi
Tattadartha kriyā loke yathā dṛṣṭā tathaiva sā (99)

सत् अद्वैतात् पृथक् कृते - having separated the '*Sat*' non-dual *Brahman*; भूमि आदि रूपिणि द्वैते - the duality in the form of the earth etc..; तत् तदर्थ - for the sake of these; क्रिया लोके - the transactions in the world; यथा - as; दृष्टा - were seen; सा - those; तथा एव - will remain the same.

Although the world of earth etc., is being discarded from the non-dual Pure Existence (as an illusion), the transactions in the world would continue to be the same as were seen earlier i.e., this knowledge will not disturb the life of the man of knowledge. (99)

Why the knower of the non-dual *Brahman* does not refute the philosophy of dualism?...

साङ्ख्यकाणादबौद्धाद्यैर्जगद्भेदो यथा यथा ।
उत्प्रेक्ष्यतेऽनेकयुक्त्या भवत्वेष तथा तथा ।।१००।।

Sāṅkhya kāṇāda bauddhā dyair jagad bhedo yathā yathā
Utprekṣyate 'nekayuktyā bhavatveṣa tathā tathā (100)

साङ्ख्य काणाद बौद्ध आद्यैः- by the *Sāṅkhyāna-s, kāṇāda, bauddhā-s* etc.; जगद् भेदः- the duality in the world; अनेक युक्त्या - by many logical ways; यथा यथा - as and when; उत्प्रेक्ष्यते - is imagined; भवतु - let it be so; एष - this; तथा तथा - as they please.

The *Sāṅkhyāna, the Kāṇada, the Bauddhā-s* and the many propounders of duality have established the duality in the world by many seemingly logical arguments. Let it be so. Let them imagine the duality as they please (i.e., there is no point in wasting our energy to refute the differences in the duality, all of which are illusions). (100)

Because...

अवज्ञातं सदद्वैतं निश्शंकैरन्यवादिभिः ।
एवं का क्षतिरस्माकं तदद्वैतमवजानताम् ।।१०१।।

Avajñātaṁ sadadvaitaṁ niśśaṁkair anya vādibhiḥ
Evaṁ kā kṣati rasmākaṁ taddvaitam avajānatām (101)

अन्यवादिभिः- by the dualists; निश्शंकैः- confidently; सत् अद्वैतम् - the *Sat* non-dual; अवज्ञातम् - is disregarded; तद् द्वैतम् अवजानताम् - the believers of the duality; एवम् - therefore; का - what; क्षतिः- loss; अस्माकम् - to us.

The dualists have so confidently rejected the non-duality of the *Brahman* (although proved according to the logic supported in the scriptures), what are we going to lose if we do not regard their standpoint of duality? (i.e., there is no loss for the knowers of the non-dual *Brahman*). (101)

The disregard to the duality is in fact a boon for the joy of freedom while living...

द्वैतावज्ञा सुस्थिता चेदद्वैते धीः स्थिरा भवेत् ।
स्थैर्ये तस्याः पुमानेष जीवन्मुक्त इतीर्यते ।।१०२।।

Dvaitā vajñā susthitā ced advaite dhīḥ sthirā bhavet
Sthairye tasyāḥ pumāneṣa jīvanmukta itīryate (102)

द्वैत अवज्ञा - the disregard for the duality; सुस्थिता - firm; चेत् - if; अद्वैते - in the non-dual; धीः- the intellect; स्थिरा - firm; भवेत् - abides; स्थैर्ये तस्याम् - by the firmness of this understanding; एषः- this; पुमान - person; जीवन्मुक्तः- liberated while living; इति ईर्यते - is thus called.

The disregard to the duality with conviction is indeed good, because it will help the person to get established in the non-dual *Brahman*. The person with firm abidance in the non-dual *Brahman* is called as *Jīvan Muktaḥ* i.e., liberated while living! (102)

This state of a liberated person while living is described by Lord *Kṛṣṇa* in *Gītā* ...

एषा ब्राह्मी स्थितिः पार्थ नैनां प्राप्य विमुह्यति ।
स्थित्वाऽस्यामन्तकालेऽपि बह्मनिर्वाणमृच्छति ।।१०३।।

Eṣā brāhmī sthitiḥ pārtha naināṁ prāpya vimuhyati
Sthitvā' syām antakāle'pi brahma nirvāṇa mṛcchati (103)

एषा - this; ब्राह्मी स्थितिः- the state of the knowledge of non-dual *Brahman*; पार्थ - O' Arjuna; एनाम् प्राप्य - having gained this; न - not; विमुह्यति - is not deluded; स्थित्वा - having established; अस्याम् - in this; अन्तकाले अपि

- even at the time of the knowledge of *Brahman*; ब्रह्म निर्वाण - the supreme state of freedom; ऋच्छति - one attains.

O' Arjuna, once the supreme state of absolute freedom is attained through the knowledge of the real nature of the non-dual *Brahman*, one is never deluded again in the illusion of the world. (103)

The real meaning of 'the last moment' is discussed...

सदद्वैतेऽनृते द्वैते यदन्योन्यैक्यवीक्षणम् ।
तस्यान्तकालस्तद्भेदबुद्धिरेव न चेतरः ।।१०४।।

Sadadvaite'nṛte dvaite yadanyo nyaikya vīkṣaṇam
Tasyānta kālas tadbheda buddhi reva na cetaraḥ (104)

सत् द्वैते अनृते द्वैते - having realised the non-dual *Brahman* and that the duality is an illusion; यद् - that; अन्योन्य ऐक्यं वीक्षणम् - seeing oneness without a second; तस्य अन्तकालः- the last moment of this ignorance; तद् भेद बुद्धिः एव - that understanding alone; न च इतरः- and not any other meaning.

The meaning of the word 'the last moment' means that the moment when the realisation of - the world to be an illusion and the *Brahman* to be real, and the wrong perception of the oneness of the two is fully discriminatingly understood; and not the usual meaning of the death of the body. (104)

Now taking the usual meaning of the word 'the last moment' to be the death of the body, what is the conclusion?...

यद्वान्तकालः प्राणस्य वियोगोऽस्तु प्रसिद्धितः ।
तस्मिन् कालेऽपि न भ्रान्तेर्गतायाः पुनरागमः ।।१०५।।

Yadvānta kālaḥ prāṇasya viyogo'stu prasiddhitaḥ
Tasmin kāle'pi na bhrānter gatāyāḥ punarā gamaḥ (105)

यदि - or; अन्तकालः- the last moment; प्राणस्य वियोगः - departure of life from the body; अस्तु - may be taken; प्रसिद्धितः- as popularly known; तस्मिन् काले अपि - at that time also; न - not; भ्रान्तेः गतायाः - once the delusion is gone; पुनः आगमः - return.

Even if we take the popular meaning of the word 'the last moment' meaning the departure of the life force from the body, even at that time if the delusion is gone, it is for good. (105)

The meaning is further explained...

नीरोग उपविष्टो वा रुग्णो वा विलुठन् भुवि ।
मूर्छितो वा त्यजत्वेष प्राणान् भ्रान्तिर्न सर्वथा ।।१०६।।

Nīroga upaviṣṭo vā rugṇo vā viluṭhan bhuvi
Mūrchito vā tyajatveṣa prāṇān bhrāntirna sarvathā (106)

नीरोग - being healthy; उपविष्टो वा - or in a sitting posture; रुग्णो वा - or being diseased; विलुठन् भुवि - or rolling on the earth (due to pain); मूर्छितो वा - or under coma; त्यजतु एष - may he leave this; प्राणान् - the life force; भ्रान्तिः- delusion; न - not; सर्वथा - at all.

May he (the man of knowledge) leave the life from the body in a healthy or sitting posture, or in a diseased condition or while rolling on the floor because of the pain, or while being in coma, he will not attain delusion thereafter at all. (106)

How his knowledge will not be forgotten is explained...

दिने दिने स्वप्नसुप्त्योरधीते विस्मृतेऽप्ययम् ।
परेद्युर्नानधीतः स्यात्तद्वद्विद्या न नश्यति ।।१०७।।

Dine dine svapna suptyo radhīte vismṛte' pyayam
Pare dyur nāna dhītaḥ syāt tadvad vidyā na naśyati (107)

दिने दिने अधीते - whatever is studied daily; स्वप्न सुप्त्योः - during the dream and the deep sleep; विस्मृते अपि - although forgotten; अयम् - this; परे द्युः- the next day; न अनधीतः स्यात् - is not forgotten; तद् वत् - in the same way; विद्या - the knowledge; न नश्यति - is not lost.

Whatever is studied every day and forgotten during the dream and the deep sleep states, is not forgotten or lost on the next day. (Similarly, the knowledge about the illusion of the world and the non-dual *Brahman* is not lost after death). (107)

Another reason why the knowledge is not lost...

प्रमाणोत्पादिता विद्या प्रमाणं प्रबलं विना ।
न नश्यति न वेदान्तात्प्रबलं मानमीक्ष्यते ।।१०८।।

Pramāṇo tpāditā vidyā pramāṇaṁ prabalaṁ vinā
Na naśyati na vedāntāt prabalaṁ māna mīkṣyate (108)

प्रमाणः उत्पादिता विद्या - the knowledge born of a proper means of knowledge; प्रबलम् प्रमाणम् विना - without stronger means of knowledge; न नश्यति - is not destroyed; वेदान्तात् - more than *vedānta*; मानम् - means of knowledge; न ईक्ष्यते - is not seen.

The knowledge born out of the *vedānta* way of investigation cannot be destroyed without any stronger and valid means of knowledge. And there is no stronger means of knowledge than the *vedānta*. (Therefore, the *Brahma Jñāna* cannot be lost if it is born of the *Vedānta Prakriyā*). (108)

Now the chapter is concluded...

तस्माद्वेदान्तसंसिद्धिं सदद्वैतं न बाध्यते ।
अन्तकालेऽप्यतो भूतविवेकान्निर्वृत्तिः स्थिताः ॥१०९॥

Tasmād vedānta saṁsiddhiṁ sada dvaitaṁ na bādhyate
Antakāle'pyato bhūta vivekān nirvṛttiḥ sthitāḥ (109)

तस्मात् - therefore; वेदान्त संसिद्धिम् - the one proved by the authority of *vedānta*; सत् अद्वैतम् - the non-dual *Brahman*; न - not; बाध्यते - is denied; अतः- therefore; अन्तकाले अपि - even at the last moment; भूत विवेकात् - by the discrimination of the five elements; निर्वृत्तिः - self abidance; स्थिता - is firmly attained.

Therefore, the knowledge born out of the authority of the *Vedānta* is not denied, and the non-dual *Brahman* is never 'nothing'. Hence, the knowledge attained even at the last moment leads to firm abidance in the Self. (109)

OM TAT SAT

Summary

Verse No.	Subject matter covered
1	*Pratijña* - One can know the *Sat* by the discrimination of the five great elements.
2 - $5_{1/2}$	Five elements and their qualities.
$5_{1/2}$ - 9	Five senses and their locations, functions etc..
10 - 11	Types of activities, their organs of action and their locations.
12 - 16	Mind as an inner instrument, its function, modifications and effects of modifications as sin, merit etc..
17	The objects, their senses etc., are the effects of elements. Here the first discrimination concludes.
18 - 19	In the *upaniṣadik* statements, *'Sadeva somya idamagra āsīt'*, the meaning of the word *'idam'* includes total creation along with the scriptures. The C.U. is quoted.
20 - 21	*'Ekam-eva-advitīyam'*, The three types of differences are explained.
22 - 25	Absence of these differences in '*Sat*' (Pure Existence) and their reasons.

26 - 33	*'ASat vāda'*, (The theory of non-existence, its fallacy, the views of *Gauḍapādācārya* and *Śaṅkarācārya*). The error of understanding in *'ASat vāda'*.
34 - 35	The 'names and forms' of the world is an illusion but not that of Brahman.
36 - 37	Possibility of duality when we say '*Sat* was' and its negation.
38 - 40	The fallacy of duality with reference to 'time', and the Absolute non-dual *Brahman* is established.
41 - 44	How the space is non-existent although without form unlike Brahman?
45	The Existence, being self-effulgent, does not need any authority for its proof of being.
46	Similarity of Existence and the witness.
47 - 51	The *māyā*, it being a superimposition on Brahman, her nature being indescribable etc., and the impossibility of duality on account of *māyā*.
52 - 53	The possibility of duality due to the effect of *māyā* i.e., the world and its negation.
54 - 58	Presence of *māyā* is generalised or localised on *Brahman* and its nature.
59	Creation of illusory world by *māyā*.
60 - 62	The first of the creation is space and its nature.

63 - 64 The illusory power of *māyā* awards reality to space and the 'Existence' becomes concealed i.e., the space becomes an object and the 'Existence' becomes its quality.

65 - 66 The cause of erroneous knowledge and its correction by right thinking.

67 Discrimination of 'Existence' from 'Space'.

68 - 71 The illusion of space on *Brahman* and its simultaneous appearance.

72 - 76 The obstacles in the experience of this knowledge and the remedy, to lead to the experience of Brahman.

77 - 82 Having discriminated between 'Existence' and 'Space', a similar line of thinking is developed with reference to air to conclude its illusoriness.

83 - 86 Air being manifest, it is other than unmanifest *māyā.* So air is 'Existence' i.e., other than *māyā.* This fallacy is rejected to conclude the air as an illusion.

87 - $90_{1/2}$ Discrimination between 'Existence' and 'Fire' and fire being illusory.

$90_{1/2}$ - $921_{/2}$ Discrimination between 'Existence' and 'Water', to prove the illusoriness of water.

$92_{1/2}$ - $94_{1/2}$ Discrimination between 'Existence' and 'Earth', to prove Earth being an illusion.

$94_{1/2}$ - 97	Discrimination between 'Existence' and the *'Brahmāṇḍa'* along with its contents to prove their illusoriness.
98	The result of the discrimination conducted so far with reference to total creation.
99	The vision and the behaviour of the man of wisdom.
100 - 101	No need to defend the Non-duality or to discard duality.
102 - 106	The state of *jīvan mukta* - liberated while living.
107 - 109	No fear of fall from the state of Reali*Sat*ion.

* * *

3

१५

Chapter III

PAÑCA KOŚA VIVEKAḤ

or

THE DIFFERENTIATION OF THE FIVE SHEATHS

After the analysis of the principle (*tattva*) was done in chapter I, the second chapter dealt with the analysis of the five great elements which consitute the world of manifestation. The author now proceeds to expound the significance and nature of the five sheaths or *pañca kośā-s* in which is 'hidden' the *Brahman*.

This subject is dealt within the *Taittiriya Upaniṣad*, where, the student approaches the teacher (his father) and asks him to tell him what

Brahman is. The teacher says that *Brahman* is the subject of investigation (*Jijñāsā*). He initiates the disciple on this path of enquiry by the statement: The *Annamaya kośa* is *Brahman*. Contemplate on that. The student does accordingly and comes to the conclusion that the *annamaya kośa* cannot be *Brahman*.

The teacher next asks him to contemplate on the *Prāṇamaya kośa* as being *Brahman*. In this way, by slow and steady enquiry, step by step, the student comes to discover that the *Brahman* cannot be any of the five *kośa-s*. It is other than the five sheaths.

This is the theme of this chapter...

गुहाहितं ब्रह्म यत्तत्पञ्चकोश विवेकतः ।
बोद्धुं शक्यं ततः कोशपञ्चकं प्रविविच्यते ।।१।।

Guhāhitaṁ brahma yat tat pañcakośa vivekataḥ
Boddhuṁ śakyaṁ tataḥ kośa pañcakaṁ pravi vicyate (1)

गुहाहितम् - hidden in the *guhā* refered in the *Taittiriya Upaniṣad*; यत् - that which; ब्रह्म - the *Brahman*; तत् - that; पञ्च कोश विवेकतः- through the discrimination of the five sheaths; बोद्धुम् - knowing; शक्यम् - is possible; ततः - therefore; कोश पञ्चकम् - the five sheaths; प्रविविच्यते - are separately described and discriminated from the *Ātman*.

That *Brahman*, which is hidden in the five sheaths (as refered in T.U.) can be realised as one's own nature, by the discrimination of five sheaths. Therefore, these five sheaths are described and separated from *Brahman*. (1)

Guhāhitam Brahma yat tat: This *Brahman* which is the core of the five *kośa-s*.

The *Taittiriya upaniṣad* says, 'He who knows that this *satyam, jñānam, anantaṁ, Brahma* resides in the cave of one's personality...'

Pañca kośa vivekataḥ boddhum śakyam: This (*Brahman*) can be known by the process of discrimination (*viveka*) of the five sheaths.

Tataḥ pañca kośa pañcakam pravivicyate: Therefore, the discussion and analysis is now being taken up regarding the validity of each *kośa* and what its status is vis-a-vis *Brahman*.

The word *guhā* is normally used as referring to the intellect (in the cave of the intellect). But *Vidyāraṇya svāmi* says that *guhā* does not refer to the *vijñānamaya kośa* alone, but all the five *kośa-s* put together. That which is the substratum of the five *kośa-s* and that which is hidden under the covering of the five *kośa-s....*, the *guḥa*, is the *Brahman*. Therefore, to understand what *Brahman* is, it is necessary to carry out a systematic process of discrimination into the nature of the five *kośa-s*. Only that knowledge which is gained by such enquiry and discrimination will have strength and stability to stand the test of time and stress.

The five *kośa-s* are...

देहादभ्यन्तरः प्राणः प्राणादभ्यन्तरं मनः ।
ततः कर्ता ततो भोक्ता गुहा सेयं परम्परा ।।२।।

Dehād abhyan taraḥ prāṇaḥ prāṇād abhyan taraṁ manaḥ
Tataḥ kartā tato bhoktā guhā seyaṁ paramparā (2)

देहात् - with reference to gross body; अभ्यन्तरः- subtler; प्राणः- the vital air sheath; प्राणात् - with reference to *prāṇaḥ*; मनः- the mind; अभ्यन्तरम् - is subtler or inner; ततः- subtler or inner than the mind; कर्ता - the intellectual sheath; ततः- subtler than the intellectual sheath; भोक्ता - the bliss sheath; सा इयम् - this is that; गुहा परम्परा - the outer and inner cave sequence.

Subtler than the gross body is the vital air sheath. Subtler than the vital air sheath is the mental sheath. Subtler than this mental sheath is the intellectual sheath. Subtler than intellectual sheath is bliss sheath. This is the cave sequence in that order. (2)

Dehāt abhyantaraḥ prāṇaḥ : The external most *kośa* is the gross body supported by the *Prāṇamaya kośa*, which is inner to gross body, *Prāṇāt abhyantaraṁ manaḥ* : Subtler than the *Prāṇamaya kośa* is the *Manomaya kośa, Tataḥ kartā* : Subtler than the *Manomaya kośa* is the *Vijñānamaya kośa* where there is *kartṛtva abhimāna. Tataḥ bhoktā* : The last and the most subtle is the *Ānandamaya kośa* where *bhoktṛtva abhimāna* operates.

Sā iyaṁ guhā paramparā : In this way, the five *kośa-s* in this specific sequence and relationship of *parā* and *aparā*... higher-lower, more subtle-less subtle, is the 'cave' or *guhā* (that 'covers' the *ātman*).

The five *kośa-s* are usually represented as layers, one inside the other (antar) and the *Ātman* lodged at the innermost point of the core.

But the real meaning of antar is support, that which supports the latter; *Annamaya kośa* is supported by the *prāṇamaya kośa*; the *prāṇamaya kośa* by the *manomaya kośa* (when the mind is calm, the respiration is steady; when the mind is agitated, the respiration goes faster). The *manomaya kośa* is supported by the *vijñāna-maya kośa*, because the convictions determined by the intellect will alone express through the *manomaya kośa.* The *vijñānamaya kośa* is supported by the *Ānandamaya kośa*, because the purpose of all decisions and convictions is for the sake of gaining happiness. *Bhoktṛtva abhimāna* is in the *Ānandamaya kośa.*

This successive nature of the *kośa-s* according to their degree of subtlety is termed *paramparā* (param + apara), param being the higher, and aparam- the lower, *sā iyam paramparā.* The five *kośa-s* are thus in this sequence and relationship.

These five *kośa-s* in this sequence and successive degree of subtlety, put together is called *guhā* (the cave).

Now the teacher proceeds to define each *kośa* and to show how it cannot be the *Ātman*...

पितृ भुक्तान्न जाद्वीर्याज्जातोऽन्नेनैव वर्धते ।
देहःसोऽन्नमयो नात्मा प्राक् चोर्ध्वं तदभावतः ।।३।।

Pitṛ bhuktā nnajād vīryā jjāto' nnenaiva vardhate
Dehaḥ so'nnamayo nātmā prāk cordhvaṁ tada bhāvataḥ (3)

देहः- the gross body; पितृभुक्तात् अन्नजात् - from the food eaten by the father and mother; वीर्यात् - from the seed; जातः- is born; अन्नेन - by the food; एव - alone; वर्धते - grows; सः- that; अन्नमयः- is the food sheath; आत्मा - the *Ātmā*; न (भवति)- cannot be; प्राक् ऊर्ध्वं च - before and after its birth and death; तद् - of the gross body; अभावतः- being absent.

The gross body is born of the seeds of the parents which (seeds) are in turn the result of the food consumed by them. It grows on food. This gross body cannot be *Ātmā* because of its prior and later absence. (3)

How is the gross body formed? The parents eat food. The essence of the food is converted into seed in each parent. The father initiates the process of body construction which is carried out by the material received from the mother. Thus...

Pitṛ bhuktā annajāt vīryāt jātaḥ dehaḥ annena eva vardhate : Out of the food eaten by the parents and the seeds that are produced thereafter, is born, the body. It (the body) grows only on the food.

This body which was created at a particular point of time, is born out of food, is maintained in the food, and goes back to the food.

Saḥ ayam annamayaḥ : (Therefore) It is called *Annamaya kośa.* Thus, we do not have any ownership of this body; it is the product of someone else.

Na ātmā: It is not *Ātmā*. Why?

Prāk ūrdhvaṁ tat abhāvataḥ : Before, and after, there was a time when this body did not exist; and there will be a time when this body will not exist. That which has come in between, how can that be the *Ātmā*?

The point that the gross body cannot be *Ātman* is further explained...

पूर्वजन्मन्यसन्नेतज्जन्म संपादयेत्कथम् ।
भाविजन्मन्यसत्कर्म न भुञ्जीतेह सञ्चितम् ।।४।।

Pūrva janma nyasann etaj janma saṁpādayet katham
Bhāvi janman yasan karma na bhuñjī teha sañcitam (4)

पूर्व - earlier; जन्मनि - in the birth; असत् - is non-existent; एतत् - this; जन्म - birth; कथम् - how can; संपादयेत् - lead; भावि - in the future; जन्मनि - birth; असत् - is not going to exist; इह - in this life; सञ्चितम् - the accumulated; कर्म - actions; न - not; भुञ्जीत - will experience.

This body was non-existent in the last life. How can it conduct this life? And this body will not exist in the next life. Therefore, the accumulated *karma* of this life will not be experienced by it in the next life. (Therefore, the gross body cannot be *Ātmā*). (4)

Pūrva janmani asat etat janma katham sampādayet : This body was not existing in the previous birth. How then can this body in this (the present) birth, take the *karma phala* from the previous life?

Bhāvi janmani asat na bhunjīteha sañcitam : (In the same way), this body will not be there in the next birth. So, it cannot enjoy (or suffer) the *sañcita karma* accumulated by this body in this birth.

This is a powerful line of thought to prove that the *Annamaya kośa* is not the *Ātmā.*

The *sañcita karma* which we have brought with us into the present birth, was not produced in this body which we are occupying in this birth, but in another body in the previous birth. This body is only the place where the carried-over *sañcita karma* is to be exhausted. In the meanwhile, more *āgāmi karma* is gathered, to exhaust which, another body will be needed. And so the cycle goes on.

Thus, in these two *śloka-s*, two points are established : (a) that the gross body cannot be the *Ātmā*, because of the nature of its biography; and (b) the body is not for the sake of the body per se; but for the owner of the body who has to be someone different from the body.

On these two counts, the *Annamaya kośa* cannot be the *Ātmā*.

How and why *Prāṇamaya kośa* cannot be *Ātmā*?...

पूर्णो देहे बलं यच्छन्नक्षाणां यः प्रवर्तकः ।
वायुः प्राणमयो नासावात्मा चैतन्यवर्जनात् ।।५।।

Pūrṇo dehe balaṁ yacchan akṣāṇāṁ yaḥ pravartakaḥ
Vāyuḥ prāṇamayo nāsau ātmā caitanya varjanāt (5)

यः वायुः- that vital air; देहे - in the gross body; पूर्णः- fully pervaded; बलम् - strength and energy; यच्छन् - offering; अक्षाणाम् - of the faculties like eyes etc.; प्रवर्तकः- is the propeller; असौ - this is; प्राणमयः- is the vital air sheath; चैतन्य - consciousness; वर्जनात् - being devoid of; आत्मा - the *Ātmā*; न (भवति)- cannot be.

That air which is occupying the whole body, giving energy to the senses and different faculties, and is thus the propeller of the activities, is called the vital air sheath. This also cannot be *Ātmā,* being devoid of consciousness. (5)

Dehe vāyuḥ pūrṇaḥ : The whole body is pervaded by the *prāṇa vāyu* or the vital air. (There are more than 600 *prāṇā-s* controlling the complete functioning of the body and constituting the *Prāṇamaya kośa*).

Yaḥ akṣāṇāṁ balaṁ yacchan pravartakaḥ : The *prāṇa vāyu* gives energy and strength to all the sense organs. It pervades and prompts all activities, good and bad.

Prāṇamayaḥ na asau ātmā : This is the *prāṇamaya kośa*. However, this *prāṇamaya kośa* is not the *Ātmā*. Why?

Caitanya varjanāt: Because it is devoid of knowledge, or consciousness.

The *jñānendriya-s* are knowledge oriented, but the *karma-endriyas* are inert. All the bhoga is through the *jñānendriya-s.*

The *prāṇamaya kośa* is inert and under the control of the *manomaya kośa*. Therefore, it cannot be the *Ātmā*, because it does not contain any trace of consciousness.

What about *manomaya kośa*?...

अहन्तां ममतां देहे गेहादौ च करोति यः ।
कामाद्यवस्थया भ्रान्तो नासावात्मा मनोमयः ।।६।।

Ahantāṁ mamatāṁ dehe gehādau ca karoti yaḥ
Kāmādya vasthayā bhrānto nāsā vātmā manomayaḥ (6)

यः- that which; देहे - in the body; गेहादौ - in the house etc..; च - and; अहन्ताम् - 'I-ness'; ममताम् - 'my-ness'; करोति - does; असौ - that; मनोमयः- is the mental sheath; कामादि - desire etc..; अवस्थया - by these modifications; भ्रान्तः-deluded; आत्मा - the *Ātmā*; न (भवति)- cannot be.

That which identifies with the body, house etc., as 'I' and 'mine' is mental sheath. It is under delusion and with modifications like desire etc., cannot be *Ātmā*. (6)

Yaḥ dehe gehe ādau ca ahantāṁ mamatāṁ karoti : That which identifies itself with the body, house etc., as 'I' and 'mine'. *Manomayaḥ kāma ādi avasthayā bhrāntaḥ* : is the *Manomaya kośa.* Through the modifications called *kāma, krodha, moha, mada, mātsarya* etc., the mind is totally under the influence of delusion.

Na sa ātmā : This cannot be the *Ātmā* because *Ātmā* does not have *ahantā, mamatā* nor *kāma, krodha* etc..

Now what is the position of *Vijñānamaya kośa*?...

लीना सुप्तौ वपुर्बोधे व्याप्नुयादानखाग्रगा ।
चिच्छायोपेतधीर्नात्मा विज्ञानमयशब्दभाक् ।।७।।

Līnā suptau vapurbodhe vyāpnuyād ānakhā gragā
Cicchāyo peta dhīr-nātmā vijñāna maya śabda bhāk (7)

चिच्छाया - the *cidābhāsa;* उपेत - alongwith; धीः- intellect; सुप्तौ - in the deep sleep; लीना - unmanifest; बोधे - in the waking state; आनख अग्रगा - from the head up to the tip of the nail; वपुः- the gross body; व्याप्नुयात् - occupies; विज्ञानमय - the intellectual sheath; शब्दभाक् - is called; आत्मा - the *Ātmā*; न (भवति)- cannot be.

The intellect, occupying the total body from the top to the toe during waking state, and getting unmanifest during deep-sleep state, associated with reflection of Consciousness, is the meaning of Intellectual Sheath. This is also not *Ātmā.* (7)

Līnā suptau vapuḥ bodhe vyāpnuyāt ānakh-āgragā : That which is totally absorbed in the deep-sleep state and that which occupies the total gross body from the head up to the (toe) nail when the waking state comes up.

Cicchāyā upeta dhīḥ vijñānamaya śabda bhāk na Ātmā : The intellect along with the reflection of consciousness, is called the *Vijñānamaya kośa.*

That is (also) not the *Ātmā* because it is also changeable i.e., appears and disappears.

The *Manomaya kośa* and *Vijñānamaya kośa* belong to the *antaḥkaraṇa,* and therefore, there is likelihood of being confused between the two. The difference between them is being explained...

कर्तृत्वकरणत्वाभ्यां विक्रियेतान्तरिन्द्रियम् ।
विज्ञानमनसी अन्तर्बहिश्चैते परस्परम् ।।८।।

Kartṛtva-karaṇatvā-bhyāṁ vikriye-tāntarin driyam
Vijñāna-manasī antar-bahiś-caite parasparam (8)

अन्तः इन्द्रियम् - the inner instrument of knowledge; कर्तृत्व करणत्वाभ्याम् - being 'doership' and 'instrumental'; विक्रियेत् - are subject to modifications; एते - these two; विज्ञान मनसी - the intellectual and mental sheaths; परस्परम् - between themselves; अन्तःबहिःच - inner and outer.

The inner instrument, is further divided into intellect and mind, as per their functional diversity; the former is associated with doership while the latter being instrument of knowledge; and are subtle and grosser in that sequence. (8)

Although the *manomaya kośa* and the *vijñānamaya kośa* seem to be the same, there is a distinct difference in the field of their functioning. In the *vijñānamaya kośa*, there is *kartṛtva abhimāna* (the sense of doership), while in the *manomaya kośa*, there is *karaṇatva abhimāna*, or the instrument of knowledge. (For example : The carpenter can be compared to the intellect and his tools to the mind).

Kartṛtva karaṇatvābhyām vikriyet antarindriyam : The modification of the *antaḥkaraṇa* (the inner organ or mind stuff) which deals with the instrumental part is called *manomaya kośa*; that which is associated with doership because of the association with the reflected Consciousness in the mind stuff is the *vijñānamaya kośa.* When there is no reflection of Consciousness in the mind stuff, it only becomes the instrument of functioning. Joy and sorrow (*sukha* and *duḥkha*) are experienced through the mind, but the one who functions through the mind is *in* the intellect. The stronger the personality, the stronger the ego, the stronger is the identification with the *vijñānamaya kośa*, and stronger are the reactions of the individual.

Vijñāna manasī antar bahiś caite parasparam : The area of operation of the *vijñānamaya kośa* and *manomaya kośa* are internal and external respectively; and former is inner while the latter is exterior to it.

The *Ānandamaya kośa* is taken for discussion...

काचिदन्तर्मुखा वृत्तिरानन्दप्रतिबिम्बभाक् ।
पुण्यभोगे भोगशान्तौ निद्रारूपेण लीयते ।।९।।

Kāci-dantar-mukhā vṛttir-ānanda-prati-bimba-bhāk
Puṇya-bhoge bhoga-śāntau nidrā-rūpeṇa līyate (9)

काचिद् वृत्तिः- some rare thought; पुण्य भोगे - at the time of experiencing the fruit of good act; अन्तर्मुखा - becomes introvert; आनन्द - bliss; प्रतिबिम्ब भाक् - associated with the reflection of; भोग शान्तौ - after that experience is over; निद्रा रूपेण - in the form of deep sleep; लीयते - becomes unmanifest (this is called bliss sheath).

Some thought while experiencing the result of a good deed, having become introvert gets the reflection of the blissful Self, and after this experience is over, becomes unmanifest in deep sleep, is called bliss sheath. (9)

Often the *Ānandamaya kośa* is mistaken to be Para-*Brahman*. It is not so. What is *Ānandamaya kośa* and its manifestations are stated in this *śloka.*

Although the mind has the ability to reflect the Consciousness fully, this reflection is not complete and perfect because of the agitations due to desire and the mala (dirt) of ignorance. When the object of desire is obtained, at that very moment, the mind attains 'agitation-less-ness' ... perfect stability without any movement.

kācit vṛttiḥ antarmukhā ānanda pratibimba bhāk: The *vṛtti* or thought is no more extroverted because of agitations. It turns inward, and is able to be in association with the light and bliss of reflected Consciousness to the fullest extent. Such a fully blissful reflection of Consciousness in the mind stuff is called *Ānandamaya kośa.*

Punya bhoge: This *Ānandamaya kośa* is able to manifest because of the result of good deeds in the past (*puṇya karma*). When this result fructifies, the individual is in a state of fulfilment.

Bhoga śāntau nidrā rūpeṇa līyate: When the desire fulfilment is over, the *Ānandamaya kośa* goes back to its source and is unmanifest in the form of deep sleep. In this way, the *Ānandamaya kośa* is expressed as *puṇya-bhoga* or blissful disposition or as total absorption in deep sleep state (when all except the *Prāṇamaya kośa* are absorbed).

Can this *Ānandamaya kośa* be *Ātmā*?...

कादाचित्कत्वतोनात्मा स्यादानन्दमयोऽप्ययम् ।
बिम्बभूतो य आनन्द आत्माऽसौ सर्वदा स्थितेः ।।१०।।

Kādācit-katvato na-ātmā syād ānanda mayo'-pyayam
Bimba-bhūto ya ānanda ātmā'sau sarvadā sthiteḥ (10)

अयम् - this; आनन्दमयः- bliss sheath; अपि - also; कादाचित् कत्वतः- being momentary; आत्मा - the *Ātmā*; न - not; स्यात् - be; यः- that which; आनन्दः- bliss; बिम्ब भूतः- is independent of reflection; असौ - this; सर्वदा स्थितेः- being ever present; आत्मा - is the *Ātmā*.

This bliss sheath also being momentary, cannot be *Ātmā*. This bliss of the pure Self being ever present is the *Ātmā*. (10)

Ayam ānanda mayaḥ api : Although the *ānandamaya kośa* is of the nature of *ānanda* or bliss, there is a difference between this *ānanda* and the *ānanda* of the *Ātman*.

Kadā cit katvataḥ : This *ānanda* of the *ānandamaya kośa* is not reflected all the time. It comes and goes for fleeting moments (*kṣaṇe*), because it is *ānanda* only at the level of the thought (*vṛtti ānanda*). Therefore, *ātmā na syāt*: it cannot be *Ātmā*.

Bimbabhūtaḥ yaḥ ānandaḥ asau sarvadā sthiteḥ ātmā : The *ānanda* of the *ānandamaya kośa is pratibimba*, is only a reflection of the *ānanda* of its origin (bimba), the Pure Self. It is dependent on many conditionings. On the other hand, the bliss of the *Ātmā* is ever present, under all circumstances.

The natural state of everyone is essentially that of bliss. But the individual falls from this state when he gets caught in the grip of: (a) Knowing an object (*jānāmi*) (b) then desiring it (*icchāmi*) and then, (c) doing something to fulfill that desire (*karomi*).

It is for the individual to decide whether the *kartṛtva abhimāna* (*vijñānamaya kośa*) should join the three external *kośa-s* (relatively easier), or whether it should form an alliance with its source, the *ānandamaya kośa*. In the latter choice, there is only one way, namely, to surrender the ego at the feet of the Lord. When this happens, the *jñāna mudrā* happens. *Jñāna mudrā* symbolises that by which the surrender to the Absolute Bliss is made.

A possible doubt is raised...

ननु देहमुपक्रम्य निद्रानन्दान्त वस्तुषु ।
मा भूदात्मत्वमन्यस्तु न कश्चिदनुभूयते ।।११।।

Nanu deham upakramya nidrā nandānta vastuṣu
Mā bhūdā-tmatvam-anyastu na kaścid-anubhūyate (11)

ननु - now a doubt is raised; देहम् उपक्रम्य - starting from the gross body; निद्रा आनन्द अन्त वस्तुषु - upto the bliss of deep sleep i.e., upto bliss sheath; आत्मत्वम् - being *Ātmā*; मा - may not; भूत् - be; अन्यः- the other; तु - indeed; कश्चित् - something else; न - not; अनुभूयते - is not experienced.

Now there is a doubt. Let the five sheaths starting from the gross body to the bliss sheath be not *Ātmā*, however, there is nothing else that can be experienced. (Therefore, there is 'nothing' called *Ātmā*)! (11)

Nanu deham upakramya nidrā nandānta vastuṣu : "I have a question, Sir." You said that, none of the five sheaths beginning from the *annamaya kośa* upto the *ānandamaya kośa* can be the *Ātmā*. This can be appreciated. Then *antaḥ tu kaścit na anubhūyate* : Other than these five *kośa-s*, what other experience is left? There seems to be nothing remaining to be known.

This doubt itself is turned around by the teacher to provide the answer...

बाढं निद्रादयः सर्वेऽनुभूयन्ते न चेतरः ।
तथाऽप्येतेऽनुभूयन्ते येन तं को निवारयेत् ।।१२।।

Bāḍhaṁ nidrādayaḥ sarve 'nubhūyante na cetaraḥ
Tathā'-pyete'nubhūyante yena taṁ ko nivārayet (12)

बाढम् - you are correct; निद्रादयः- from the gross body upto the bliss sheath; अनुभूयन्ते - are experienced; च - and; न - not; तथापि - however; सर्वे - all; एते - these five sheaths; येन - that by which; अनुभूयन्ते - are experienced; तम् - to that conscious witness; कः- who; निवारयेत् - will deny.

(To reply to this doubt) You said it! Yes, all these five sheaths are experienced and none other than these is experienced. However, that by whom these sheaths are experienced, to him, who can reject? (12)

Bādhaṁ nidrādayaḥ sarve anubhūyante : What you say is true! Namely, that all the five sheaths, the gross body etc., fall within the purview of the objects of experience.

Itaraḥ na ca : And then you also said that there is nothing else to be experienced.

Tathā yena ete api anubhūyante tam ko nivārayet : Your doubt itself provides the answer. When you say that the five *kośa-s* fall within the field of experience, whose experience are you talking about? This means, there is an experiencer who is other than these five *kośa-s*, who cannot fall within the experience. Therefore, how can we deny that by which the five *kośa-s* are experienced?

Now, why cannot the *Ātmā* be experienced?...

स्वयमेवानुभूतित्वाद्विद्यते नानुभाव्यता ।
ज्ञातृज्ञानान्तराभावादज्ञेयो न त्वसत्तया ।।१३।।

Svaya-mevā-nubhūti-tvād-vidyate nānu-bhāvyatā
Jñātṛ-jñānān-tarā bhāvād-ajñeyo na tva-sattayā (13)

स्वयम् एव - the *Ātmā* being itself; अनुभूतित्वात् - of the nature of experience; अनुभाव्यता - the object of experience; न - not; विद्यते - is; ज्ञातृ ज्ञानान्तर अभावात् - there being no other knower and knowledge; अज्ञेयः- cannot be known objectively; न तु - not indeed; असत् तया - because of non-existence.

The Self being of the nature of experience, there is no possibility of its becoming an object of experience. There being absence of difference between the knower and the known, it is unknowable, not because it is absent, and therefore, it is unknown! (13)

Svayam eva anubhūtitvāt : The *Ātmā* cannot become the object of experience like the *pañca kośa-s* are, because the *Ātmā* itself is of the nature of experience (*anubhūti*).

Jñatṛ jñāna antar abhāvāt anubhāvyatā na vidyate : It cannot become an object of experience. To know this *Ātmā,* which is of the nature of experience, there is no other (second) *Ātmā* required; because this *Ātmā* cannot be known (as an object of knowledge).

Ajñeyaḥ tu na asattayā : However, it should not be hastily concluded from the above, that because the *Ātmā* cannot be known as an object of knowledge, it does not exist, lack of experience is not lack of existence.

To summarise the sequence of the argument presented in this *śloka* as to why the *Ātma tattva* cannot be known:

a) *Ātma tattva* is itself of the nature of experience.

b) Therefore, it cannot be an object of experience.

c) Because it cannot be known as an object of experience, it is called *ajñeya.*

d) There is no second *Ātmā* required to know the first (and only) *Ātmā.*

e) But that does not mean that the *Ātmā* is non-existent.

From the above, it follows that the *Ātma tattva* cannot be objectified, because the subject can never become the object. All attempts to know the Truth through the instrument of the intellect only indicates that the *Vijñānamaya kośa* is functioning too strongly, and are bound to fail.

How the *Ātma tattva* cannot be known as an object of experience, is illustrated by some examples...

माधुर्यादि स्वभावानामन्यत्र स्वगुणार्पिणाम् ।
स्वस्मिंस्तदर्पणापेक्षा नो न चास्त्यन्यदर्पकम् ।।१४।।

Mādhuryādi-svabhāvānām-anyatra sva-guṇār piṇām
Svasmiṁ-stad-arpaṇā-pekṣā no na cā-stya nyadar-pakam (14)

अन्यत्र - to other objects; स्वगुण अर्पिणाम् - those who lend their qualities; माधुर्य आदि स्वभावानाम् - to those who have the qualities in them such as sweetness etc..; स्वस्मिन् - in themselves; तद् अर्पण अपेक्षा - the expectation of getting or borrowing these qualities; न उ - is never required; अन्यत् - the other lending sweetness etc., to the sugar; अर्पकम् - any lender; न - not; अस्ति - is.

The sweet objects such as sugar etc., lending their essential sweetness to other objects (such as sweet-meats), do not depend for sweetness on other objects, and there is no other object other than sugar that has inherent sweetness. (14)

Mādhuryādi svabhāvānām anyatra svaguṇa arpiṇām : Sugar which is sweet by nature, can lend its sweetness to other objects which are not sweet by themselves.

Svasmin tad arpaṇam apekṣā na : However, sugar does not expect to be sweet on account of some object, whether or not there is any object (like rice or milk) to be sweetened, sugar will continue to be sweet because that is its nature.

In the same way, the *Ātma tattva,* which is of the nature of *anubhava* or experience, does not depend on any other object of experience.

If there is no object for experience, what will happen to the *Ātmā*?

Anyad arpakam na asti : The sugar does not depend on other objects for receiving the sweetness. Its sweetness is beyond cause and effect. So also, the *Ātma tattva* is beyond the realm of cause and effect, and therefore, beyond the realm of intellectual understanding.

This is further explained...

अर्पकान्तरराहित्येपि अस्त्येषां तत्स्वभावता ।
मा भूत्तथाऽनुभाव्यत्वं बोधात्मा तु न हीयते ।।१५।।

Arpakāntara-rāhityepi astyeṣāṁ tat svabhāvatā
Mā bhūttathā-'nubhāvyatvaṁ bodhātmā tu na hīyate (15)

अर्पकान्तर - another lender of sweetness etc..; राहित्ये - being not present; अपि - although; एषाम् - of the sugar etc..; तत् - that sweetness; स्वभावता - by nature; अस्ति - is; तथा - in the same way; अनुभाव्यत्वम् - the *Ātman* being the object of knowledge; मा - may not; भूत् - be; बोधात्मा - the essential nature of being knowledge; तु - indeed; न - not; हीयते - is destroyed.

Although there is no other object for lending sweetness of sugar etc., they have this sweetness inherently. Similarly, the *Ātmā* may not become an object of experience, it will not lose its essential nature called knowledge or experience. (15)

Arpakāntara rāhitye api eṣām tat svabhāvatā asti : Even if, there is no other object to be sweetened, the nature of sugar to be sweet continues.

Tathā anubhāvyatvam mā bhūt : In the same way, the *Ātmā* does not fall in the purview of an experience. Therefore, when all the five *kośa-s* are rejected and when there is nothing to experience, the *Ātmā* will continue to be. Let there be no possibility of experience for the *Ātmā*, nothing will happen to it.

For, *bodhātmā tu na hīyate* : this *bodhātmā*, which is of the nature of Consciousness, Pure Knowledge, is never denied. It is self existing, *svayambhū*.

To support this point, the *Upaniṣads are cited in the next three śloka-s...*

स्वयं ज्योतिर्भवत्येष पुरोऽस्माद्भासतेऽखिलात् ।
तमेव भान्तमन्वेति तद्भासा भास्यते जगत् ।।१६।।

Svayaṁ jyotir-bhavatyeṣa puro'smād bhāsate 'khilāt
Tameva bhāntam-anveti tad-bhāsā bhāsyate jagat (16)

एषः- this *Ātmā*; स्वयं ज्योतिः- self effulgent; भवति - is; अस्मात् अखिलात् पुरः- before all these five *kośaḥ*; भासते - is self illumined; तम् एव - his alone; भान्तम् - light; अनु - later; एति - all the world comes into being; तद् भासा - by this light; जगत् - the world; भास्यते - is illumined.

This *Ātmā* is self illumined. Even before the creation of these five sheaths (world), it is self effulgent. After his light, comes the world into existence. By his light of Consciousness, the world is illumined. (16)

Eṣa svayam jyoti bhavati : The *upaniṣad-s* (B.U. 4.3.9, Nrpt.U. 2, M.U. 2.2.11, K.U. 5.15, S.U. 6.14) declare that this *Ātma tattva* is of the nature of self- effulgence. It does not require any other object to illumine it.

Asmāt akhilāt puraḥ bhāsate : Before the manifestation of all the five *kośa-s*, the Self is Self-illumined.

Tameva bhāntam anveti tat bhāsā jagat bhāsyate : The world of names and forms is illumined by the *Ātma tattva* alone (*tam eva*) and by the light of this Consciousness (the *Ātma tattva*), that which is inert and which is of the nature of constant change i.e., the world, is illumined.

Some more quotations from the *upaniṣad-s* are given...

येनेदं जानते सर्वं तत्केनान्येन जानताम् ।
विज्ञातारं केन विद्याच्छक्तं वेद्ये तु साधनम् ।।१७।।

Yenedaṁ jānate sarvaṁ tatkenānyena jānatām
Vijñātāraṁ kena vidyāt-śaktaṁ vedye tu sādhanam (17)

येन - that by which; इदम् - this world; सर्वम् - all; जानते - knows; तम् - to that; अन्येन - by other; केन - how and by whom; जानताम् - will one know?; विज्ञातारम् - to the knower; केन - by which knower; विद्यात् - will be known; साधनम् - the means of knowledge; तु - indeed; वेद्ये - in the field of objects; शक्तम् - are capable.

That witnessing Self by whom the whole world is known, to that witness, what other thing can know? By what the Knower is known? The means of knowledge are functional in the field of objective perception. (17)

Yena idaṁ sarvaṁ jānate tat anyena kena jānatām : By this Consciousness, (*Ātmā*, witness, *caitanya*, etc..) all that falls within the purview of objects, is known. What other thing can know this *sākṣī* or witness which is knowing everything? (B.U. 4.5.15)

Vijñātāram kena vidyāt: How can one know the knower? Because, Knower alone is the Knower! (K.U. 6.13)

Sādhanam tu vedye śaktam : The mind can function only in the objective experience. When functioning through the instrument of knowledge, one can only know the object of knowledge, and not the Knower of the object. Thus the impossibility of the subject ever becoming the object is establised. Furthermore, the *Ātmā* is of the nature of self-existence, self-experience, self-illumination. It is, therefore, incorrect to say that because, unlike the *pañca kośa-s*, the *Ātmā* cannot be the object of knowledge, it is non-existent. The *Ātmā* is not only ever present, but it is because of the *Ātmā* that everything is known and is existent.

स वेत्ति वेद्यं तत्सर्वं नान्यस्तस्यास्ति वेदिता ।
विदिता विदिताभ्यां तत्पृथग्बोध स्वरूपकम् ।।१८।।

Sa vetti vedyaṁ tat sarvaṁ nānyas tasy-āsti veditā
Viditā-viditābhyāṁ tat pṛthag-bodha-svarūpakam (18)

सः- that *Ātmā*; तत्सर्वम् - all that; वेद्यम् - which is known; वेत्ति - knows; तस्य - of his; वेदिता - knower; अन्यः- other; न - not; अस्ति - is; तत् - that; बोध स्वरूपकम् - of the nature of Pure knowledge; विदित अविदिताभ्याम् - from the known and the unknown; पृथक् - is different.

He, the Self, knows all that is objective. There is none who can know the Self. The Self being of the nature of Pure Knowledge, is other than the categories of known or not known. (18)

Saḥ tatsarvaṁ vedyaṁ vetti tasya anya veditā na asti : The *Ātma tattva* knows all that can be known i.e., the knower, known and the knowledge. And to know The knower, there is no other knower, otherwise we will end up in the fallacy of regress infinitum.

Tat bodha svarūpakam : The reason is that the *Ātma tattva* is of the nature of pure knowledge, not of that knowledge which is the opponent of ignorance. 'It is other than the known and the unknown.' (Ke.U. I.3). Known is always the effect and the unknown is always a cause. So the Truth is other than cause and effect. The known is manifest, and the unknown is unmanifest. Therefore, the Truth is beyond the manifest and unmanifest. To reflect on this is itself a contemplative exercise.

In spite of this clear statement, the student can still insist : "Unless I experience *Ātmā*, I cannot believe that it exists!". To such a student, the teacher gives a reply in a somewhat sarcastic vein...

बोधेऽप्यनुभवो यस्य न कथञ्चन जायते ।
तं कथं बोधयेच्छास्त्रं लोष्टं नरसमाकृतिम् ।।१९।।

Bodhe'pya-nubhavo yasya na kathaścana jāyate
Taṁ kathaṁ bodhaye-cchāstraṁ loṣṭaṁ nara-samā-kṛtim (19)

बोधे अपि - although experienced; यस्य - he to whom; अनुभवः- experience; कथञ्चन - in any way; न - not; जायते - is gained; नर समाकृतिम् -

to the one like the shape of human; तम् - to that; लोष्टम् - mud; शास्त्रम् - the scriptures; कथम् - how; बोधयेत् - can instruct.

He who although conscious of his being, yet is unable to experience his being conscious, to such a dull witted (mud doll) one, how can the scriptures instruct? (19)

Yasya bodhe api anubhavaḥ kathañcana jāyate : He who knows very clearly that he is conscious, if he still doubts his own existence, he must be dull witted indeed. To such a mud doll of human form, how can the scriptures help?

There is no doubt that one IS; there is no doubt that one is ALIVE; there is no doubt that one LOVES oneself the most. That is *Ātmā*. Nevertheless, the doubting student does not give up his doubt, "I have understood everything that you said, but I still cannot comprehend this *Ātmā*."

The teacher tries to clarify through another beautiful example...

जिव्हा मेऽस्ति न वेत्युक्तिर्लज्जायै केवलं यथा ।
न बुध्यते मया बोधो बोद्धव्य इति तादृशी ।।२०।।

Jivhā me'sti na vetyuktiḥ-lajjāyai kevalaṁ yathā
Na budhyate mayā bodho boddhavya iti tādṛśī (20)

मे जिव्हा - my tongue; अस्ति - is; न वा - or not; इति - thus; उक्तिः- statement; यथा - as; केवलम् - only for; लज्जायै - causes shame; मया - by me; बोधः- the knowledge; न - not; बुध्यते - is known; बोद्धव्यः - want to know; इति - such statements; तादृशी - is of similar kind (shameful).

A statement like, 'Do I have a tongue or not?' is in reality a matter of shame. Similarly, I do not experience my being consciousness; therefore, I must experience consciousness, such statements are of the same category. (20)

Yathā jihvā me asti vā na iti ukti kevalam lajjāyai : If someone asks, 'Please tell me if I have a tongue or not!', such a statement is something to be ashamed of, because, if the tongue is, there cannot be this doubt; and if the tongue is not, the question can never be asked.

Tādṛśī mayā bodhaḥ na budhyate boddhavyaḥ iti : Similarly, the statement that, 'I do not know that I am conscious' is foolish (meaningless). For, unless one is Conscious, one will not have even this doubt. Therefore, the statement that I must realise that I exist, that I am Conscious, and I must do *sādhanā* to realise this nature of myself, that I am this *Ātma tattva* is equally shameful.

Then what is the purpose of this knowledge?...

यस्मिन्यस्मिन्नस्ति लोके बोधस्तत्तदुपेक्षणे ।
यद्बोधमात्रं तद्ब्रह्मेतिएवं धीर्ब्रह्मनिश्चयः ।।२१।।

Yasmin-yasminn-asti loke bodhas-tat-tad-upekṣaṇe
Yad-bodha-mātraṁ tad-brahmeti-evaṁ dhīr-brahma-niścayaḥ (21)

लोके - in the world; यस्मिन् यस्मिन् - whatever; बोधः- objective knowledge; अस्ति - is; तत् तत् - that object; उपेक्षणे - having dropped; यद् - that which; बोध मात्रं - the pure knowledge; तद् - that; ब्रह्म - is *Brahman*; इति - thus; एवं - in this manner; धीः- understanding; ब्रह्मनिश्चयः- is experience of *Brahman*.

From the objective knowledge. when the object of knowledge is rejected, whatever, Pure Knowledge is left, that is *Brahman*. This is called the vision of *Brahman*.(21)

Loke yasmin yasmin bodhaḥ asti tat tat upekṣaṇe : From every object of knowledge and every experience i.e., from the objective knowledge, reject the object of knowledge then that Pure Knowledge which is not the knowledge of something but knowledge itself, that is what is called *Brahman*.

Iti evaṁ dhīḥ brahma niścayaḥ : To get established in this knowledge is called *Brahmānubhūti.* Whatever be the object of knowledge or experience (in the three states of consciusness), the Consciousness is reflected. (*Pratibodha viditam mattam* : in and through every modification of the mind, the Consciousness is reflected) (Ke.U. II.4). The object is to be rejected, not the knower of the object. The Consciousness which is illuminating the presence of the object as well as its absence, continues to be.

In this way, the *abhyāsa* is to be done by withdrawing attention from the objects and experience of the outer world; on the life that is permeating through each and every cell of the body. Thus, when the object of knowledge is dropped, what remains is the Pure Knowledge, which is without involvement in the objective manifestation of the knower and the known. This Pure Knowledge 'I am', in this, there is neither tension, nor effort.

This understanding (*dhī*) is called *Brahman.* The attention will not be on the world of names and forms (*alankāra buddhi* is an example of ornament) but on that Consciousness because of which, subject-object relationship is ever possible (*suvarṇa buddhi*). This is the real *dhī*, this is *Brahman*, this is *Brahmāsmi dhī*, this is *Brahma anubhūti.*

पञ्चकोश परित्यागे साक्षिबोधावशेषतः ।
स्वस्वरूपं स एव स्याच्छून्यत्वं तस्य दुर्घटम् ।।२२।।

Pañca-kośa parityāge sākṣi-bodhā-vaśeṣataḥ
Sva-svarūpaṁ sa eva syāt-śūnyatvaṁ tasya durghaṭam (22)

पञ्चकोश - the five sheaths; परित्यागे - having rejected (through discrimination); साक्षि बोध - the witnessing Consciousness; अवशेषतः- being left; स एव - that witnessing Consciousness alone; स्व स्वरूपम् - one's own essential nature; स्यात् - is; तस्य - of this witness; शून्यत्वम् - being nothingness; दुर्घटम् - is impossible.

Having rejected the five sheaths, the witnessing consciousness that remains, is our own real nature. That is *Brahman*. It is impossible to deny its existence, as nothing. (22)

Pañcakośa parityāge : (Applying the same principle as explained above), when the five *kośa-s* are rejected by proper discrimination, *sākṣi bodha avaśeṣataḥ svasvarūpa sa eva syāt* : what remains is the *sākṣi* or witness which is of the nature of Pure Consciousness. That is what is called our own essential nature. *Tasya śūnyatvam durghaṭam* : Therefore,to say that after negating the five *kośa-s*, nothing is left; that nothingness is an impossibility. The argument that because *Sākṣi* cannot be known, it does not exist, is fallacious. *Śūnyatvam* is the ultimate confusion.

How this *Sākṣi* cannot be 'an absence', but it is of the nature of 'presence' is explained...

अस्ति तावत्स्वयं नाम विवादाविषयत्वतः ।
स्वस्मिन्नपि विवादश्चेत् प्रतिवाद्यत्र को भवेत् ।।२३।।

Asti tāvat-svayaṁ nāma vivādā-viṣaya-tvataḥ
Svasminn-api vivādaś-cet prativādy-atra ko bhavet (23)

स्वयं नाम - the meaning of the word 'I myself'; तावत् अस्ति - is popularly known; विवाद - doubt or discussion; अविषयत्वतः- cannot be a topic; स्वस्मिन् अपि - about one's own nature also; विवादः चेत् - if there is any doubt; अत्र - then in this discussion; प्रतिवादी - opponent; कः- who; भवेत् - will be.

The meaning of the word *'svayam'* is clearly known to everyone, that it means oneself. There is no doubt or discussion on this topic. If one wants to doubt and argue about one's own presence, then with whom will he argue? (23)

Svayam nāma tāvat asti vivādaḥ aviṣayatvataḥ : The very meaning of this word *svayam* is 'I'. This is known to everyone without any doubt and there is no place for any argument or controversy about it; this 'I' cannot become the subject of logic or doubt.

Svasmin api vivādaḥ cet atra prativādi ko bhavet : If, however, one still has a doubt about one's own being, if one is there or not, in that case with whom can one argue? His very presence is in doubt!! Therefore, this thought that after the rejection of the *pañca kośa-s*, nothing is left, is an impossibility. The very process of doubting proves one's existence.

But such an impossible thought can occur once in a while, when?...

स्वासत्त्वं तु न कस्मैचिद्रोचते विभ्रमं विना ।
अत एव श्रुतिर्बाधं ब्रूते चासत्त्ववादिनः ।।२४।।

Svāsattvaṁ tu na kasmai-cid-rocate vibhramaṁ vinā
Ata eva śrutir-bādhaṁ brūte cā-sattva-vādinaḥ (24)

विभ्रमम् विना - unless deluded; स्व - one's own; असत्त्वम् - non-presence; तु - indeed; कस्मैचित् - to none; न - not; रोचते - is acceptable; अतः एव - therefore; श्रुतिः च - the scriptures also; असत्त्व वादिनः- of those who propose the non-existence; बाधं ब्रूते - declares negation.

Unless deluded, none will ever accept one's own absence. Therefore, the scriptures declare the negation of those who emphasise the non-existence. (24)

Vibhramaṁ vinā sva asattvaṁ kasmai cit na rocate : Only under the spell of delusion, can one have peculiar thought fixation that one is not there. Otherwise, no one can experience one's own absence or non-existence.

Ata eva śrutiḥ ca asattva vādinaḥ bādham bhrūte : And therefore, the *śruti-s* also condemn those who advocate *śūnyatva* - that there is nothing left after the five *kośa-s* are rejected.

How does the *Śruti* condemn the *śūnyavādins*?...

असदब्रह्मेति चेद्वेद स्वयमेव भवेदसत् ।
अतोऽस्य मा भूद्वेद्यत्वं स्वसत्त्वं त्वभ्युपेयताम् ।।२५।।

Asad-brahmeti ced-veda svayam-eva bhaved-asat
Ato'sya mā bhūd-vedyatvaṁ sva-sattvaṁ tvabhyu peyatām (25)

असत् ब्रह्म इति - *Brahman* is non-existent; वेद - one knows; चेत् - if; स्वयम् एव - he himself; असत् - non-existent; भवेत् - will be; अतः- therefore; अस्य - of the self; वेद्यत्वम् - objectively knowable; मा - may not; भूत् - be; स्वसत्त्वम् - one's own existence; तु - indeed; अभ्युपेयताम् - has to be accepted.

If someone says that the *Brahman* is non-existent, he attains self-denial. Therefore, the Self may not become an object of knowledge or experience, yet one must accept one's own existence. (25)

Brahma asat iti cet veda : If someone asserts that *Brahman* is non-existent, *svayam eva asat bhavet*: It will only lead to his own non-existence (T.U. II.6). This means that one cannot say that after the *pañca kośa-s* are rejected, nothing is left, for the inference will be that one is denying one's own existence, one's own presence.

Ataḥ asya vedyatva mā bhūt sva sattvam tu abhyu-peyatām : Therefore, the *Ātmā* may not become an object of knowledge like the *pañca kośa-s*, but one must recognise one's own presence. The ever-present-existence, that I am. That is called *Brahman*, not the *pañca kośa-s*.

The next question that follows the acceptance that the *Ātmā* is and that it is not the object of knowledge is, what is the essential nature of this *Ātmā* which one cannot objectify?...

कीदृक्तर्हीति चेत्पृच्छेदीदृक्ता नास्ति तत्र हि ।
यदनीदृगतादृक्च तत्स्वरूपं विनिश्चिनु ।।२६।।

Kīdṛk-tarhīti-cet-pṛcched-īdṛktā nāsti tatra hi
Yad-anī-dṛg-atādṛk-ca tat-svarūpaṁ viniś-cinu (26)

तर्हि - in that case; कीदृक् इति - what is the nature of Self; चेत् - if; पृच्छेत् - is asked; ईदृक्ता - 'like this-ness'; हि - indeed; तत्र - in the Self; न अस्ति - is not; यद् - that; अनीदृक् - unlike this-ness; अतादृक् - unlike that; च - and; तत् - that; स्वरूपम् - one's essential nature; विनिश्चिनु - come to realise.

Now, if one wants to know that 'like what' is the *Ātmā*; this 'like-what-ness' is not applicable to *Ātmā*. That which is unlike this or that, is the nature of *Ātmā*. Come to discover it! (26)

Tarhi kīdṛk iti cet pṛcchet īdṛktā tatra na asti : Then if you ask the question, what is the nature of *Ātmā*, it is not possible to describe that the *Ātmā* is like 'this' or 'this' (*īdṛk*).

Yad anīdṛk tādṛk ca tat svarūpam viniścinu : Nor is it possible to conjecture it is like 'that' or 'that' (*tādṛk*). In this way, by negating 'this' as well as 'that' you establish your own essential nature.

What is the meaning of *īdṛk* and *tādṛk*?...

अक्षाणां विषयस्त्वीदृक्परोक्षस्तादृगुच्यते ।
विषयी नाक्षविषयः स्वत्वान्नास्य परोक्षता ।।२७।।

Akṣāṇāṁ viṣaya-stvī-dṛk-parokṣas-tādṛg-ucyate
Viṣayī nākṣaviṣayaḥ svatvān-nāsya parokṣatā (27)

अक्षाणां विषय - the object of senses; तु - indeed; ईदृक् - the word *īdṛk* i.e.,'like this' means; परोक्षः- the directly unknown thing; तादृक् - like that; उच्यते - is called; विषयी - the seer *Ātmā*; न - neither; अक्षविषय - an object of knowledge; स्वत्वात् - being one's own nature; न - nor; अस्य - of the *Ātmā*; परोक्षता - the indirectness.

The objects of senses is meant by the word 'like this', which are directly perceived. '*Tādṛg*' refers to the things (such as *dharma*, heaven etc..) known indirectly through scriptures. The knower of the objects is not an object of knowledge for senses. Being 'Itself', there is no indirectness in his being i.e., known without means of knowledge. (27)

Akṣāṇāṁ viṣayaḥ tu īdṛk ucyate : Whatever is known through the sense perception is referred to by the term *īdṛk*. *Ātmā* is like this or this, as if we are trying to spell out *Ātmā* in the form of *śabda, sparśa, rūpa, rasa, gandha.*

Parokṣaḥ tādṛk (ucyate) : The term *tādṛk* refers to that knowledge gathered from the scriptures, and not directly experienced (e.g. heaven is like that etc..).

In other words, *pratyakṣatva* is called *īdṛk* and *parokṣatva* is called *tādṛk*. Therefore, when it is said that *Ātmā* cannot be defined in terms of like 'this' or like 'that', it means that the *Ātmā* is neither the object of sense perception nor is it something other than me. It is of my own nature.

Viṣayī akṣa viṣaya na : *Ātmā* being the knower (*viṣayī*), it cannot become the object of knowledge.

Svatvāt asya parokṣatā na : Ātmā being the Self cannot fall within the purview of *parokṣata, tādṛktā.*

Therefore, *Ātmā* cannot be defined in terms of like 'this' or like 'that'.

How can it be proved that this *Ātmā* is *Brahma-svarūpa*?

The teacher takes up this thought for development first by stating that the *Ātmā* is *aparokṣa, svayam-prakāśa*, next by describing the nature of *Brahman*, and followed by deducting the nature of *Brahman* in *Ātmā* and thus establishing the identity of the *Ātmā* and *Brahman*...

अवेद्योऽप्यपरोक्षोऽतः स्वप्रकाशो भवत्ययम् ।
सत्यं ज्ञानमनन्तं चेत्यस्तीह ब्रह्मलक्षणम् ।।२८।।

Avedyo-'pya-parokṣo-'taḥ sva-prakāśo bhava-tyayam
Satyaṁ jñānam-anantaṁ ceti-astīha brahma-lakṣaṇam (28)

अयम् - this *Ātmā*; अवेद्य - unknowable; अपि - although; अपरोक्षः- is immediate; अतः- therefore; स्वप्रकाशः- self illumined; भवति - is; सत्यम् - existence; ज्ञानम् - knowledge; अनन्त - unconditioned; च - and; इति - this; ब्रह्म लक्षणम् - the indicative definitions of *Brahman*; इह - in this *Ātmā*; अस्ति - is.

This *Ātmā*, although unknowable, but being self-illumined, is immediate. The essential natureof *Brahman*, namely Existence-Knowledge-Bliss are seen here in case of *Ātmā*. (28)

Ayam avedya api aparokṣa (san) ataḥ sva-prakāśaḥ bhavati : Although the *Ātmā* cannot become the object of knowledge, it is *aparokṣa* of the nature of one's own being. Therefore, it is self-illumined and self-existing (*svayambhū*). This is the nature of the *Ātmā*.

Satyam jñānam anantam ca it iha brahma lakṣaṇam : Now regarding the nature of the *Brahman*, it is *Satyam* (Existence), *Jñānam* (Knowledge), *Anantam* (Bliss) (*Satyam jñānam anantam brahma yo veda nihitam guhāyām* -T.U. 2.1).

The nature of *Brahman* can also be deduced in the *Ātmā*. Therefore, *Ātmā* which is *aparokṣa* and *svaprakāśa* is nothing but the

Parabrahman Paramātmā. In this way, *Brahmātma aikya bodha* takes place through the *pañca kośa viveka*.

How the *Ātmā* is *Brahmansvarūpa*, and how each and every aspect of the *Brahman* can be deduced in the *Ātmā* is further explained...

सत्यत्वं बाधराहित्यं जगद्बाधैकसाक्षिणः ।
बाधः किंसाक्षिको ब्रूहि न त्वसाक्षिक इष्यते ।।२९।।

Satyatvaṁ bādha-rāhityaṁ jagad-vādhaikasākṣiṇaḥ
Bādhaḥ kiṁ-sākṣiko brūhi na tva-sākṣika iṣyate (29)

सत्यत्वम् - the Existence; बाध राहित्यम् - cannot be negated; जगत् बाधैक साक्षिणः- of the witness of the negation of the world (as in deep sleep etc.); बाधः- absence; किं - who; साक्षिकः- the witness; ब्रूहि - tell; असाक्षिकः- without the witness; तु - the negation; न - not; ईष्यते - acceptable.

The existence means that which is immune to negation. That which is the witness of the negation of the world, who will know the negation of this witness? And the absence, without which the knower of the absence is not proved. (29)

Satyatvaṁ bādha rāhityaṁ : Taking the quality of *satyam* first; *satyatvam* (Existence) is that which cannot be denied.

Jagat bādhaika sākṣiṇaḥ : Every denial of the world (the *pañca kośa-s*) can be established only if there is a witness to the negation. Therefore, the two qualities of Existence are:

a) That which cannot be denied and
b) That which is the witness of every denial (*bādha*).

Bādhaḥ kiṁ sākṣikaḥ brūhi : Who can deny this Existence which is the witness of the denial or rejection of the world of plurality?

This *sākṣi,* which is ever present, is the nature of *Brahman.* This can be deduced in the *Ātmā* also.Therefore, the satyam of the *Brahman* is fully established in the satyam of the *Ātmā-tattva* in the form of 'ever present *sākṣi*'.

Asākṣikaḥ bādhaḥ na iṣyate : Because, without the *sākṣi,* the negation cannot be established.

This point is illustrated by an example...

अपनीतेषु मूर्तेषु ह्यमूर्तं शिष्यते वियत् ।
शक्येषु बाधितेष्वन्ते शिष्यते यत्तदेव तत् ।।३०।।

Apanītesu mūrteṣu hyamūrtaṁ śiṣyate viyat
Śakyeṣu bādhite-ṣvante śiṣyate yattadeva tat (30)

मूर्तेषु अपनीतेषु - when the objects with form are removed (from a room); अमूर्तम् - the formless; वियत् - space; शिष्यते - is left behind; हि - certainly; शक्येषु बाधितेषु - when all that can be negated is negated; अन्ते - after that; यत् - that which; शिष्यते - is left un-negated; तत् एव - that indeed; तत् - is the*Ātmā.*

When the objects with forms are removed (from a place), the formless space is left behind. (Similarly), all that can be negated is negated, at the end of it, whatever is left un-negated, that indeed is *Ātmā.* (30)

Mūrteṣu apanīteṣu amūrtaṁ viyat śiṣyate hi : When objects (with form) are removed, the space which has no shape or dimensions remains. Space cannot be removed, it is only possible to remove the object. The space which can never be removed is always left behind.

Yat śakyeṣu bādhiteṣu śiṣyate tat eva tat : In the same way, when the *pañca kośa viveka* is carried out, the five *kośa-s* can be rejected but the *Ātmā* which is the substratum supporting all the *kośa-s* can never be denied. Therefore, *Ātmā* is *satya svarūpam* like the *Brahman.*

सर्वबाधे न किञ्चिच्चेद्यन्न किञ्चित्तदेव तत् ।
भाषा एवात्र भिद्यन्ते निर्बाधं तावदस्ति हि ।।३१।।

Sarva bādhe na kiñcic-ced-yanna kiñcit-tad-eva tat
Bhāṣā evātra bhidyante nirbādhaṁ tāva-dasti hi (31)

सर्वबाधे - when everything is negated; न - not; किञ्चित् - is left behind; चेत् - is objected; यत् - that; न किञ्चित् - 'really nothing'; तद् एव - that indeed; तत् - is *Brahman*; अत्र - in this expression; भाषा एव - only language; भिद्यन्ते - differs; निर्बाधम् - the non-negated *Ātmā*; तावत् अस्ति हि - is always present indeed.

If one objects that when everything (the five sheaths) is negated, nothing is left, then that "really nothing" is *Brahman*. In this expression, only language differs. The non-describable *Ātmā* is ever present indeed. (31)

To the obstinate student who refuses to be convinced that the *Ātmā* is, the teacher says:

Sarva bādhe yat na kiñcit, tat na kiñcit tat eva tat : If you keep on saying that after denying all the *pañca kośa-s,* nothing remains, then whatever you mean by 'nothing' (*na kiñcit*), 'that' is *Ātmā.*

Bhāṣā evātra bhidyante nirbādhaṁ tāvat asti hi : You are only getting lost in words. What I call *Ātmā,* you call 'nothing'. This 'nothing', this *Ātmā* which can never be denied (*nirbādhaṁ*) is called *Ātma tattva* and it is ever present (*asti hi*).

This ever present, never deniable Existence, which is the nature of the *Brahman*, is also the nature of the *Ātman.*

To support this point again, the *śruti* is cited...

अत: एव श्रुतिर्बाध्यं बाधित्वा शेषयत्यदः ।
स एष नेति नेत्यात्मेत्यतद्व्यावृत्तिरूपतः ।।३२।।

Ataḥ eva śrutirbādhyaṁ bādhitvā śeṣaya-tyadaḥ
Sa eṣa neti netyātmeti-atad-vyāvṛtti rūpataḥ (32)

अतः- therefore; एव - certainly; स - this *Ātmā*; एष न इति न इति - not this, not this, in this way; आत्मा - *Ātmā*; इति - is; श्रुतिः- the scriptural statement; अतद् व्यावृत्ति रूपतः- by negating the not-self; बाध्य बाधित्वा - having negated all that can be negated; अदः- the Self; शेषयति - is left behind (to comprehend as Self).

Therefore, this is not *Ātmā*, in this way, the *upaniṣad*, by the method of negating the non-Self; and having negated all that which can be negated; indicates the one which is left behind, un-negated, as *Ātmā.* (32)

Ataḥ eva śrutiḥ sa eṣa na iti na iti : And therefore, when the *śruti vākya* says *Ātmā* is not this, not this...

Ātmā atad vyavṛtti rūpataḥ : In this way, by the process of denial or negation (*niṣedha*), all that is not *Ātmā* (*atat* - not *Ātmā* as opposed to *tat* - that *Ātmā*) is rejected.

Bādhyaṁ bādhitvā adaḥ śeṣayati: After having rejected that which can be rejected, what is left behind is called the *Ātma tattva.*

Thus the *śruti mātā* does not create *Ātmā*, but by again and again denying and rejecting all that we are holding on to, as not Truth, helps in revealing the *Ātma tattva* to the seeker, as his own essential nature.

Now, what is that which can be rejected, and what is that which cannot be rejected?...

इदं रूपं तु यद्यावत्तत्त्यक्तुं शक्यतेऽखिलम् ।
अशक्यो ह्यनिदंरूपः स आत्मा बाधवर्जितः ।।३३।।

Idaṁ-rūpaṁ tu yadyāvat-tat-tyaktuṁ śakyate-'khilam
Āśakyo hyanidaṁ-rūpaḥ sa ātmā bādha-varjitaḥ (33)

इदम् रूपम् - all that is objectified; यद् यावद् - such as body, mind etc.; तत् अखिलम् - all that; त्यक्तुम् शक्यते - can be negated; अनिदम् रूपः- that which is not known objectively i.e., subjective Self; अशक्यः- is not possible to be negated; हि - therefore; बाध वर्जितः- that which cannot be negated; स - that; आत्मा - is *Ātmā.*

All that can be objectified (such as body, mind etc.) can also be negated. However, that which is not known objectively i.e., the Subjective Self, cannot be negated. Therefore, that which cannot be negated is *Ātmā.* (33)

Idaṁ rūpaṁ tu yat yāvat tat akhilam tyaktum śakyate : Idaṁ means all that can be included in the purview of objective perception begining with and including one's own gross body. Whatever be it the external world can become the object of our knowledge - those that fall under the purview of five senses: *śabdha, sparśa, rūpa, rasa, gandha* followed by the instruments of perception and the *pañca kośa-s,* they can be rejected.

Aśakyaḥ hi anidaṁ rūpam : That which cannot become the object of perception cannot be rejected.

Bādha varjitaḥ sa ātmā : In the subject-object relationship, objects can be rejected, but not the subject. That which cannot be negated, that is *Ātmā,* the *sākṣi.*

In deep sleep, everything is rejected except that one thing which cannot be rejected - that is the Pure Self.

A question can be asked: 'In deep sleep, there is still one thing that is not rejected namely, ignorance'. Ignorance is absence of knowledge. Absence means that which is not. Even that absence is illumined by the presence of the *Ātma tattva.*

Now the second *Brahma lakṣaṇam* namely *Jñānaṁ,* is dealt with...

सिद्धं ब्रह्मणि सत्यत्वं ज्ञानत्वं तु पुरेरितम् ।
स्वयमेवानुभूतित्वादित्यादिवचनैः स्फुटम् ।।३४।।

Siddhaṁ brahmaṇi satyatvaṁ jñānatvaṁ tu pureritam
Svayam-evā-nubhū-titvā-dityādi-vacanaiḥ sphuṭam (34)

ब्रह्मणि - in the *Brahman*; सत्यत्वम् - the existence aspect; सिद्धम् - is thus confirmed; ज्ञानत्वम् - the knowledge aspect; तु - already; पुरा - earlier (in *śloka* 13); स्वयम् एव अनुभूतित्वात् - '*svayam eva anubhūti-tvāt*'; इत्यादि - etc..; वचनैः- by these words; स्फुटम् - clearly; ईरितम् - is declared.

In this way, the Existence, which is the nature of *Brahman* is proved to be also that of *Ātmā.* And the knowledge aspect (of *Brahman*) is already proved to be similar in *Ātmā* earlier (*śloka* 13) by the words like '*Svayam-evānubhūti tvāt*' etc.. (34)

Siddhaṁ brahmaṇi satyatvaṁ : In this way, the *satyatvaṁ* (Beingness) is established in the *Brahman* which is also seen in *Ātmā.*

Jñānatvaṁ tu purā īritam svayam eva anubhūti-tvāt: Regarding the second *lakṣaṇam* of *Brahman*, namely *jñānam,* this has already been discussed earlier (in *śloka* 13 ante) where it is said, *svayam eva anubhūti-tvāt,* that *Ātmā* is of the nature of Self-knowledge, Self-awareness. Therefore, the *jñāna lakṣaṇam* of *Brahman* is also established in the *Ātmā.*

Now the third *lakṣaṇam* of *Brahman* - *Ānandatva* is taken up...

न व्यापित्वाद्देशतोऽन्तो नित्यत्वान्नापि कालतः ।
न वस्तुतोऽपि सार्वात्म्यादानन्त्यं ब्रह्मणि त्रिधा ।।३५।।

Na vyāpitvāt deśato'nto nityatvān-nāpi kālataḥ
Na vastuto'pi sārvātmyād-ānantyaṁ brahmaṇi tridhā (35)

व्यापित्वात् - being omnipresent; देशतः- due to space; अन्त - limitation; न - is not; नित्यत्वात् - being ever present; कालतः- due to time; अपि - limitation; न - is not; सार्वात्म्यात् - being all pervading; वस्तुतः- due to objective difference; अपि - limitation; न - not; ब्रह्मणि - in the *Brahman*; त्रिधा - the three types; आनन्त्यम् - absence of these limitations.

There is total absence of three types of limitations in *Brahman*, (i) being omni present : no limitation due to space (ii) being ever present : no limitation due to time and (iii) being all pervading : there is no limitation due to differences in objects. (35)

Brahmaṇi ānantyam tridhā : In the *Brahman anantatva* (*anantatva*, absence of limitations) is described in three ways; limitation due to space (*deśataḥ*),time (*kālataḥ*) and object (*vastutaḥ*).

Vyāpitvāt deśataḥ antaḥ na : The *Brahman* is all pervading, the limitation of space is totally absent in the *Brahman*.

Nityatvāt na kālataḥ api : *Brahman* being *nityatvāt*, eternal, there is no limitation of time on the *Brahman*. Therefore *Brahman* is *ananta*.

Sārvātmyāt vastutaḥ api na : There is no limitation of objects. *Brahman* is present in all objects being the material cause, or *upādāna kāraṇa*.

In this way, all the three types of limitations or *pariccheda* are totally absent in the *Brahman*, therefore, the *Brahman* is *anantam*, infinite.

What has been stated here on the basis of scriptural statements is now proved by logical explanation...

देशकालान्यवस्तूनां कल्पितत्वाच्च मायया ।
न देशादिकृतोऽन्तोस्ति ब्रह्मानन्त्यं स्फुटं ततः ।।३६।।

Deśa-kālānya-vastūnāṁ kalpita-tvācca māyayā
Na deśādi-kṛto-'ntosti brahmā nantyaṁ sphuṭaṁ tataḥ (36)

देश - space; काल - time; अन्य - other; वस्तूनाम् - of these things; मायया - by *māyā*; कल्पितत्वात् - being imagined and projected; च - and; देशादि - the space etc.; कृतः- created (limited); अन्तः- limitation; न - not; अस्ति - is; ततः- therefore; ब्रह्म - the *Brahman*; आनन्त्यम् - the limitation-lessness; स्फुटम् - is very clear.

The time, space and objects being the projections of *māyā* are imaginary, hence, there cannot be a real limitation due to space etc.. Therefore, the *Brahman* is proved clearly to be devoid of any limitations. (36)

Deśa kāla anya vastūnām māyayā kalpitatvāt: Time, space and vastu (object) are only concepts of the mind. Space is not something solid that can be described, it is only a concept of the mind. Time is another concept, and object is that which is governed by space and time. That which is governed by concepts of the mind cannot be real. That is also *kalpanā mātra* i.e., conceptual.

Deśādi kṛtaḥ antaḥ brahmaṇi na asti: So these limitations of space etc., which are only conceptual cannot limit the *Brahman*, which is the substratum of all concepts and imagination. (e.g. limitations of East, West etc., do not touch space.

Tataḥ brahma ānantyaṁ sphuṭaṁ : Therefore, it is distinctly clear that *Brahman* is *anantam* without the imposition of any limitation.

Now the student raises another peculiar doubt: There may not be limitations on *Brahman* on accouct of space, time and object; but there is the limitation of *jīvatva* and *Īśvaratva*. So, how can *Brahman* be termed *ananta*?

सत्यं ज्ञानमनन्तं यद्ब्रह्म तद्वस्तु तस्य तत् ।
ईश्वरत्वं च जीवत्वमुपाधिद्वयकल्पितम् ।।३७।।

Satyaṁ jñānam-anantaṁ yad-brahma tad-vastu tasya tat
Īśvaratvaṁ ca jīvatvam-upādhi-dvaya-kalpitam (37)

यत् - that which; सत्यम् - Existence; ज्ञानम् - Knowledge; अनन्तम् - devoid of any kind of limitations; ब्रह्म - *Brahman*; तद् - that; वस्तु - reality; तस्य - of that reality; तत् - that; ईश्वरत्वम् - the *Īśvarahood*; जीवत्वम् च - and the *jīvahood*; उपाधि द्वय - these two conditionings; कल्पितम् - is imagined and projected.

The *Brahman*, which is Existence-Knowledge and devoid of limitations is the reality. Of this reality, the *Brahman*, the status of *Īśvara* and *jīva* are two projected imagined conditioning. (37)

Yat satyam jñānam anantam brahma tad vastu : From the absolute standpoint, *Brahman* which is Existence, Knowledge, and Infinity (unlimited) is the Reality.

Tasya tat Īśvaratvam jīvatvam ca upādhi dvaya kalpitam : But are not the *jīvatva* and *Īśvaratva* limitations in the same *Brahman*?

The teacher explains that these two *upādhi-s* i.e., limitations are only imagined and proceeds to explain how...

शक्तिरस्त्यैश्वरी काचित्सर्ववस्तुनियामिका ।
आनन्दमयमारभ्य गूढा सर्वेषु वस्तुषु ।।३८।।

Śaktir-asty-aiśvarī kācit-sarva-vastu-niyāmikā
Ānanda-mayam-ārabhya gūḍhā sarveṣu vastuṣu (38)

काचित् - some inexplicable; ऐश्वरी - divine; सर्व वस्तु - all things and beings; नियामिका - controller; शक्तिः- power or potentiality; अस्ति - is; आनन्दमयम् आरभ्य - starting from bliss sheath; सर्वेषु - in all; वस्तुषु - objects of this world; गूढा - is hidden.

There is some inexplicable divine power, which is the controller of all the things and beings, and it is hidden in all the beings, in the five sheaths starting from the bliss sheath. (38)

Kācit aiśvarī śaktiḥ asti, sarva vastu niyāmikā : There is some (*kācit*) divine power which cannot be defined (*anirvacanīya*) and which is called *māyā*, which controls all the things and beings in this world. Which things and beings?

Ānanda mayam ārabhya sarveṣu vastuṣu gūḍhā : Begining from the *ānandamaya kośa*, this *māyā* or divine power is inherent in the total world, which is under its control.

How does one know that there is such a *śakti* (power)? How the presence of *māyā śakti* inferred, is explained in *śloka* 39...

वस्तु धर्मा नियम्येरन् शक्त्या नैव यदा तदा ।
अन्योन्य धर्म सांकर्याद्विप्लवेत जगत्खलु ।।३९।।

Vastu-dharmā niyamyeran śaktyā naiva yadā tadā
Anyonya-dharma-sāṅkaryād-viplaveta jagat-khalu (39)

वस्तु धर्माः- the qualities of the object; यदा - if; शक्त्या - by this *māyā* power; न - not; एव - at all; नियम्येरन् - controlled; तदा - then; अन्योन्य - mutual; धर्म सांकर्यात् - admixture of the qualities; जगत् - the world; विप्लवेत - will result in chaotic state; खलु - indeed.

If the qualities of the different objects are not controlled by this power, then there will be mutual admixture of qualities of things, and the world will sink in the state of chaos indeed! (39)

Vastu dharmā yadā śaktyā na eva niyamyeran : Every object in the world has its own quality like the earth has smell (*gandha*), water being liquid has taste etc.. These qualities which are governed by certain precise principles, constitute the *vastu dharma* of each object. Had there been no power or *śakti* exercising proper control over these objects, *tadā anyonya dharma sāṅkaryāt* : there would be total chaos, resulting from the mixture (*sāṅkarya*) of the qualities of different things and beings.

Therefore, it can be inferred that there is a Power which is keeping Nature running in an orderly, cosmic manner.

Jagat viplavet khalu : But for that, everyone knows, that the world would not have been an orderly manifestation. The laws of Nature are so well defined and precisely manifested that one can trust Nature more than anything else.

Now another doubt is raised: If the *māyā śakti* is other than Consciousness (*Brahman*), is it inert?

चिच्छायावेशतः शक्तिश्चेतनेव विभाति सा ।
तच्छक्त्युपाधिसंयोगाद्ब्रह्मैवेश्वरतां व्रजेत् ।।४०।।

Cicchāyā-veśataḥ śaktiś-cetaneva vibhāti sā
Tac-chaktyu pādhi-saṁyogāt-brahmaive śvaratāṁ vrajet (40)

सा - that; शक्तिः- power; चित् छाया वेशतः- being associated with the reflection of consciousness; चेतना इव - as if Consciousness; विभाति - appears; तद् शक्तिः- that power; उपाधि - conditioning; संयोगात् - in association with; ब्रह्म - the *Brahman*; एव - alone; ईश्वरताम् - the *Īśvarahood*; व्रजेत् - attains.

This power in association with the reflection of the Consciousness, appears as Consciousness. Conditioned by this power, the *Brahman* alone has attained the status of *Īśvara*. (40)

Sā śaktiḥ cicchāyā veśataḥ cetana iva vibhāti : When the *cetana* (Consciousness) is functioning through the conditioning of *māyā*, this *māyā śakti* starts manifesting as if, it is Consciousness.

Tat śaktiḥ upādhi saṁyogāt brahma eva Īśvaratām vrajet: Therefore, when *Brahman* is referred with reference to the conditioning of the *māyā*, the *Īśvaratva* is manifested in the *Brahman*. This is how the *Īśvaratva,* as one of the apparent limitations of *Brahman* comes about, because of the conditioning of this *sarva niyāmikā śakti* called *māyā.*

Now the second limitation of *Brahman*, the *jīvatva* is explained, also the question as to how the one and the same *Brahman* can have two limitations...

कोशोपाधिविवक्षायां याति ब्रह्मैव जीवताम् ।
पिता पितामहश्चैकः पुत्रपौत्रौ यथा प्रति ।।४१।।

Kośo-pādhi-vivakṣāyāṁ yāti brahmaiva jīvatām
Pitā pitāmahaś-caikaḥ putra-pautrau yathā prati (41)

कोश उपाधि विवक्षायां - with reference to the five sheaths; ब्रह्म एव - the Brahma alone; जीवताम् - the status of *jīva*; याति - attains (is clearly understood); यथा - as; एकः- one; पुत्र - son; पौत्रौ प्रति - for the grandson; पिता - father; पितामहः- grandfather; च - and.

With reference to the five sheaths, the *Brahman* alone attains the statusof *jīva*, as the same person attains the status of father and grandfather with reference to his son and grandson respectively. (41)

Having defined *Īśvaratva* with reference to *Brahman* and *māyā*, the teacher says, *Brahma eva jīvatām yāti kośa upādhi vivakṣāyām* : The same *Brahman* also attains *jīvatva.* How?

We have already seen that the *pañca kośa-s* are illumined by the *Ātmā*, and that the *Ātmā* is nothing but the *Brahman*. Therefore, the

Brahman when it is in association with the limitations of the *pañca kośa-s*, is called the *jīva.* The same *Brahman* in association with the conditioning of *māyā* is called *Īśvara.* How can the same *Brahman* have two *upādhi-s* simultaneously?

Yāthā ekaḥ putra pautra prati pitā pitāmaḥ : Just as the same individual can simultaneously be father to his son, and grandfather to his grandson; in the same way, to support the *pañca kośa-s* in one place becomes the *jīvatva*, and to support the *māyā* in another, becomes the *Īśvaratva*; both are possible simultaneously in the *Brahman*.

Now, if the *Brahman* is seen without reference to the *pañca kośa* or *māyā upādhi*, then the *Brahmatva* will be seen to be one and the same. This is stated in the next *śloka*.

पुत्रादेरविवक्षायां न पिता न पितामहः ।
तद्वन्नेशो नापि जीवः शक्तिकोशाऽविवक्षणे ।।४२।।

Putrā-dera-vivakṣāyāṁ na pitā na pitāmahaḥ
Tad-van-neśo nāpi jīvaḥ śakti-kośā'vivakṣaṇe (42)

पुत्र आदेः- of the son etc.; अविवक्षायां - without reference; न पिता - neither father; न पितामहः- nor grandfather; तद् वत् - in the same way; शक्ति - the divine power *māyā*; कोशा - the five sheaths; अविवक्षणे - when not referred; न ईशः - neither *Īśvara*; न जीवः अपि - nor is the *jīva*

Without reference to the son etc., the person is neither father nor grandfather. Similarly, without the conditioning of *māyā* and five sheaths, neither there is *Īśvara* nor *jīva* (but *Brahman* alone is!) (42)

Putrādeḥ avivakṣāyām : When we refer to a person without reference to son or grandson, *Na pitā na pitāmaḥ* : Then he is neither father nor grandfather. This 'non-related' person (Devadatta!) is the reality. He does not suffer. But the father and the grandfather are not the reality, they are conditioned by their fatherhood and grand-fatherhood and therefore suffer. When the *upādhi* of the *pañca kośa-s,*are rejected and one is able to look at the body, mind and intellect with detachment, one is in a state of *niṣṭhā*, meditation, and can understand what is *Ātmā*.

"From the relative standpoint, there is no answer to any question; from the Absolute standpoint, there is no question to be answered!"

Tadvat śakti kośā aviva kṣaṇe na īśaḥ na api jīvaḥ : In the same way, (as Devadatta is the reality and not the father or the grandfather), their is neither *Īśvara* nor *jīva*, both are only in relation to each other like the *putratva* and *pitṛtva*. The two are born simultaneously in mutually dependent relationship. Then it is only by rejecting, by proper discrimination, the *upādhi* of the *jīva*, the *pañca kośa-s*; and the *upādhi* of the *Īśvara*, the *māyā*, that one discovers one's own essential nature.

In the first stage, the limitations of the *pañca kośa-s* are rejected and the seeker gets firmly established in the conviction that he is someone other than the five *kośa-s*.

Then comes the knowledge that what is left after the rejection of the five *kośa-s*, is my own essential nature, the *Ātmā*, which is itself *Brahma svarūpa*. Once this knowledge takes place, there is no more need to struggle about the limitation of *māyā*. Or alternatively, the *māyā* can be destroyed by surrendering one's individuality to the power of the Lord. Where individuality is not, totality loses its meaning; when the *jīvatva* is denied, the process of denying the *Īśvaratva* also takes place.

The fruit of this study and practise is...

य एवं ब्रह्म वेदैष ब्रह्मैव भवति स्वयम् ।
ब्रह्मणो नास्ति जन्मातः पुनरेष न जायते ।।४३।।

Ya evaṁ brahma vedaiṣa brahmaiva bhavati svayam
Brahmaṇo nāsti janmātaḥ punareṣa na jāyate (43)

यः- he who; एवम् - as discussed in this chapter; ब्रह्म - the *Brahman*; वेद - knows; एषः- he; स्वयम् एव - he himself; ब्रह्म - the *Brahman*; भवति - attains; ब्रह्मणः- of the *Brahman*; जन्मः- birth; न - not; अस्ति - is; अतः- therefore; एषः -this realised one; पुनः- again; न - not; जायते - is born.

He who thus recognises the *Brahman* as indicated in this chapter (by discrimination of the five sheaths); comes to be *Brahman*. The *Brahman* is not born. Therefore, he is never again born. (43)

This *śloka* summarises the total thought in this chapter.

He who knows the *Brahman* in this way i.e., by following the method of *pañca kośa viveka*, as explained in this chapter, comes to realise that this *Brahman* is 'I'.

He is *Brahman* himself. For, he cannot know the *Brahman* by being other than *Brahman*. This is the basic difference between *aparā vidyā* (material knowledge) and *parā vidyā* (spiritual knowledge). In *aparā vidyā*, the knower does not become the known, the two are always separate; but in *parā vidyā*, the knower of the *Brahman* does not remain someone other than the *Brahman* (*Brahmavit brahmaiva bhavati svayam*). The knower-known difference stands totally cancelled.

Brahmajñānam is that knowledge where the knower and the known are both absent and there is only Pure, undivided Knowledge. Once one comes to discover this essential nature of oneself, this *Brahmatva*, there is no question of rebirth for him. The *Brahmavit* transcends the limitations of birth and death. He attains immortality (*amṛto bhavati*). This is how *pañca kośa viveka* has to be practised.

Following are a few **guidelines** for this practise:

1. *Pañca kośa viveka* is an entirely subjective excercise. It cannot be objective when one is dealing with one's own *pañca kośa*. Therefore, this *viveka* is not to be applied on others. *Vedānta* i.e., this *viveka* is applied on oneself, and while dealing with others, one deals in an atmosphere of love and understanding.

2. *Pañca kośa viveka* is not a mere intellectual jugglery. Then one gets lost in the forest of clever words (*śabda jālam mahāraṇyam citta bhramaṇa kāraṇam*).

3. How does one know that the *pañca kośa viveka* is proceeding in the right direction? By certain indicators such as:

(a) *Vairāgya* or dispassion : The attachments to the *pañca kośa-s*, to the body, to the mind, intellect will become minimal and as the seeker goes deeper and deeper with his own personality, he will attain tranquility without effort. Tranquility comes when all wordly things, all the *kośa-s* are devalued.

(b) Freedom from *sukha-duḥkha* : Arrival of *sukha* or *duḥkha* depends on the *prārabdha*. But whether one allows oneself to become *sukhi* or *duḥkhi* is one's choice. To the extent that one accepts and practises this choice, one has separated oneself from the *pañca kośa-s*. The *Manomaya kośa* is *kāraṇātmaka*, the instrument of knowledge which registers that something is *duḥkham* or *sukham*. It is the *vijñānamaya kośa* which determines whether one gets identified with the *duḥkham* or *sukham*. To maintain this distinction every moment of our life is the result of the practise of *pañca kośa viveka*.

(c) Frequency of thoughts with reference to *annamaya kośa, prāṇamaya kośa* become less; and with reference to *vijñānamaya kośa*, the *kartṛtva abhimāna* becomes less intense.

(d) Identification with the *Ānandamaya kośa*, the *bhoktṛtva abhimāna* gets less and joyful experiences are surrendered at the feet of the Lord. Meditation is no longer something that 'was enjoyed'.

In this way, the more the contemplation on the *pañca kośa viveka* and the more one applies it to every encounter in this world, the more established one becomes in the spiritual way of life. It is no more a part-time occupation, but an all-time preoccupation. Half hearted spirituality is neither here nor there.

OM TAT SAT

Summary

Verse No.	Subject matter covered
1	*Pañca kośa viveka* leads to the knowledge of *Brahman*
2 - 10	The *Pañca kośa-s* in our personality - their names, description and how each *kośa* cannot be the *Ātmā*
11	Doubt that when all the *kośa-s* are rejected, nothing remains; and hence *Ātmā* is non-existent.
12 - 13	Clarification that *Ātmā* cannot become the object of knowledge because it is *Anubhava svarūpa;*
14 - 15	like the sweetness of sugar.
16 - 17	This is supported by the *śruti vākya-s*
18	*Ātma tattva* is of the nature of pure knowledge and beyond cause-effect relationship.
19 - 20	To doubt the existence of *Ātmā* is as absurd as doubting one's own existence.
21- 22	*Brahmānubhūti* is that which remains after rejecting every object of experience and the *pañcakośa-s.*
23 - 25	Argument of non-existence of *Ātmā* or *Śūnyatva* has no basis and is condemned by the *śruti-s.*

26 - 27	Nature of *Ātmā* cannot be defined in terms of *idṛk* or *tādṛk* (this or that). It is *aparokṣa.*
29 - 33	How *Ātmā* has the same characteristics as *Brahman* i.e., *satyam*, *jñānam*, anantam...it cannot be denied (*sat-svarūpa*).
34	It is also *jñāna svarūpa.*
35 - 36	Its anantattva is established by freedom from limitations of time, space and object.
37- 42	The limitations of *jīvatva* and *Īśvaratva* on *Brahman* and how they can exist simultaneously is explained.
43	He who understands and practices this *Pañca kośa viveka* and discovers his essential nature, transcends the limitations of birth and death.

* * *

4

१५

Chapter IV

DVAITA VIVEKA

or

THE DIFFERENTIATION OF DUALITY

Introduction

This chapter which deals with the analysis and discrimination of duality is the fourth in the first section of five chapters of *Pañcadaśī* dealing with '*Sat-viveka*'. The first chapter dealt with '*Tattva viveka*' (That-ness), that Pure Consciousness which is present everywhere. In the second chapter, the discrimination on the basis of the *pañca mahā bhuta-s* was discussed. The third chapter covered the theme of discrimination on the basis of the *pañca kośa-s,* the *Guhā* where the *Paramātmā* resides. The *pañca kośa viveka* leads one to one's own essential nature.

In this way, the entire *Pañcadaśī* is developed with *viveka* i.e., discrimination as the basis. For, without a highly developed faculty of discrimination, it will not be possible to arrive at a point of 'thoughtlessness' in which alone the Truth is revealed.

Perhaps it is appropriate at this point to pause and analyze the mind so that the meaning, method and purpose of discrimination will be clearly understood.

Mind has two aspects: *vikāra* (modification) and *vicāra* (discrimination). Both fall under the category of thoughts. When one is unable to understand clearly whether a particular thought is a *vikāra* or a *vicāra,* two consequences follow:

a) a *vikāra* is taken to be *vicāra* and,

b) one becomes proud of the *vicāra* (which is really *vikāra.* e.g. anger is *vikāra* but one can justify it as *vicāra*).

This kind of mix-up shuts off the possibility for correction or improvement. Besides, *vikāra* aspect of thought leads to regression to the level of matter, whereas *vicāra* lifts one to the kingdom of the Spirit.

When *vicāra* is predominant in the individual's thoughts, he is called a decent person; the 'decency' lies in the fact that discrimination is more important to him than whims and fancies and outbursts. He is a *yogi* who can withstand the onslaughts of *kāma* and *krodha* under the shield of *vicāra* (B.G. V. 23)

In this way, when one observes one's own mind, step by step it will be possible to separate these two aspects of the thought, to know when the *vikāra* aspect overpowers one, and to guard oneself against a similar fall again.

Equal degree of watchfulness needs to be exercised to see that *vicāra* does not deteriorate into *vikāra.* The litmus test is, if thought begets thought, it is a *vikāra*, it is 'worrying'. It becomes an addiction, a habit; an exhausting effort.

True *vicāra* on the the other hand is a hobby of thinking, it leads to cessation of thoughts – to rejuvenating *ānanda.* To such an individual, with sharp and subtle intellect, is the Truth revealed (K.U. III.12). To one with such a vision, there will appear nothing but divinity in the world. He will transcend all sense of duality and be one with That, One without a second.

ईश्वरेणापि जीवेन सृष्टं द्वैतं विविच्यते ।
विवेके सति जीवेन हेयो बन्धः स्फुटीभवेत् ।।१।।

Īśvareṇ-āpi jīvena sṛṣṭaṁ dvaitaṁ vivicyate
Viveke sati jīvena heyo bandhaḥ sphuṭī-bhavet (1)

ईश्वरेण - by the *Īśvara*; सृष्टम् - created; द्वैतम् - world of duality and dualism; जीवेन - by the *jīva*; अपि - also (created world); विविच्यते - is being described separately; विवेके सति - having discriminated; जीवेन - by the *jīva*, हेयः- worthy of discarding; बन्धः- bondage on account of the world; स्फुटी भवेत् - will be clearly known.

The world of duality and dualism created by *Īśvara* and *jīva* is being described separately. Having discriminated, one clearly understands that the world of *jīva* and the bondage thereof is worthy of discard. (1)

The chapter opens in the traditional style of defining the subject matter or theme or *viṣaya* of the chapter and the purpose (*prayojana*) of studying this theme. These are two aspects of *anubhandha catuṣṭaya.*

The *viṣaya* being dealt with is *Dvaitam vivicyate* : There are two types of duality which is going to be analysed critically for proper understanding.

These two kinds of dualities are :

1. *Īśvareṇa sṛṣṭam* : The duality created by *Īśvara* - by Him who is keeping *Māyā* under his control (who is called *māyāpati, māyāvi or maheśvara*) and;

2. *Jīvena api*: The other is *dvaita*m created by *jīva* who is under the control of conditioning called *antaḥkaraṇa.*

To analyse and understand these two types of dualities is the subject matter of this chapter.

What is the *prayojana* of this analysis?

Viveke sati jīvena heyaḥ bandhaḥ sphuṭī bhavet : When this discrimination is carried out thoroughly and completely, then it will be clear to the *jīva* as to what it is, that is keeping it in bondage and thereafter, the *jīva* will be able to reject the limitations that have created the sense of bondage.

Once this clear vision is gained, then it would be clear that this *Īśvara Tattva* pervading the entire manifested world is none other than 'I'. (Ref. I.U.1) The vision will be that of *Bhagavān Kṛṣṇa,* that everything and every experience is, 'strung on me like rows of gems on a string'. (B.G. VII. 7)

Such a vision born out of discrimination will see only divine joy in every situation, in every being. The world will sit lightly on one's shoulders. Such an individual will attain a high degree of detachment. He will be neither overjoyed nor depressed, he neither creates tension nor is he tense, he is free from fear and anxiety and obsessions. (Ref.: B.G. 12.5)

This discrimination has to be on the basis of the authority of the scriptures (*śreyasa mārga*) and not on one's likes and dislikes, whims and fancies (*preyasa mārga*). This *śreyasa mārga* is what Arjuna asked for from Lord *Kṛṣṇa* again and again. (B.G.III.2; V.1 etc.).

In the next few *śloka-s*, the author quotes the scriptures in support of *Īśvara sṛṣṭi*

मायां तु प्रकृतिं विद्यान्मायिनं तु महेश्वरम् ।
स मायी सृजतीत्याहुः श्वेताश्वतरशाखिनः ।।२।।

Māyāṁ tu prakṛtiṁ vidyāt-māyinaṁ tu maheśvaram
Sa māyī sṛjatī-tyāhuḥ śvetāśvatara-śākhinaḥ (2)

मायाम् - to the *māyā*; तु - indeed; प्रकृतिम् - material cause of the world; विद्यात् - is to be known; मायिनम् - to the wielder of *māyā*; तु - indeed; महेश्वरम् - the *Maheśvara*; सः- he; मायी - the *Īśvara*; सृजति - creates the world; इति - thus; श्वेताश्वतर शाखिनः- the knowers of *Śvetāśvatara* branch of *Kṛṣṇa Yajurveda*; आहुः- is said.

The *māyā* is the material cause of the world indeed, and the wielder of *māyā* is called *Maheśvara*. This *Īśvara* creates the world, is the declaration of the followers of *Śvetāśvatara* branch of *Kṛṣṇa Yajur Veda*. (2)

Iti prāhuḥ śvetāśvatara śākhinaḥ : The *śvetāśvatara upaniṣad* states as follows (4.10)...

Māyāṁ tu prakṛtiṁ vidyāt māyinaṁ tu Maheśvaram : *Māyā* is the material cause of this world. He who is the controller of *māyā* is called *Maheśvara.*

Saḥ māyī sṛjati: That *Maheśvara* creates the world.

When *dvandva* or dualism (pairs of opposites) is transcended, there is nothing to keep the *dvaita* alive in the mind. The knower-known merger or *advaita siddhi* takes place.

Having quoted one authority to establish the *Īśvara kṛta dvaita*, the author quotes from the *Ṛg veda* (the *aitereya Upaniṣad*).

आत्मा वा इदमग्रेऽभूत्स ईक्षत सृजा इति ।
संकल्पेनासृजल्लोकान्स एतानिति बह्वृचाः ।।३।।

Ātmā vā idam agre 'bhūt sa īkṣata sṛjā iti
Saṁkalpenā sṛjallokān sa etāniti bahvṛcāḥ (3)

इदम् - This world; अग्रे - before creation; आत्मा - the Self; वै - indeed; अभूत् - was; सः- he; ईक्षत - contemplated; सृजै - 'I should create', इति - in this manner; सः- he; एतान् लोकान् - these (fourteen) worlds; संकल्पेन - by thought; असृजत् - created; इति - thus; बह्वृचाः- the knowers of (*aitereya* branch of) *Ṛg veda* say.

Before the creation of the world, the *Ātmā* alone was (as existence). He contemplated that "I should create". In this way, He created this world of fourteen *loka-s*. This is declared by the knower of *Aitereya Upaniṣad* of *Ṛg Veda*. (3)

Idaṁ agre ātmā vā abhūt : Before (in time) this world was (*idam* in *Vedāntic* thought means this world including oneself); there was only *Ātman*. (Ref also I.U.7).

Saḥ īkṣata sṛjā iti : He (the Lord) thought, 'Let me create, manifest'. In this way...

Saḥ etān lokān saṅkalpena asṛjata : The *Īśvara* created all the fourteen worlds (*lokān*) just by His will (*saṅkalpa-mātra*).

Iti baha vṛcā : This is what the *Aitereya Upaniṣad* explains.

Now the third authority of *Taittirīya Upaniṣad* is cited...

खंवाय्वग्निजलोर्व्योषध्यन्नदेहाः क्रमादमी ।
संभूता ब्रह्मणस्तस्मादेतस्मादात्मनोऽखिलाः ।।४।।

Khaṁ-vāyvagni-jalorvyoṣadhi-annadehāḥ kramādamī
Saṁbhūtā brahmaṇas-tasmād-etasmādātmano-'khilāḥ (4)

तस्मात् - from that; एतस्मात् - from this; आत्मनः- from the Self; ब्रह्मणः- from the *Brahman*; अमि - these; खम् - space; वायु - air; अग्निः- fire; जल - water; उर्वी - earth; औषधी - plants; अन्न - food; देहाः- body; अखिलाः- all these; क्रमात् - in this sequence; संभूताः- are born.

From this *Ātmā* – which is the nature of *Brahman*, all these space, air, fire, water, earth, plants, food, bodies etc., are born in the same order. (4)

Tasmāt estasmāt ātmanaḥ brahmaṇaḥ : From that, this *Ātmā*, which is of the nature of *Brahman*...

Amī khaṁ vāyuḥ agni jala urvi oṣadhi anna deha akhilaḥ kramāt sambhūtaḥ : these, namely, the space, air, fire, water, earth, trees, plants, different types of bodies, etc. were manifested in succession.

बहु स्याम हमेवातः प्रजायेयेति कामतः ।
तपस्तप्त्वाऽसृजत्सर्वं जगदित्याह तित्तिरिः ।।५।।

Bahu syāma ham-evātaḥ prajāyey-eti kāmataḥ
Tapas-taptvā-'sṛjat-sarvaṁ jagad-ity-āha tittiriḥ (5)

अहम् - I; एव - alone; बहुस्याम - become many; अतः- therefore; प्रजायेय - should be born; इति - thus. कामतः- desiring; तपः- tapas; तप्त्वा - having done the *tapas*; सर्वम् - all; जगत् - world; असृजत् - created; इति - in this way; तित्तिरिः- knower of *Taittirīya* branch of *yajurveda*; आहः- declare.

I alone should become many. Therefore, I should be born. Desiring this, He performed *tapas*. Having performed the *tapas*, the total world was created. This is how, the knower of *Taittirīya* branch of *Yajurveda* declare. (5)

Aham eva bahusyām ataḥ prajāyeya iti kāmataḥ tapas taptvā : In this way, after the *Paramātmā* started thinking "Let me become many", and therefore, he became many.

Having such a desire he did *tapasyā.* Because *Paramātmā* is of the nature of Pure Knowledge, therefore this *tapasyā* was also *jñānātmaka.*

Tapasyā is rejection. For the *jīva*, rejection is of the *ahaṁkarā.* For *Īśvara*, rejection is of non-dual existence, and appearing to take on duality.

Sarvam jagat asṛjat : In this way, he created the total world of names and forms.

(*Iti taittiri aha* :- Thus said the *Taittirīya Upaniṣad*)

Now *Vidyāraṇya svāmī* quotes from the *Chāndogya Upaniṣad (sāma veda) : The theory of creation is explained in the upaniṣad-s in a variety of ways, but one should not digress from the main purpose in trying to analyse which theory is more correct. The whole purpose of dealing with creation is not to prove that there is creation, but to develop the perception to experience the divine presence.*

In the Śvetāśvatara Upaniṣad, the prakṛti and māyā created the world, in the Aitereya Upaniṣad, the world was created by sankalpa mātra (by thought alone); in the Taittirīya Upaniṣad, it was as a result of tapasyā, that the world including the five great elements was created.

इदमग्रे सदेवासीद्बहुत्वाय तदैक्षत ।
तेजोऽबन्नाण्डजादीनि ससर्जेति च सामगाः ।।६।।

Idam-agre sad-evāsīd-bahutvāya tad-aikṣata
Tejo'bannāṇḍa jādīni sasarjeti ca sāmagāḥ (6)

इदम् - this world; अग्रे - before creation; सत् - existence; एव - alone; आसीत् - was; तत् - that *Brahman*; बहुत्वाय - for becoming many; ऐक्षत - contemplated; तेजः- fire; अप् - water; अन्न - earth; अण्डजादिनि - born out of egg etc.; ससर्ज - created; इति - thus; च - and; सामगाः- knowers of *Sāmaveda* (said).

Before the creation of the world, Existence alone was. That *Brahman* contemplated for becoming many. In this way, created the fire, water, earth and creatures born out of egg etc.. Thus, the knowers of *Sāma Veda* say! (6)

Idaṁ agre sat eva āsīt : Before the world of plurality of names and forms became manifest, there was only pure non-manifested existence.

That is, nothing is created out of non-existence; and that which is existence need not be created! This means that, the world is Existence, and other than Existence, nothing else is!

Tat bahutvāya aikṣata : This sat vastu desired "Let me become many". Thus the *Paramātma Tattva*, which is one without a second imagined or desired to become many, like the ocean "wanting" to become many waves!

Tejaḥ apa anna aṇḍajādīni sasarja : With the birth of that desire, the three great elements- fire, water and earth; and beings born out of eggs etc., were created.

Sāmagāḥ ca iti : And the *Sāma veda* (*Chāndogya Upaniṣad*) says thus.

Now the *Atharvaṇa veda (Muṇḍakopaniṣad)* is cited –

विस्फुलिङ्गा यथा वह्नेर्जायन्तेऽक्षरतस्तथा ।
विविधाश्चिज्जडा भावा इत्याथर्वणिकी श्रुतिः ।।७।।

Visphuliṅgā yathā vahner jāyante 'kṣaratastathā
Vividhāścijjaḍā bhāvā ityāthar vaṇikī śrutiḥ (7)

यथा - as; वह्नेः- from the fire; विस्फुलिङ्गाः- sparks; जायन्ते - are created; तथा - in the same way; अक्षरतः- from the immutable *Brahman*; विविधाः- many; चित् - conscious; जडाः- insentient; भावाः- things and beings; इति - thus; आथर्वणिकी श्रुतिः- *Atharvaṇa veda* (says)

As many sparks are created from the fire, so from the Immutable *Brahman*, many insentient and sentient things and beings are born. Thus, declare the *Atharvaṇa Veda*. (7)

Yathā vahneḥ visphuliṅgā jāyante : Just as many sparks are born when fire becomes manifest...

Tathā akṣarataḥ vividhāḥ cit jaḍā bhāvā jāyante : In the same way, from the *Paramātma tattva* which is immutable (*Akṣara*), the different sentient and insentient things and beings are born.

Iti atharvaṇikī śrutiḥ : The Atharvaṇa Veda (M.U. 2.1.1) states thus.

Now the *Vājasaneya Śruti* i.e., the *Bṛhadāraṇyaka Upaniṣad* is quoted:

जगदव्याकृतं पूर्वमासीद्व्याक्रियताधुना ।
दृश्याभ्यां नामरूपाभ्यां विराडादिषु ते स्फुटे ।।८।।

Jagad-avyākṛtaṁ pūrvam-āsīd-vyākriyatādhunā
Dṛśyābhyāṁ nāma-rūpābhyāṁ virāḍādiṣu te sphuṭe (8)

जगत् - this world; पूर्वम् - before manifestation; अव्याकृतम् - unmanifest *Īśvara*; आसीत् - was; अधुना - now during manifestation; दृश्याभ्याम् - in the form of seen; नामरूपाभ्याम् - by way of names and forms; व्याक्रियत - became expanded; ते - these names and forms; विराडादिषु - in the total gross world called *virāṭ*; स्फुटे - are evident.

The world was unmanifest *Īśvara* before manifestation. Now during manifestation, (the *Īśvara*) became expanded as names and forms in the objective world. They are distinctly clear in the gross world called *Virāṭ*. (8)

विराण्मनुर्नरो गावः खराश्वाजावयस्तथा ।
पिपीलिकावधि द्वन्द्वमिति वाजसनेयिनः ।।९।।

Virāṇ-manur-naro gāvaḥ kharā-śvā jāvayas tathā
Pipīlikā vadhi dvandvam iti vājasa neyinaḥ (9)

विराट् - The self identified with total gross world is *vaiśvānara*; मनुः- the *manu*; नराः- human beings; गावः- cows; खराः- the donkeys; अश्वाः- the horses; अजाः- goats; अवयः- sheep; तथा - and; पिपीलिकावधि - up to ants; द्वन्द्वम् - the pairs of males and females; इति - thus (were created); वाजसनेयिनः- those who know the *vājasaneya* branch (say).

The *Virāṭ* identified with total gross world includes - *Manu*, human beings, cows, donkeys, horses, goats, sheep and up to ants, in the form of pairs. This is accepted by the followers of *Vājasaneya* branch of *Veda* i.e., *Bṛhadāraṇyaka Upaniṣad* (9)

Iti vājasaneyinaḥ : The *Bṛhadāraṇyaka Upaniṣad* states thus:-

Jagat pūrvam avyākṛtam āsīt : Before the world's creation, there was only Pure Consciousness or unmanifest *ParaBrahman*.

Adhunā dṛśyābhyāṁ nāma rūpābhyāṁ vyākriyata : Thereafter, now during manifested creation, the same *Paramātmā* expanded in the form of names and forms. *Vyākaraṇa* means "expansion". In relation to grammar, it signifies the derivation of many words (nouns and verbs) from one *dhātu* or root. In the present context, *vyākriyata* is used to indicate that the original *tattva*, the *sat* vastu, Pure Consciousness became expanded, that is, it became many without the loss of oneness.

Before creation, it was only *Īśvara tattva*; after creation, the same *Paramātmā* expresses as name and form and objectifies itself (*dṛśyābhyām*).

Te virāḍādiṣu sphuṭe : These names and forms came into being distinctively as the total gross world called *virāṭ*. The creation extended further when the total gross body is owned by the consciousness called *Vaiśvānara*. (The individual owner of the individual gross body is called *viśva*).

Manuḥ naraḥ gāvaḥ kharāḥ aśvaḥ ajāḥ avayaḥ tathā pipilikāvadhi : The son of *Vaiśvānara*, *Mānas putra- Manu*, children of *Manu* i.e., *manuṣya*- human beings, cattle, donkeys, horses, goats, sheep, and so on up to the small ant.

In this way, the totality and the individuality were created as explained in the *Bṛhadāraṇyaka Upaniṣad.*

Dvandvam : Then, all the creations enumerated above are always in the form of pairs (male-female).

In this way, up to this *śloka*, the authority of all the four *veda*-s is quoted to show how the world came into being and in the form of *dvaita*m. The second aspect of creation is the *jīva*, which is also created by the *Paramātmā.*

How is the *Sarvajña Sarva śaktimān, Sarva vyāpī Paramātmā* reduced to *alpajña, alpa śaktimān, alpa vyāpī sukhī-duḥkhi jīvātmā*? This subject is taken up from the next *śloka*...

कृत्वा रूपान्तरं जैवं देहे प्राविशदीश्वरः ।
इति ताः श्रुतयः प्राहुर्जीवत्वं प्राण धारणात् ।।१०।।

Kṛtvā rūpāntaraṁ jaivaṁ dehe prāviśad-īśvaraḥ
Iti tāḥ śrutayaḥ prāhur jīvatvaṁ prāṇa dhāraṇāt (10)

ईश्वरः- The *Īśvara*; जैवम् - in the form of *jīva*; रूपान्तरम् - changing the nature; कृत्वा - having done so; देहे - in the body; प्राविशत् - entered; इति - in this way; ताः श्रुतयः- these scriptures; प्राहुः- declare; प्राणधारणात् - by wielding the *prāṇa*; जीवत्वम् - the *jīvahood* (is attained).

The *Īśvara* having reduced to the status of *jīva* entered the body. In this way, by supporting the *prāṇa*, the *jīvahood* is attained by *Īśvara*. So say the scriptures. (10)

Īśvara : The *Paramātma Tattva* when referred with reference to the world is called the creator of the world or *Īśvara*.

Jaivaṁ rūpāntaraṁ kṛtva : He assumed change in the form, as *jīva*. What is the 'change' referred to? *Paramātmā* is *Sat-Cit-Ānanda*. *Īśvara* is *Sarvajña, sarva śaktimān, sarva-vyāpī*. Therefore, the change in the *jīvahood* is in the form of *alpajña, alpa śaktimān* and *alpa-vyāpī*.

Dehe prāviśat : Thus having changed into *alpatva*, he entered the individual bodies.

Iti tāḥ śrutayaḥ prāṇah : All the *upaniṣad-s* quoted earlier thus state that after creating different names and forms and different bodies, *Īśvara* entered the body and attained *jīvātma bhāva*.

How is this body sustained?

Prāṇadhāraṇāt : Having entered the body, *Īśvara* became its owner and sustains it by the *prāṇā-s*

This thought reaches its completion in the next *śloka*, where the *jīva* is defined in a most beautiful way. This clear understanding of who is the *jīva* is essential for spiritual *sādhanā*.

Without knowing who is doing the *sādhanā* and for what purpose, the *Sādhanā* will only be a groping in the dark.

चैतन्यं यदधिष्ठानं लिङ्गदेहश्च यः पुनः ।
चिच्छाया लिङ्गदेहस्था तत्संघो जीव उच्यते ।।११।।

Caitanyaṁ yada-dhiṣṭhānaṁ liṅga-dehaś-ca yaḥ punaḥ
Cicchāyā liṅga-dehasthā tatsaṁgho jīva ucyate (11)

चैतन्यम् - Consciousness; यद् - that; अधिष्ठानम् - substratum; यः- that; च - and; लिङ्ग देहः- the subtle body; पुनः- and also; लिङ्ग देह स्था - reflected in the subtle body; चित् छाया - the reflected/conditioned consciousness; तत्संघः- that assemblage; जीवः- the *jīva*; उच्यते - is called.

The *jīva* is an assemblage of the substratum – the Pure Consciousness, the subtle body and the Consciousness reflected in the subtle body. (11)

Tat sanghaḥ jīva ucyate : The combination or assemblage of three factors is called the *jīva*. These three are :

1. *Yat adhiṣṭhānaṁ caitanyaṁ* : The substratum called Pure Consciousness

2. *Liṅga dehaḥ* : The subtle body and,

3. *Yaḥ ca punaḥ liṅga dehasthā cit chāyā* : The reflection of Consciousness in the subtle body.

The substratum or Pure Consciousness or *śuddha* caitanya is without limitation. On this limitless substratum is introduced the element of limitation called *antaḥkaraṇa* or subtle body.

Third, in this *antaḥkaraṇa* is the reflection of Pure Consciousness. These three factors together is called as *jīva.*

This can be explained by the example of the reflection of an electric bulb in a glass of water. The glass container is the gross body in which is contained the water of thoughts (*antaḥkaraṇa*). In this water of *antaḥkaraṇa* is reflected the light of consciousness. The *Śuddha caitanya* which was infinite and unlimited when referred with reference to the *antaḥkaraṇa* becomes the *jīva*, a finite limited expression.

From this can be inferred the spiritual *sādhanā*, which is to undo the limitation and transcend it. *Īśvara sṛṣṭi* created the human beings, the *jīva sṛṣṭi* creates all limiting relationships of father, mother etc.. To stay established in *Īśvara sṛṣṭi* as human beings and to ignore and rise above all other relationships which limit and shackle is the *sādhanā* to go back to the source.

What is the factor that reduced the infinite *adhiṣṭhānam*, the *śuddha caitanya* to the finitude of the *jīva*? This point is explained...

माहेश्वरीतु माया या तस्या निर्माणशक्तिवत् ।
विद्यते मोहशक्तिश्च तं जीवं मोहयत्यसौ ।।१२।।

Māheśvarītu māyā yā tasyā nirmāṇa śaktivat
Vidyate moha śaktiś-ca taṁ jīvaṁ mohayaty-asau (12)

माहेश्वरी - of the *Maheśvara*; तु - indeed; या - that; माया - *māyā*; तस्याः- of that *māyā*; निर्माण शक्तिवत् - the power of creation; मोह शक्तिः- the power of delusion; च - and; विद्यते - is; असौ - this power of delusion; तम् - to that; जीवम् - *jīva*; मोहयति - deludes.

As the Divine potentiality *māyā* has the power of creation, so also it has the power of delusion. This power of delusion deludes the *jīva.* (12)

Yā māheśvarī māyā tasyā nirmāṇa śaktivat : That power which is called *māyā* of *Maheśvara*, like its power to create the world (vide *śloka* 2 ante)...

This *māyā* is called *saṁkalpa* in *Aitereya Upaniṣad, tapasyā* in *Taittirīya Upaniṣad, ikṣaṇa* in *Chāndogya Upaniṣad* and expansion in *Bṛhadāraṇyaka Upaniṣad.* Like that *nirmāṇa śakti* (the Power to create), this *māyā* has another *śakti* aspect.

Moha śaktiḥ ca vidyate asau taṁ jīvaṁ mohayati : It is called the Power of delusion. This moha *śakti* deludes the *jīva* and that delusion is the cause for the *Paramātmā* being reduced to the level of the *jīvātmā.* The same moha *śakti* creates the duality of *jīva* and *jagat*. Thus *Paramātmā* becomes divided into the seer who is limited by the seen, and the seen which is limited by the seer. Limitation means mutual dependence. In the *jīvātma bhāva,* the sense of limitation, and the limitation, exist in mutual appreciation. So the Conditioned Consciousness gets deluded into believing.

Māyā is defined in different ways : According to *Sāṁkhya* philosophy, it is the power of the Lord as 'other' than *Paramātmā*; so the philosophy ends in *dvaita*. According to *Vedānta, māyā* means (*mā* + *yā*) 'That which is not', that imaginary power is invoked to explain the world. According to *Sant Jñāneśvara,* (*Miyate anayā iti māyā*), it is that which expresses measured knowledge. This definition does not allow the existence of ignorance, *avidyā* etc. (*Āmṛtānubhava* VII), that it is conditioned. This classic spiritual comparison of this *moha* is the parrot on the *nalika* (a stick inside a rotating tube). To eat the fruit suspended from the tube, the parrot has to sit on it, and it rotates, the parrot holds on to the tube fearing it will fall, and forgetting its own power to fly away at its own free will. And the bird is easily caught.

In the same way, the *jīva* himself holds on to the world and deludes himself that God has created bondage.

What are the consequences of the *jīvatma bhāva*? The next *śloka* answers this point, and concludes the theme of *Īśvara sṛṣṭi.*

मोहादनीशतां प्राप्य मग्नो वपुषि शोचति ।
ईशसृष्टमिदं द्वैतं सर्वमुक्तं समासतः ।।१३।।

Mohād-anīśatāṁ prāpya magno vapuṣi śocati
Īśa-sṛṣṭam-idaṁ dvaitaṁ sarvam-uktaṁ samāsataḥ (13)

मोहात् - due to this delusion; अनीशताम् - loss of *Īśvarahood* i.e., the power of control of *māyā*; प्राप्य - having attained; वपुषि - in the body; मग्नः- identified, that *jīva*; शोचति - suffers (and enjoys); ईश सृष्टम् - created by *Īśvara*; इदम् द्वैतम् - this world of duality; सर्वम् - all this; समासतः- in short; उक्तम् - is discussed.

The *jīva* loses the *Īśvarahood* due to this power of delusion and thereafter gets identified with individual body and suffers the experience of limited existence. This is in short, the duality created by the *Īśvara*. (13)

Mohāt anīśatāṁ prāpya : Because of the *Moha śakti*, the *jīva* imagines that he has no freedom and no power. (*Īśatāṁ* means *Īśvaratva*, the status of being the Lord, the Powerful, free; *anīśatāṁ* means the loss of status of *Īśvaratva*, the loss of freedom). How freedom is lost?

Vapuṣi magnaḥ śocati : Because the *jīva* got identified with the gross body. And thereafter, he is subjected to misery. The whole downfall starts with this *moha līlā* which is so fantastic and unconquerable that it sees valuable gems in stone pieces, wife in an assemblage of bones, blood, fat etc., and considers this body made of the five great elements as "I" the *Ātmā*.

Īśa sṛṣṭam idaṁ sarvam dvaitaṁ samāsataḥ uktaṁ : This identification with the body and then undergoing all the consequent experiences is called 'duality' which is created by *Īśvara*, has been described briefly so far (from *śloka* 2- 13).

Now begins the discussion on the *dvaita* created by the *jīva* (*jīva sṛṣṭi dvaitam*). When this is understood, it will become obvious that there is no misery in God's creation, all the misery is only in the *jīva's* creation!...

सप्तान्नब्राह्मणे द्वैतं जीवसृष्टं प्रपञ्चितम् ।
अन्नानि सप्त ज्ञानेन कर्मणाऽजनयत्पिता ।।१४।।

Saptānna brāhmaṇe dvaitaṁ jīvasṛṣṭaṁ prapañc itam
Annāni sapta jñānena karmaṇā 'janayat pitā (14)

सप्त अन्न ब्राह्मणे - In sapta anna *Brāhmaṇa* of *Bṛhadāraṇyaka upaniṣad*; जीव सृष्टम् - created by *jīva*; द्वैतम् - world of duality; प्रपञ्चितम् - is exhaustively discussed; पिता - the all creator *jīva*; ज्ञानेन - by knowledge; कर्मणा - by *karma*; सप्त अन्नानि - the seven foods; अजनयत् - created.

In the *saptānna brāhmaṇa* of *Bṛhadāraṇyaka upaniṣad*, the world of duality created by *jīva* is discussed exhaustively. The *jīva* created seven types of foods with the help of knowledge and action. (14)

Saptānna brāhmane jīva sṛṣṭaṁ dvaitam prapañ citam : In the *Saptānna Brāhmaṇa* (a chapter) in *Bṛhadāraṇyaka upaniṣad*, the duality created by the *jīva* is exhaustively explained. What has been said in that *Upaniṣad* is given in the second line of this *śloka* upto *śloka* 16.

Pitā jñānena karmaṇā sapta annām ajanayat : (In this context) It is the *jīva* who creates the duality - by the two methods of knowledge and action, he created seven types of Anna or food. The *karma* and the knowledge determine the type of embodiment that the *jīva* takes. Action is born according to one's knowledge. (ref. K.U. V.7 *yathā karma yathā śrutam*).

The seven kinds of food are explained...

**मर्त्यान्नमेकं देवान्ने द्वे पश्वन्नं चतुर्थकम् ।
अन्यत्त्रितयमात्मार्थम् अन्नानां विनियोजनम् ।।१५।।**

*Martyānna mekaṁ devānne dve paśvannaṁ caturthakam
Anyat tritayam ātmārtham-annānāṁ viniyojanam (15)*

मर्त्यान्नम् - the food of the mortals; एकम् - is one; देवान्ने - the foods of the gods; द्वे - are two; पश्वन्नम् - the food of the animals etc.; चतुर्थकम् - is the fourth; अन्यत् - the remaining; त्रितयम् - three types; आत्मार्थम् - for the self (i.e. *jīva*); अन्नानाम् - of the foods; विनियोजनम् - purposeful classification.

There is but one food for the mortals, two for the Gods, the fourth is that for animals, and the remaining three are considered to be for *jīva*. This is the classification of foods. (15)

Martyānnam ekaṁ : One kind of food is meant for mortals;

Devānne dve : for the Gods, there are two types;

Paśvānnaṁ caturthakam : the fourth kind is for the animals;

Anyat tritayam ātmārtham : The remaining three are intended for the *Ātmā* or *jīva*.

Annānāṁ viniyojanam : In this way, the seven types of food are classified in seven categories. These seven types of food which symbolize the respective fields of experiences are declared as the *jīva sṛṣṭi prapañca* in the *upaniṣad*.

Which are these seven foods are explained now...

**व्रीह्यादिकं दर्शपूर्णमासौ क्षीरं तथा मनः ।
वाक्प्राणाश्चेति सप्तत्वमन्नानामवगम्यताम् ।।१६।।**

*Vrīhy-ādikaṁ darśa-pūrṇa māsau kṣīraṁ tathā manaḥ
Vāk prāṇāśceti saptatvam annānām avagamyatām (16)*

व्रीह्यादिकम् - Wheat etc.; दर्शपूर्णमासौ - the *yāga* called *darśa* and *pūrṇamāsa*; क्षीरम् - the milk; तथा - and; मनः- the mind; वाक् - speech; प्राणः- vital air; च - and; इति - thus; अन्नानाम् - of the food; सप्तत्वम् - the seven types; अवगम्यताम् - should be understood.

For our understanding, the seven types of foods are wheat etc.; *darśa and pūrṇamāsa yāga*; milk, similar, mind, speech and vital air. (16)

Vrīhyādikaṁ : The food for human beings *(martyānnam)* consists of grains such as rice, wheat, barley etc.. *Darśa pūrṇam āsou* : food for the *deva-s (devānna)* is of two types of *yajña - darśa yāga and pūrṇamāsa yāga* (certain types of rites to be done on *Amāvāsya* i.e., new moon and *Pourṇimā* i.e., full moon days). These are offerings to support the *deva loka* or *pitṛ loka* through different types of *pūjā, karmā-s, yāga-s, yajña etc.. Tatha ksīraṁ :* Milk etc. is the food for the animals. They consume food as created by the Lord without modification.

Manaḥ vāk ca prāṇāḥ : The remaining three types of food for the *Ātma tattva* are : the mind, speech and the vital air.

Without the mind, *prāṇa śakti* and *vāk śakti, jīva* cannot exist. And the *jīvātmā* is living only in association with the *vāk, prāṇa* and mind. When the *jīvātmā* departs from the body, he carries with him the package of the mind containing all the impressions and the *vāsanā-s* in this life on to the next life, where he unfolds it for his new life.

So, for the *jīvātmā*, the mind, *prāṇāḥ* and speech are the field of experience. For the animals, it is raw food as created by God; for the *devā-s* it is *yajña*, and for the human beings, it is food created and modified by different processes. *Iti annānām saptatvam avagamyatām*: Thus all the seven types of food are created by the *jīvātmā* for his own enjoyment.

But then, are not these seven types of food created by *Īśvara*? How are they called the *jīva sṛṣṭi*?

ईशेन यद्यप्येतानि निर्मितानि स्वरूपतः ।
तथापि ज्ञानकर्माभ्यां जीवोऽकार्षीत्तदन्नताम् ।।१७।।

Īśena yadyapy-etāni nirmitāni svarūpataḥ
Tathāpi jñānakarmābhyāṁ jīvo'kārṣīttadannatām (17)

यद्यपि - although; एतानि - these seven types of foods; ईशेन - by the *Īśvara*; स्वरूपतः- from his own being; निर्मितानि - are created; तथापि - even then; जीवः- the *jīva*; ज्ञानकर्माभ्याम् - by the knowledge and *karma*; तद् - to these; अन्नताम् -objects and instruments of enjoyments; अकार्षीत् - made.

Although these seven types of food are created by *Īśvara* from His essential nature, the *jīva* has attributed utility and enjoyment by his knowledge and actions. (17)

Yadyapi etāni īśena svarūpataḥ nirmitāni : Although these foods are, indeed, created by *Īśvara, tathā api jīvaḥ jñāna karmābhyām tat annatām akārṣīt* : however, the same objects are converted into *bhogya vastu* (objects of enjoyments by the *jīva* by the process of *jñāna* and *karma* (vide *śloka* 14 ante).

Thus, every field of experience (the seven types of foods) has two aspects - the *Īśvara śṛṣṭi* i.e. the creation by the Lord; and second, as the *bhogya* vastutva - i.e. enjoyment of objects for the *jīva.* The latter aspect associated with the world is *jīva's* creation. It is *kārya* from the Lord's point of view. Doubtless, everything is created by the Lord. But everything is accepted by the *jīva* as its own *bhogya vastu.* It is in the involvement in the *bhoga* aspect that the *jīva's* problems begin.

These two aspects, namely the *kāryatva* from *Īśvara's* point of view, and the *bhogyatva* from the *jīva's* point of view are further explained...

ईशकार्यं जीवभोग्यं जगद्द्वाभ्यां समन्वितम् ।
पितृजन्या भर्तृभोग्या यथा योषित्तथेष्यताम् ।।१८।।

Īśakāryaṁ jīvabhogyaṁ jagad dvābhyāṁ samanvitam
Pitṛjanyā bhartṛbhogyā yathā yoṣit tathe ṣyatām (18)

जगत् - This world i.e. food etc.; ईशकार्यम् - being created by *Īśvara*; जीवभोग्यम् being experienced by *jīva*; द्वाभ्याम् - by two (i.e. effect and object of experience); समन्वितम् - endowed with; यथा - as; योषित् - a woman; पितृजन्या - created by father; भर्तृभोग्या - object of experience for husband; तथा - similarly; इष्यताम् - know about the world (i.e. seven types of food).

This world is associated with these two aspects viz., (i) it is a creation (i.e. effect of *Īśvara* and (ii) a field of experience for the *jīva*. Just as a woman is created by her father and is an object of experience for the husband, so is the case of these seven types of foods. (18)

Jagat dvābhyām samanvitam : The seven types of food that are being discussed with reference to *jīva sṛṣṭi*, each of them is associated with two aspects. *Īśa kāryam jīva bhogyam* : (i) It is created by God, and (ii) the same thing accepted by the *jīva* as the field of experience for itself.

Yathā pitṛjanyā yoṣit bhartṛ bhogyā : Just as a woman is created by the parents - she is the *kārya* from the parent's point of view; at the same time, she is the field of experience for the husband.

Tathā iṣyatām : In the same way, everything in the world has these two aspects. Everything that is created by the Lord is thus 're'created into the field of experience by the *bhoga buddhi* of the *jīva*.

The clear understanding of this demarcation between these two aspects in every experience in life will and should lead to a weakening of attachment to the world. With such a vision, it will be possible to stay in the Lord's creation and be free from all attachments to both - *Īśa sṛṣṭi* and *jīva sṛṣṭi*.

How these two aspects *Īśa kāryam* and *jīva* bhogyam are both associated with the same experience is now explained...

मायावृत्त्यात्मको हीशसंकल्पः साधनं जनौ ।
मनोवृत्त्यात्मको जीवसंकल्पो भोगसाधनम् ।।१९।।

Māyā vṛttyā tmako hīśa saṁkalpaḥ sādhanaṁ janau
Mano vṛttyātmako jīv asaṁkalpo bhoga sādhanam (19)

ईशसंकल्पः- The contemplative thought of *Īśvara*; हि - indeed; मायावृत्त्यात्मकः- is the manifestation of *māyā* as effects; जनौ - for the creation of this world; साधनम् - is an instrument; जीव संकल्पः- the contemplative thought of *jīva*; मनोवृत्त्यात्मकः- is the mainifestation of mind's modification; भोग साधनम् - is the instrument of experience.

The contemplative thought of *Īśvara*, which is of the nature of *māyā* is the cause for the creation of this world. The contemplative thought of *jīva*, which is of the nature of the modifications of the mind, is the cause for the experience for the *jīva*. (19)

Sādhanam janau : for the creation of the world, i.e. for the *Īśa Kārya* aspect of every object, two factors have together been the cause;

(i) *Īśa saṅkalpaḥ* - the desire in the Lord for creation to become many (vide *śloka* 5 ante); and

(ii) *Māyā vṛtyātmakaḥ* - the modifications in the *prakṛti* or *māyā* (vide 2 ante).

Bhoga sādhanaṁ : for the *jīva bhogyaṁ* aspect, the cause is *mano vṛtyātmakaḥ jīva saṅkalpaḥ* : the *saṅkalpa* or desire in the mind of the *jīva* for the enjoyment of that object (which has been created by the Lord).

An illustrative example would be the discovery by the scientist (*Īśa kārya*) and its application by the technologist (*jīva bhogya*). So also, everything is created by the Lord, and then in everything is discovered a field of experience by the *jīva*! For example, so many children are born in the world (God's *sṛṣṭi*) and it makes no difference to the individual, but when one child happens to be born to one's own child or grandchild, then a whole field of experience opens up, of joys and sorrows (*jīva bhogyaṁ*). So all problems arise with *jīva sṛṣṭi*.

This is now explained through an example...

ईशनिर्मितमण्यादौ वस्तुन्येकविधे स्थिते ।
भोक्तृधीवृत्तिनानात्वात्तद्भोगो बहुधेष्यते ।।२०।।

Īśanirmita maṇyādau vastu nyekavidhe sthite
Bhoktṛ dhīvṛtti nānātvāt tadbhogo bahu dheṣyate (20)

ईशनिर्मित - created by the *Īśvara*; मणि - diamond; आदौ - etc.; वस्तुनि - object; एक विधे - of onc kind; स्थिते - is; भोक्तृ धीवृत्ति - the understanding of the experiencer to enjoy; नानात्वात् - being of many types; तद्भोगः- the experience of that object; बहुधा - of many types; ईष्यते - is accepted to be.

The object created by *Īśvara*, such as a diamond, gem etc., is of one kind. However, depending on the multitude of its utility by the enjoyer (*jīva*), the same object is experienced in many ways. (20)

Īśa nirmita maṇi ādau vastuni eka vidhe sthite : Objects created by God such as diamonds and other gems remain the same, they do not change. However...

Bhoktṛ dhī vṛtti nānātvāt : the thoughts of a person looking at them will differ depending on...

Tat bhogaḥ bahudhā īṣyate : the value that the individual gives to that object, and how he intends to use that object within his field of experience.

The simile continues to show how the same gem can be experienced in three different ways...

हृष्यत्येको मणिं लब्ध्वा क्रुध्यत्यन्योह्यलाभतः ।
पश्यत्येव विरक्तोऽत्र न हृष्यति न कुप्यति ।।२१।।

Hṛṣya ty eko maṇiṁ labdhvā krudhya ty anyo hyalā bhataḥ
Paśyaty-eva virakto-'tra na hṛṣyati na kupyati (21)

एकः- a person; मणिम् - the diamond; लब्ध्वा - having got; हृष्यति - becomes happy; अन्यः- the other person; हि - while; अलाभतः- having not gained; क्रुध्यति - becomes angry; अत्र - in this diamond; विरक्तः- a person of dispassion; पश्यति - sees; एव - only; न - not; हृष्यति - becomes happy; न - not; कुप्यति - becomes angry.

If one becomes happy having got the diamond, the other becomes angry for not getting it. While a man of dispassion only sees the diamond, but neither he becomes happy nor angry. (21)

Ekaḥ maṇim labdhvā hṛṣyati : one person may feel happy when he gets a precious gem;

Anyaḥ hi alābhataḥ krudhyate : another not being able to obtain it gets frustrated and angry;

Virakta atra paśyati eva: a third individual who is not interested in this (or any other) gem, he (also) sees the same gem, but;

Na hṛṣyati na kupyati, he is neither elated nor is he angry (with disappointment). For such an indifferent person, the object can cause neither joy nor sorrow.

Continuing this analysis –

प्रियोऽप्रिय उपेक्ष्येश्चेत्याकारा मणिगास्त्रयः ।
सृष्टा जीवैरीशसृष्टं रूपं साधारणं त्रिषु ।।२२।।

Priyo'priya upekṣye śceti ākārā maṇigās trayaḥ
Sṛṣṭā jīvair-īśa-sṛṣṭaṁ rūpaṁ sādhāraṇaṁ triṣu (22)

मणिगाः- With reference to the diamond; प्रियः- liking; अप्रियः- disliking, उपेक्ष्यः- indifference; च - and; इति - these; त्रयः- three; आकाराः- shapes i.e., differences; जीवैः- by the *jīva*; सृष्टाः- are created; त्रिषु - among these three differences; साधारणम् - common; रूपम् - shape/form; ईशसृष्टम् - is created by *Īśvara.*

Liking, disliking and indifference are the three kinds of differences created by *jīva.* The common aspect of the same diamond is created by *Īśvara.* (22)

Maṇigāḥ priyaḥ apriyaḥ upekṣya ca iti trayaḥ ākārāḥ jīvaiḥ sṛṣṭāḥ : With reference to the same gem liking, disliking and indifference, these three responses, or shapes of thought (*ākārāḥ*), are created by the *jīva* (not by *Īśvara*). The gem *Triṣu sādhāraṇam rūpam īśa sṛṣṭam* is the common denominator on which these three shapes are created by the *jīva.*

This *jīva's* creation of the different shapes on *Īśvara's* creation is explained further through an example...

भार्या स्नुषा ननान्दा च याता मातेत्यनेकधा ।
प्रतियोगिधिया योषिद्भिद्यते न स्वरूपतः ।।२३।।

Bhāryā snuṣā nanāndā ca yātā māte tyanekadhā
Pratiyogi dhiyā yoṣid bhidyate na svarūpataḥ (23)

योषित् - woman; प्रतियोगि धिया - with reference to the relative; भार्या - wife; स्नुषा - daughter-in-law; ननान्दा - sister-in-law; याता - wife of brother in law; माता - mother; इति - in this way; अनेकधा - in many ways; भिद्यते - is differentiated; स्वरूपतः- essentially; न - not.

A woman can be differentiated with reference to a relative as wife, daughter-in-law, sister-in-law, wife of a brother-in-law, mother etc., in many ways but essentially, she cannot be differentiated (she being one). (23)

Yoṣit pratiyogi dhiyā anekadhā bhidyate : The (same) woman gets differentiated into many-ness (many relationships) according to the point of reference, according to the buddhi of the *jīva.*

Bhāryā, snuṣā, nanāndā, yātā, mātā : Such as the wife, daughter-in-law, sister-in-law, wife of husband's brother, or mother. *Iti* : In this way, different names are superimposed on the same woman depending on the point of reference in relationship.

One does not suffer being a human being, but all suffering starts when *ākārā-s* are assumed on oneself as husband, wife, father, son etc.. In *svarūpataḥ*, in essence, one is the same; it is when one spilts one's personality into superimposed shapes that the conflict of 'mine' and 'yours' or 'his' begins.

A peculiar doubt is now raised with reference to the above example of the many-ness on the same woman...

ननु ज्ञानानि भिद्यन्तामाकरस्तु न भिद्यते ।
योषिद्वपुष्यतिशयो न दृष्टो जीवनिर्मितः ।।२४।।

Nanu jñānāni bhidyantām akarastu na bhidyate
Yoṣid vapuṣya tiśayo na dṛṣṭo jīva nirmitaḥ (24)

ननु - A doubt is raised; ज्ञानानि - the knowledges of the woman being a wife etc., भिद्यन्ताम् - may they be differenct; आकारः- the shape difference; तु - indeed; न - not; भिद्यते - are seen to be different; योषित् वपुषि - in the woman's body; जीव निर्मितः- created by *jīva*; अतिशयः- additional specifications; न - not; दृष्टः- are seen.

A doubt is raised. Let there be differences in the knowledge about woman (such as wife, mother etc.) but one is not able to see any additional and specific difference created in the body of the woman, by the *jīva.* (24)

Nanu jñānāni bhidyatām ākārastu na bhidyate : Now, one can agree that, with reference to one and the same individual, the understanding can be different. Nevertheless, one does not see any difference in the woman, whether she is a mother, or mother-in-law, or wife etc..

Yoṣit vapuṣi jīva nirmitaḥ atiśayaḥ na dṛṣṭaḥ : In the body of the woman, the many-ness that has been created by the *jīva* cannot be seen as something special. There are no distinctive features to distinguish whether she is a mother, daughter, etc., at any particular time !

This doubt is cleared in the next *śloka*...

मैवं मांसमयी योषित्काचिदन्या मनोमयी ।
मांसमय्या अभेदेऽपि भिद्यते हि मनोमयी ।।२५।।

Maivaṁ māṁsa mayī yoṣit kācid anyā mano mayī
Māṁsa mayyā abhede'pi bhidyate hi mano mayī (25)

एवम् - Like this; मा - don't conclude; मांसमयी - made of muscles; योषित् - woman's body; काचित् - something; अन्या - is different; मनोमयी - the mental understanding of mother etc.; मांसमय्याः- from the muscular; अभेदे - not different; अपि - although; मनोमयी - the mental figure; भिद्यते - is different; हि - indeed.

The answer is - don't conclude like this. The woman's body made of muscles etc. is different and the mental understanding of the woman as mother, wife etc. is different. Although, the gross muscular body may not be different, but the mental perception of that woman (as mother etc.) is certainly different. (25)

Mā eva : It is not so. Do not say that there is no difference or special characteristic created in the woman which can demarcate the *Īśvara sṛṣṭi* from *jīva sṛṣṭi.*

Māṁsa-mayī yoṣit kācid : The woman made of flesh and bones which is the Lord's creation is one thing *mano-mayī anyā*: the woman seen as mother, sister etc. is something else. It is different and more subtle, more in the mind than what you apparently see as the physical body.

Māṁsamayyā abhede api mano mayī bhidyate hi : Although the physical body made of flesh and bones remains the same, the differences lie in how she sees herself and others see her role in their mutual relationship and respective points of reference. These relationships are established only in the mind in the form of mental images. These types of differences in the same object exist only in *jīva sṛṣṭi* and never in *Īśvara sṛṣṭi* (where the concept of "mind" has no existence).

A further doubt is raised on another aspect of the same example...

भ्रान्तिस्वप्नमनोराज्यस्मृतिष्वस्तु मनोमयम् ।
जाग्रन्मानेन मेयस्य न मनोमयतेति चेत् ।।२६।।

Bhrānti svapna manorājya smṛtiṣ vastu mano mayam
Jāgran mānena meyasya na mano maya teti cet (26)

भ्रान्ति - delusion; स्वप्न - dream; मनोराज्य - imagination; स्मृतिषु - in the memory etc.; मनोमयम् - mental thought only; अस्तु - may be accepted; जाग्रन्मानेन - with reference to the waking experience; मेयस्य - of the direct object of perception; मनोमयता - mental thought only; न - not; इति चेत् - if argued in this way.

The mentation can be acceptable with reference to delusion, dream, imagination, memory etc.. However, with reference to the direct object during the experience of the waking world, how can one accept the mental thought to be real? (26)

Bhrānti svapna manorājya smṛtiṣu astu manomayam : In delusion, dreaming, imagining, fantasizing and memory, the objects can be accepted as being caused by the mind; but the doubt is –

Jāgrat mānena meyasya na mano mayatā iti cet : In the waking state (when all the faculties are alert), when one is seeing the woman directly in flesh and blood, is it possible that she is only imagination (*manomayī*)?

The teacher replies to this question in the next few *śloka-s...*

बाढं माने तु मेयेन योगात्स्याद्विषयाकृतिः ।
भाष्यवार्तिककाराभ्यामयमर्थ उदीरितः ।।२७।।

Bāḍhaṁ māne tu meyena yogāt syād viṣayā kṛtiḥ
Bhāṣya vārtika kārābhyām ayam artha udīritaḥ (27)

बाढं - Yes it is true that object is real in waking state; माने - in the thought of knowledge; विषयाकृतिः- the shape of the thought; तु - certainly; मेयेन - by the objects of knowledge; योगात् - in relation to; स्यात् - is; अयम् - this; अर्थः- meaning; भाष्य वार्तिक काराभ्याम् - by the *bhāṣyakāra śaṅkarācārya* and *sureśvarācārya*; उदीरितः- is declared.

Certainly one can. The thought of an object in the mind results when the object of the thought comes in contact with the mind. This is declared to be so by both, *Śaṅkarācārya* and *Sureśvarācārya*. (27)

Bāḍhaṁ : Yes! Doubtless there is truth in what you say!

Māne viṣayā-kṛtiḥ tu meyena yogāt syāt : In the waking state, knowledge about any object is gained by the mind going and touching that object and assuming the shape of that object.

Ayam arthaḥ bhāṣya vārtika kārābhyām udīritaḥ : This is the meaning given by *Bhagavān Śaṅkarācārya,* the great *bhāṣyakāra,* and *Bhagavān Sureśvarācārya,* the well known *vātikakāra.* What they have stated is that, the knowledge of an object takes place only in the mind, not directly. The whole world, therefore, exists only in the mind.

Thus, in deep sleep, when the mind is totally folded up, it cannot go and establish contact with the gross waking world, including one's own gross body. It cannot take the shape of any object and hence there is no knowledge.

Continuing to cite the above mentioned *Ācāryā-s...*

मूषासिक्तं यथा ताम्रं तन्निभं जायते तथा ।
रूपादीन्व्याप्नुवच्चित्तं तन्निभं दृश्यते ध्रुवम् ।।२८।।

Mūṣā siktaṁ yathā tāmraṁ tannibhaṁ jāyate tathā
Rūpādīn vyāpnuva ccittaṁ tannibhaṁ dṛśyate dhruvam (28)

यथा - As; ताम्रम् - the copper; मूषासिक्तं - poured in the mould; तन्निभम् - of that shape; जायते - takes the shape; तथा - similarly; रूपादीन् - to forms etc.; व्याप्नुवत् - objectifying; चित्तम् - mind; ध्रुवम् - indeed; तन्निभम् - of that type of object; दृश्यते - is seen to acquire.

As copper poured in a mould takes the shape of that mould, similarly, the mind objectifying different objects like forms etc., also takes the thought of that object. (28)

In this *śloka,* the teacher quotes *Ādi Śaṅkara* from his *Upadeśa Sāhasri* 14.3 & 4 : *Yathā mūṣāsiktaṁ tāmraṁ tannibhaṁ jāyate* : When molten copper is poured into the mould of an object, it takes the shape of that mould or pattern;

Tathā rūpādīn vyāpnuvat cittaṁ tannibhaṁ drśyate dhruvam : In the same way, the mind is able to take the form of everything in this world, not only relating to colour and form, but also to *śabda, sparśa, rasa and gandha.* The mind or *cittam* is thus able to comprehend all the five types of objects, by taking the shape according to the object of knowledge.

In this way, the *manomayī ākṛti*, and gross *ākṛti*, are able to exist only because there is gross shape or *ākāra* outside. That shape is accepted by the mind when it comes in contact with the object. No speciality can be seen in the object in a gross way, because the speciality (the special 'shape') is happening at the level of the *manomayī ākṛti.* In this way, *jīva sṛṣṭi* is *manomayī* and *Īśa sṛṣṭi* is *saṅkalpamayī.*

The quotation from *Upadeśa Sāhasri* continues with an illustration to prove the same point...

व्यञ्जको वा यथाऽऽलोको व्यंग्यस्याकारतामियात् ।
सर्वार्थव्यञ्जकत्वाद्धीरर्थाकारा प्रदृश्यते ।।२९।।

Vyañjako vā yathā''loko vyaṅgyasy-ākāratā-miyāt
Sarvārtha-vya-ñjakatvād-dhīḥ arthakārā pradṛśyate (29)

यथा वा - or like; व्यञ्जकः आलोकः- the light illuminating the object; व्यंग्यस्य - of the object; आकारताम् - shape; इयात् - is taken; धीः- the thought; सर्वार्थ - all the objects of knowledge; व्यञ्जकत्वात् - being the illuminator; अर्थाकारा - of the shape of the object; प्रदृश्यते - is seen.

Or, as the light illuminating an object takes the shape of that object, so also the thought being an illuminator of all objects of knowledge, is seen to take the shape of these objects. (29)

Yathā vā vyañjakaḥ ālokaḥ vyaṅgyasya ākāratām iyāt : Or just as light by itself has no shape, but when the light rays reach an object, they take its shape, whatever it may be.

Dhīḥ sarvārtha vyañjakatvāt arthākārā pradṛśyate : The mind, being able to know everything - whether it is a gross object in terms of form, colour, sound, smell, touch or taste; or the object is in the form of an emotion, such as love, greed, passion, anger etc., or it is a concept at the level of intellect - the mind takes the shape of that particular object or *artha*.

Therefore, the conclusion reached by the examples given in these two *śloka*-s 28 and 29, is that every object has these two aspects:

a) creation of the *Īśvara*; and

b) creation of the *jīva*, wherein there is sense of enjoyership or a sense of experience associated with that object.

Now another authority, namely of *Sureśvarācārya* is given. *Sureśvarācārya* is accepted with great reverence and esteem by those who follow *Śaṅkara Sampradāya* very strictly. He is held to have interpreted *Ādi Śaṅkarā's* teachings most accurately.

मातुर्मानाभिनिष्पत्तिर्निष्पन्नं मेयमेति तत् ।
मेयाभिसंगतं तच्च मेयाभत्वं प्रपद्यते ।।३०।।

Mātur mānābhi niṣpattiḥ niṣpannaṁ meyam-eti tat
Meyābhi saṁgataṁ tac-ca meyābhatvaṁ prapadyate (30)

मातुः- From the knower (according to *śloka* 11); मानाभिनिष्पत्तिः- the means of knowledge called thought; निष्पन्नम् - born; तत् - that thought; मेयम् - to the object of knowledge; एति - goes; तत् च - and that thought; मेयाभिसंगतम् - having come in contact with the object of knowledge; मेयाभत्वम् - the shape of the object of knowledge; प्रपद्यते - attains.

A thought (i.e. mind) from the knower is born and comes in contact with the object. Having come in contact with the object of knowledge, the knowledge of the object takes place. (30)

How knowledge takes place is explained in this *śloka*...

Mātuḥ : The knower, the *jīva* which was referred to in *śloka* 11 ante, as being made compositely of the substratum or Pure Consciousness, the *Paramātmā* ; the conditioning called the *liṅga śarīra* or subtle body; and the expression of the Absolute through the limitation called *cit chāyā*; this *jīva* is referred to as *mātuḥ*.

From this *jīva* or the knower, the mind (*māna* is the *pramāṇa*) is born. (The Pure Consciousness for no reason or logic) because of its own nature and potentiality, appears as if to separate into two aspects - the knower and the known, the former being *jñāna pradhāna* and the latter being *astitva pradhāna.* This is called the mind or *antaḥkaraṇa.*

Niṣpannam tat meyam eti : Once the mind is born, it goes towards the object of knowledge. Then,

Tacca meyābhi saṁgataṁ meyābhatvaṁ prapadyate : when the mind comes in contact with the object, it takes the shape of that object (like water assuming the shape of the container). The mind flowing through the channels of the sense organs comes in contact with the sense objects and takes the respective shape. (This is called *vṛtti vyāpti*). This is the way objects are cognized.

If the gross object is understood by the mind, who understands the mental creation? This is explained...

सत्येवं विषयौ द्वौ स्तो घटौ मृण्मयधीमयौ ।
मृण्मयो मानमेयः स्यात्साक्षिभास्यस्तु धीमयः ।।३१।।

Saty evaṁ viṣayau dvau sto ghaṭau mṛṇmaya dhīmayau
Mṛṇmayo mānameyaḥ syāt sākṣi bhāsyas tu dhīmayaḥ (31)

एवम् सति - this being so; विषयौ - objects; द्वौ - two; स्तः- are; मृण्मयः- the mud pot; धीमयः- the thought pot; घटौ - pots; मृण्मयः- the mud pot; मानमेयः- is known by the means of knowledge (i.e. eyes, mind etc.); स्यात् - is; धीमयः- the thought pot; तु - indeed; साक्षिभास्यः- is illumined by witness.

This being so, the object, 'pot' is of two kinds: (i) made up of mud and (ii) made up of thought. The mud pot is known by the means of knowledge (i.e. eyes etc. and mind). The 'pot thought' is illumined by witness. (31)

Evaṁ sati viṣayau dvau staḥ mṛṇmaya dhīmayau ghaṭau : This being so, every object has these two aspects associated with it. In other words, the pot is made of two things - the mud and the mind.

Mṛṇmayaḥ mānameyaḥ syāt : The pot is made out of mud, and it is known in the mind.

The pot which is in the mind, who knows that?

Dhīmayaḥ tu sākṣī bhāsyaḥ : The witness or the *sākṣi* is the knower of the thought of the pot in the mind.

The whole world is illumined and known by the mind. When it is known by the mind, it enters one's territory with the potential to make one happy or unhappy. The freedom of choice is one's own, whether to allow that potentiality to express itself in the form of giving value to the world and seeking happiness in it, or devalue it totally and remain unborn as an individual. Then one cannot be made a *sukhi* or *duḥkhi* by anything in the world.

When one stands apart and watches the mind and its content play out this drama with every object in the external world, gradually the mind loses its potency to make one dance to its tune. The external level is God's creation and holds no problem, it is when *jīva's* creation is introduced that problems begin.

What is indicated by this analysis is, that man's creation is *dvaitam*, duality, which causes bondage. This is explained...

अन्वयव्यतिरेकाभ्यां धीमयो जीवबन्धकृत् ।
सत्यस्मिन्सुखदुःखेस्तस्तस्मिन्नसति न द्वयम् ।।३२।।

Anvaya vyatirekā bhyāṁ dhīmayo jīva bandhakṛt
Satya smin sukha duḥkhestaḥ tasmin nasati na dvayam (32)

अन्वयव्यतिरेकाभ्याम् - By the process of inclusion and exclusion; धीमयः- the thought object; जीव बन्धकृत् - is the cause of bondage for *jīva*; अस्मिन् सति - when the *jīva's* creation is considered to be real; सुखदुःखे - the joy and sorrows; स्तः- are; तस्मिन्–असति - when the *jīva's* creation is not present; द्वयम् - the two; न - are not.

By the process of enquiry consisting of "inclusion and exclusion", (it is seen) that the 'thought-object' is the cause of bondage for *jīva*. When 'thought-object' is taken to be real, both joys and sorrows result, while in their absence, both joy and sorrows exist not. (32)

Anvaya vyatirekā bhyām dhīmayaḥ jīva bandhakṛt : By this technique of association and dis-association, it can be concluded that the *jīva* comes under bondage of this world, not because of God's creation, but because of the mental images that he forms in himself about God's creation.

Asmin sati sukha duḥkhe staḥ : Furthermore, so long as this mental projection about the Lord's creation exists in an individual, he enjoys or suffers.

Tasmin asati dvayam na : On the other hand, when the mind does not accept anything in this world, there is neither joy nor sorrow. The bondage that man suffers from is because of the *jīva sṛṣṭi mānasa prapañca*, the mental projection of the world created by the *jīva*, therefore, it is "*jīva bandha kṛta*". When mental creation ceases, all binding chains are snapped, and one rises above the limitations of relative existence.

Is the *anvaya-vyatireka* technique applicable with reference to external objects? This topic is discussed now...

असत्यपि च बाह्यार्थे स्वप्नादौ बद्ध्यते नरः ।
समाधिसुप्तिमूर्च्छासु सत्यप्यस्मिन्न बद्ध्यते ।।३३।।

Asat-yapi ca bāhyārthe svapn-ādau baddhyate naraḥ
Samādhi-supti-mūrcchāsu satyapya smin-na baddhyate (33)

स्वप्नादौ - In the dream etc.; बाह्यार्थे असति अपि - although the external objects are not available; नरः- man; बद्ध्यते - is affected by (joy and sorrows); समाधि सुप्ति मूर्च्छासु - in *Samādhi*, deep sleep and while under sedation; च - and; अस्मिन् सति अपि - although the outer objects are available; न - not; बद्ध्यते - is not affected (to be happy or not).

In dream etc., man is affected by joys and sorrows, although the external objects are not available. Contrary to this, when the external objects are available, they are not able to affect a person in *Samādhi*, deep sleep or under sedation. (33)

Svapnādau bāhyārthe asati api naraḥ baddhyate : In the dream state or in the memory, there are no external objects actually present. Yet the individual experiences the joys and sorrows, although the objects are only at the level of the mind. This is one kind of perception.

Samādhi supti mūrchāsu bāhyartha sati api naraḥ na baddhyate: There is second kind of perception, which is quite the opposite - when an individual is in *samādhi* or in deep sleep plane of Consciousness, or when he has fainted or is un-conscious under medication, although all the external objects are present, the individual is not aware of them and is not influenced by their presence or absence.

The essence of the thought is that the *jīva's* bondage is created not by God but by the *jīva* alone. Therefore, the effort to release oneself from this bondage should begin from one's own end, not from the world's, nor the God's. "The mind in itself makes a heaven out of hell and a hell out of heaven". In correcting this hallucination and changing the vision lies the release.

This path was indicated by Lord *Kṛṣṇa* when he said, " Even if the most sinful man worships me and no other, he must be regarded as righteous, for he has decided firmly to change himself. (Ch. IX.30)

To emphasize the *anvaya - vyatireka* technique, two examples are given.

दूरदेशं गते पुत्रे जीवत्येवात्र तत्पिता ।
विप्रलंभकवाक्येन मृतं मत्वा प्ररोदिति ।।३४।।

Dūra deśaṁ gate putre jīvatye vātra tat pitā
Vipra laṁ bhaka vākyena mṛtaṁ matvā prarodìti (34)

दूरदेशम् - to a distant place; गते पुत्रे - when the son has gone; जीवति एव - although alive; अत्र - in his home; तत् पिता - his father; विप्रलंभक - a liar; वाक्येन - by the statement; मृतम् - dead; मत्वा - considering; प्ररोदिति - grieves and weeps.

Although the son is alive in a distant land, his father (deluded) by a statement of a liar grieves and weeps imagining his son to be dead. (34)

Dūra deśaṁ gate putre jīvati eva vipralaṁ bhaka vākyena : A son has gone to a distant place, although he is alive and well, because of the information given by a liar...

Atra tat pitā mṛtam matvā prarodìti : the boy's father believed his son to be dead, and mourns his loss. Because of the false news, the living son is considered dead, and a dead son is born in the mind of the father. This is called *vyatireka.*

A second example follows...

मृतेऽपि तस्मिन्वार्तायामश्रुतायां न रोदिति ।
अतः सर्वस्य जीवस्य बन्धकृन्मानसं जगत् ।।३५।।

Mṛte-'pi tasmin vārtāyām aśrutāyāṁ na roditi
Ataḥ sarvasya jīvasya bandha kṛn mānasaṁ jagat (35)

तस्मिन् मृते अपि - although dead; वार्तायाम् अश्रुतायाम् - having not heard about the death news; न - not; रोदिति - weeps; अतः- therefore (according to this method of inclusion and exclusion); सर्वस्य जीवस्य - for all the *jīva's*; मानसम् - mental; जगत् - duality and world; बन्धकृत् - is cause of bondage.

(In another case), Although really dead, but having not known about the death of a son, the father weeps not. Therefore, (it is concluded that) the *jīva dvaita*, which is mental projection, is the cause of bondage. (35)

Mṛte api tasmin vārtāyāṁ aśrutāyāṁ na roditi : Although the son is dead (in a distant place), not having heard that news, the father does not grieve. The mind is holding on only to the image of the living son.

These two examples show : -

Ataḥ sarvasya jīvasya bandha-kṛt mānasam jagat : Therefore, it can be concluded that the bondage of all *jīva's* is only at the level of the mind and is the creation of the mind alone. Good, bad, friend, enemy such judgments of the world are only mental projections, according to the status of the mind at a particular moment.

A doubt is raised that if it is said that, external objects carry no significance for joys and sorrows and that all experiences are in the mind only, will not this line of thinking lead to the *vijñānavāda* of the *Bauddha-s.* This is now refuted ...

विज्ञानवादो बाह्यार्थवैयर्थ्यात्स्यादिहेति चेत् ।
न हृद्याकारमाधातुं बाह्यस्यापेक्षितत्वतः ।।३६।।

Vijñāna vādo bāhyā rthavaiyarthyāt-syād iheti-cet
Na hṛdya-kāra-mādhātuṁ bāhyasy-āpekṣita-tvataḥ (36)

बाह्यार्थवैयर्थ्यात् - The outer objects being not of any consequences; इह - in this line of thinking; विज्ञानवादः- the *vijñānavāda* of buddhists; स्यात् - is the conclusion; इति चेत् - if considered to be so; न - no; हृदि - in the mind; आकारम् - shape; आधातुम् - for getting; बाह्यस्य - of the external objects; अपेक्षितत्वतः- is expected to be present.

If one concludes from the above discussions, that the external objects being of no consequence, one is talking about *Vijñānavāda* of *Bauddhā-s*, it is a wrong conclusion. Because, for the eruption of thought in the mind, an external object is essential. (36)

Bāhyārtha vaiyarthyāt vijñāna vādaḥ iha syāt, iti cet? : The *vijñāna-vādi-s* say that all the experiences are at the level of the mind and therefore the gross world is *mithyā* (unreal). It is of no consequence.

Now, if you also say that everything is only a mental projection, and is the root cause of the *jīva's* bondage, is this not likely to end up in the same *vijñāna- vāda*? If this is your doubt –

Na hṛdi ākāram ādhātuṁ bāhyasya apekṣitatvataḥ : The teacher denies this - it is not so, because for the formation of the mental image, the presence of the external object is essential.

The mental projections have their basis on the external gross world created by God. This is not *vijñānavāda* which denies the external world as *mithyā*, as null and void. This is not accepted in the *vedānta śāstra*,because, without the external objects, the internal image cannot be formed.

The same objection can be answered in yet another way...

वैयर्थ्यमस्तु वा बाह्यं न वारयितुमीश्महे ।
प्रयोजनमपेक्षन्ते न मानानीति हि स्थितिः ।।३७।।

Vaiyarthya mastu vā bāhyaṁ na vārayitu mīśmahe
Prayojana mapekṣante na mānāniti hi sthitiḥ (37)

वा - or; वैयर्थ्यम् - the outer objects may be unimportant; अस्तु - may be so; बाह्यम् - the outer objects; वारयितुम् - to deny; न - not ; ईश्महे - are able; मानानि - means of knowledge; प्रयोजनम् - purpose; न - not; अपेक्षन्ते - expect.

Or, let the external objects (i.e. God's creation) be not important at all, however, we can do nothing about their presence. The means of knowledge (senses, mind etc.), do not expect any purpose in knowing an object. (37)

Vaiyarthyam vā astu : Or, if one accepts your (the student's) argument that external objects are not required for the formation of mental images, that without the presence of the external world (God's creation), one can still become miserable, because it is all only mental;

Bāhyaṁ vārayitum na īśmahe: Nothing can be done about God's creation, only the mind is at one's own disposal.

Mānāni prayojanaṁ na apekṣante : Furthermore, by themselves, the means of knowledge viz., the mind and the sense organs, have no purpose to see or not to see etc.. Only what is seen, heard etc., in the external world can be experienced by the mind.

The sincere seeker leaves God's creation alone to take care of itself and focuses his attention on his mind which is creating the problem. Hence the *upaniṣad* says: The path is so narrow that there will be no crowd on this path!

Now a doubt is raised: If the mind is the sole culprit that creates so much havoc by creating *dvaitam*, why not control the mind?...

बन्धश्चेन्मानसं द्वैतं तन्निरोधेन शाम्यति ।
अभ्यसेद्योगमेवातो ब्रह्मज्ञानेन किं वद ।।३८।।

Bandha ścen mānasaṁ dvaitaṁ tanni rodhena śāmyati
Abhya sed yoga mevāto brahma jñānena kiṁ vada (38)

मानसम् - mental; द्वैतम् - duality or world; बन्धः- bondage; चेत् - if considered; तत् - that (mental world and duality); निरोधेन - by absorption of the mind; शाम्यति - is removed; अतः- therefore; योगः- the *yoga* of mind absorption; एव - alone; अभ्यसेत् - should be practiced; ब्रह्मज्ञानेन किम् - what is the need of knowledge of *Brahman*; वद - say what is achieved ?

If mental world, is cause for bondage, then it can be removed by absorption of mind. Therefore, one should practice the *yoga* of absorption of mind. What is the need of knowing *Brahman* ? (38)

Mānasaṁ dvaitaṁ bandhaḥ cet : The question - If the mind is responsible for creating the bondage on account of duality, then;

Tat nirodhena śāmyati : the *mānasic dvaita* can be removed by controlling the mind?

Pātanjali yoga śāstra states, "When the *vṛtti* in the mind is suspended, this ability is called *yoga*". When the thoughts are suspended, mental creation cannot take place and the bondage because of the mind ceases to exist.

Ataḥ yogam eva abhyaset brahma jñānena kim vada?: Therefore, only *yoga* needs to be practiced. Why should we talk about *Brahma jñānam? Prāṇāyāmam, Pratyāhāram* and *citta vṛtti nirodham* should be able to eliminate the *mānasic* bondage!

This expression of frustration is answered by the teacher:

तात्कालिकद्वैतशान्तावप्यागामिजनिक्षयः ।
ब्रह्मज्ञानं विना न स्यादिति वेदान्तडिण्डिमः ।।३९।।

Tātkā lika dvaita śāntau apyāgāmi jani kṣayaḥ
Brahma jñānaṁ vinā na syād iti vedānta ḍiṇḍimaḥ (39)

तात्कालिक - for the time being; द्वैत - world of duality; शान्तौ अपि - although negated; आगामि - the future; जनिक्षयः- absence of birth; ब्रह्मज्ञानम् - knowledge of *Brahman*; विना - without; न - not; स्यात् - is possible ; इति - thus; वेदान्त डिण्डिमः - is the declaration of *Vedānta.*

(By the *yoga* of absorption of mind), although there is a negation of mental world of duality, the freedom from future birth (and death) is not possible without the knowledge of *Brahman*, thus declare the *Vedānta śāstra.* (39)

Tāt kālika dvaita śāntau api : It is true that by *prāṇāyāmam* and other forms of *yoga*, the frequency of thoughts in the mind can be reduced (*Ramaṇa Maharṣi* also says this in *Upadeśa Sāram* 14). The mind can be made to quieten down. But the effect is only temporary. The moment the force of *prāṇāyāmam* is withdrawn;

Āgāmi janikṣayaḥ na : the thoughts rise again, the duality manifests again, all the limitations that were buried under by the force of *yoga sādhanā* and which had remained in hibernation in seed form, the *saṁskāra* associated with one can come out, and it is back to the old cycle of births and deaths.

Release from *mānasic dvaita's* bondage cannot be achieved through such struggle and forced effort, but only by totally erasing all impressions from the mind.

Brahmajñānaṁ vinā na syāt iti Vedānta diṇḍimaḥ : Without knowing one's own essential nature, it is not possible to get out of the cycle of repeated births and deaths, so proclaim the *śruti-s,* the *vedānta śāstra.*

The *yoga śāstra* can only deal with the path, the vehicle of bondage, but the *Vedānta śāstra* deals with the very core of one's own essential nature. When *mānasic* bondage is mentioned and discussed, it does not mean that one should only focus on the mind and its control. The utimate goal of *sādhanā* is to go beyond the mind and come to discover one's own Self. Once the source is reached, the mind will cease to be a tyranny. Let the world - God's creation be as it is. The *Īśvara sṛṣṭi* is not the obstacle for knowing the Truth. It is the *jīva sṛṣṭi* that has to be negated and conquered.

What is the approach to gain this *Brahma jñānam*?...

अनिवृत्तेऽपीशसृष्टे द्वैते तस्य मृषात्मताम् ।
बुद्ध्वा ब्रह्माद्वयं बोद्धुं शक्यं वस्त्वैक्यवादिनः ।।४०।।

Anivṛtte-'pīśa sṛṣṭe dvaite tasya mṛṣā tmatām
Buddhvā brahmā dvayaṁ boddhuṁ śakyaṁ vastvaikya vādinaḥ (40)

ईशसृष्टे द्वैते अनिवृत्ते - without disappearance of the duality and world created by the *Īśvara*; अपि - although; तस्य - of that world; मृषात्मताम् - the illusory nature; बुद्ध्वा - having ascertained; वस्तु–ऐक्यवादिनः- of *vedāntin* accepting the non-dual *Brahman*; अद्वयम् - non-dual; ब्रह्म - *Brahman*; बोद्धुं शक्यः- can be known.

It is possible for the follower of the *Advaita Vedānta* to know *Brahman* even without the disappearance of the world of duality, having once ascertained its illusory nature. (40)

Vastu aikya vādinaḥ : Those who emphasise the scriptural statement (*ekam eva advitīyam*) and live up to it, say that;

Advayaṁ brahma boddhuṁ śakyaṁ - it is possible to know the *advaita tattva.*

Īśa sṛṣṭeḥ dvaite anivṛtte api - even when the *dvaita* created by *Īśvara* is not removed, and left as it is. There is no need to meddle with the creation of the *Īśvara* to know one's own essential nature.

All that is needed to be done is - *Tasya mṛṣātmatām buddhvā*: To understand the *mithyā* aspect of *Īśvara sṛṣṭi*, the *mithyātva* lies in the differences that are perceived. The Reality is that substratum, which supports all the differences. The dualism, the dvandva is the *mithyā*. They cancel each other out. It is no use fretting about what cannot be changed, what has been going on since time immemorial (*anādi kāla*). It is wise to accept it all as *Īśvara līla*, and concentrate the attention on removing the *dvaita* in oneself. The negation of the duality created by the Lord is not spiritual advancement.

Then what should be done? By the study of the scriptures, by the *upadeśa* of the *Guru*, by knowing one's own essential nature, one should transcend the *jīva dvaita*. This is stated in the next *śloka*...

प्रलये तन्निवृत्तौ तु गुरुशास्त्राद्यभावतः ।
विरोधिद्वैताभावेऽपि न शक्यं बोद्धुमद्वयम् ।।४१।।

Pralaye tan nivṛttau tu guru śāstrādy abhāvataḥ
Virodhi dvaitā bhāve 'pi na śakyaṁ boddhum advayam (41)

प्रलये - during dissolution; तत् निवृत्तौ - when the duality is fully absent; तु - indeed; विरोधि - opposite; द्वैत - duality; अभावे - absence; अपि - also; गुरु - the teacher; शास्त्र - the scriptures; अभावतः- in the absence; अद्वयम् - the non-dual *Brahman*; बोद्धुम् न शक्यः- is not possible to be known.

In total dissolution, although there is complete absence of the world of duality, however, due to the absence of the scriptures and teacher, one is not able to realise the non-dual *Brahman*. (41)

Pralaye tat nivṛttau tu, virodhi dvaita abhāve api : At the time of the *pralaya* or final dissolution, although *Īśvara sṛṣṭi* is negated, and thereafter, there is no *dvaita*;

Guru śāstra ādi abhāvātaḥ : yet, there is no possibility in the state of the oblivion in *pralaya* to study the scriptures or to receive the *upadeśa* from the *Guru* and therefore,

Advayam boddhuṁ na śakyaṁ : there is no opportunity for gaining *advaya jñānam.*

For example - In deep sleep, which is a form of temporary daily *pralaya*, no *dvaita* operates, but once the individual comes out of that plane of Consciousness into the waking state, the *dvaita* is born again. So also in the cosmic cycle, all the *dvaita* images lie dormant only to well up again in the next cycle. Therefore, any effort to negate *Īśvara dvaita* is futile and serves no purpose for the seeker's spiritual evolution.

On the contrary, the *Īśvara*-created *dvaita* is in actuality a boon for the seeker, not an obstacle. This is now stated...

अबाधकं साधकं च द्वैतमीश्वरनिर्मितम् ।
अपनेतुमशक्यं चेत्यास्तां तद्द्विष्यते कुतः ।।४२।।

Abādhakaṁ sādhakaṁ ca dvaita mīśvara nirmitam
Apanetum aśakyaṁ ceti āstāṁ tad dviṣyate kutaḥ (42)

ईश्वर निर्मितम् द्वैतम् - the world created by the *Īśvara*; अबाधकम् - is not an obstacle of non-dual knowledge; च - but; साधकम् - is an asset for this knowledge; अपनेतुम् - worthy of removing; अशक्यम् - is impossible; च - and; इति - therefore; आस्ताम् - let this duality remain; कुतः- what for; तत् - that (duality created by the Lord) ; द्विष्यते - hate.

The Lord's creation is never an obstacle for knowing the non-dual *Brahman*, nay, it is an asset to gain *Brahma jñāna.* Further, it is impossible to negate. Therefore, let it remain as it is. Why should one hate it? (42)

Īśvara nirmitam dvaitam abādhakaṁ : God's creation, the duality created by Him is not an obstacle. Once the correct picture of *Īśvara sṛṣṭi* is got, namely,

a) that the world of plurality has been created out of joy and abundance;

b) that the Lord's creation is beyond the realm of cause and effect:

c) That 'good' and 'bad' in the Lord's creation is only in our mind.

There will be no more problems perceived in His creation. Everything that happens or exists is according to a grand design, which He alone knows.

Therefore, God's creation is not an obstacle in knowing one's own essential nature. The presence of the waves is no obstacle for the ocean to know that it is water alone. The *Paramātma* can be easily understood through His manifestations.

Not only is that, *Īśvara dvaita*m not an obstacle but *(sādhakam* ca) it is an asset too. How?

1. Birth and death are *Īśvara sṛṣṭi* . Rebirth (*punar janma*) is an asset because it offers yet another chance.

2. The coming of Saints and Sages in one's life is entirely in the realm of *Īśvara sṛṣṭi.* The meeting of the *Guru* and the *śiṣya* is according to His plan.

Apanetum aśakyaṁ : Besides, *Īśvara*-created *dvaita*m cannot be changed, cannot be removed. It cannot be challenged or destroyed.

Taking all the three aspects into account namely,

i) that *Īśvara dvaita* is not an obstacle,

ii) but it is an asset, and

iii) it cannot be changed, removed, or challenged. *Āstām tat* let *Īśvara dvaita* be, the way it is.

Kutaḥ dviṣyate : Why do you resist it so much and fret about it? Stop fighting with the Lord's creation. On the other hand, one should learn to thank Him for the worst experiences as for the best, the good and the bad being His manifestation alone!

Now the author proceeds to the *jīva dvaita* which is to be rejected...

जीवद्वैतं तु शास्त्रीयमशास्त्रीयमिति द्विधा ।
उपाददीत शास्त्रीयमातत्त्वस्यावबोधनात् ।।४३।।

Jīva dvaitaṁ tu śāstrīyam-aśāstrīyam-iti dvidhā
Upādadīta śāstrīyam ātattvasyā vabodhanāt (43)

जीवद्वैतम् - the mental world of duality created by *jīva*; तु - certainly; शास्त्रीयम् - sanctioned by scriptures; अशास्त्रीयम् - not sanctioned by scriptures; इति - in this way; द्विधा - is of two kinds; शास्त्रीयम् - scripturally accepted; आतत्त्वस्य अवबोधनात् - uptil the realization of the Truth; उपाददीत - should be practiced.

The world created by *jīva* is of two types – (i) sanctioned by the scriptures and (ii) not acceptable to scriptures. One must practice the former till the realization of the Truth. (43)

Jīva dvaitam tu dvidhā iti : The *dvaita* created by the *jīva* is of the following two types:

Śāstrīyam aśāstrīyam : One is as per sanction of the scriptures; the other is that which is not sanctioned by the scriptures.

Śāstrīyam upādadīta : The *dvaita*m created by the *jīva* at the mental level, according to the scriptures, is to be practiced, not neglected. For example, *Śaṅkarācārya* says that with the *Guru* and *Īśvara,* one should not behave in an *advaita* way.

How long should this *jīva* created *śāstrītya dvaita*m be practiced?

Ātattvasya avabodhanāt: Till one is established in one's own essential nature.

When *jīva-s* like *Ramaṇa Maharṣi* or *Ānanda Mayī Mā* are born, they have already transcended the *śāstrīya dvaitam* in their previous births and do not require a *Guru* or study of the scriptures etc..

How is this practice of *śāstrīya dvaitam* done?...

आत्मब्रह्मविचाराख्यं शास्त्रीयं मानसं जगत् ।
बुद्धे तत्त्वे तच्च हेयमिति श्रुत्यनुशासनम् ।।४४।।

Ātma-brahma-vicārākhyaṁ śāstrīyaṁ mānasaṁ jagat
Buddhe tattve tacca heyam iti śrutyanu śāsanam (44)

आत्म ब्रह्म - about *Ātmā* and *Brahman*; विचाराख्यम् - known enquiry about them; शास्त्रीयम् - is according to scriptures; मानसम् - mental; जगत् - world of duality; तत्त्वे बुद्धे - when the Truth is revealed; तत् - that (mental duality); च - indeed; हेयम् - is worthy of rejection; इति - thus; श्रुति अनुशासनम् - is the command of the scriptures.

The mental world sanctioned by the scriptures viz., – The enquiry about the *Ātmā* and the *Brahman* is also worthy of renunciation, after the Truth is realized. This is the commandment of the *Veda*s! (44)

Śāstrīya mānasaṁ jagat ātma brahma vicārākhyaṁ : The *dvaita* created by the *jīva* which is according to the scriptures, is that line of thinking which establishes the one-ness between the *Ātmā* and *Brahman*, between the *jīva* and *Paramātmā.* Such *mānasik sṛṣṭi* is contemplative thinking.

In such a practice, the mind should not entertain any modifications such as desire or the temptation of the world, even for half a moment. This practice should be maintained till one enters deep sleep or till one leaves this body till the last moment.

Dadyānnāvasaram kiñcit kāmādināṁ manāgapi ।
āsupte rāmṛteḥ kālam nayet vedānta cintayā ।।

When this habit of contemplative thought becomes one's second nature, the external objects and events become blurred in one's perception, and the mind becomes calm, quiet but very alert.

In due course, *Buddhe tattve tat ca heyaṁ iti śruti anuśāsanam* : Even this contemplation of *Śāstrīya dvaita* is to be rejected, when one comes to discover one's own essential nature (the *tattvam*). This is what the scriptures state. Once one is established in the Self, the *śāstrīya dvaita* practice drops away automatically.

To support this statement, the *śruti-s* are quoted in the next three *śloka-s:*

शास्त्राण्यधीत्य मेधावी अभ्यस्य च पुनः पुनः ।
परमं ब्रह्म विज्ञाय उल्कावत्तान्यथोत्सृजेत् ।।४५।।

Śāstrāṇya dhītya medhāvī abhyasya ca punaḥ punaḥ
Paramaṁ brahma vijñāya ulkāvat tānya thot sṛjet (45)

मेधावी - the wise one; शास्त्राणि - scriptures; अधीत्य - having studied; पुनः पुनः- again and again; च - and; अभ्यस्य - by practicing; परमं ब्रह्म - the

Supreme *Brahman*; विज्ञाय - having realized; अथ - thereafter; तानि - these scriptural study and duality; उल्कावत् - like a burning wood; उत्सृजेत् - renounce.

A wise man should renounce the scriptures and their study after having studied again and again, having practiced the knowledge and after having realized the Supreme *Brahman*, like one discards a burning coal (on the palm). (45)

This is a citation from *Amṛtanāda upaniṣad* 1.

Medhāvi śāstrāṇi adhītya : The *adhīkāri*, one who is qualified to study, should study the scriptures relating to *śāstrīya jīva davita*, and *Abhyasya ca punaḥ punaḥ* : should practice what he studies in his life again and again.

Param brahma vijñāya atha tāni ulkāvat utsṛjet : Having ultimately discovered one's own essential nature to be *Brahma svarūpa*, thereafter all those practices should be renounced, just as one throws off a piece of burning charcoal in the hand. After long study and practice, a stage is reached when the ladder by which one climbed this far is kicked off!

Second quotation from *Amṛta-bindu upaniṣad* follows...

ग्रन्थमभ्यस्य मेधावी ज्ञानविज्ञानतत्परः ।
पलालमिव धान्यार्थी त्यजेद्ग्रन्थमशेषतः ।।४६।।

Grantha mabhyasya medhāvī jñāna vijñāna tatparaḥ
Palālam iva dhānyārthī tyajed grantham aśeṣataḥ (46)

मेधावी - the wise one; ग्रन्थम् - scriptures; अभ्यस्य - having studied; ज्ञान - indirect (*parokṣa jñānam*); विज्ञान - direct immediate (*aparokṣa jñānam*); तत्परः- having attained firm abidance; ग्रन्थम् - the scriptures; अशेषतः- exclusively and totally; त्यजेत् - should renounce; धान्यार्थी - the desirer of the grains; पलालम् - husk; इव - like.

A wise man should renounce the scriptural books exclusively and totally, after having gained the indirect and direct knowledge about the Self and having attained firm abidance in the Self; as a farmer discards the husk after taking the grains. (46)

Medhāvī grantham abhyasya jñāna vijñāna tatparaḥ : The qualified student or seeker having studied, through that study, first he gets *parokṣa jñānam.* Then by reflection and contemplation, this knowledge becomes his own, not of the book or someone else. That is *aparokṣa jñānam* or *vijñānam.*

Dhānyārthī palāla iva grantham aśeṣataḥ tyajet : Thereafter, like the grain is separated from the husk, he should drop all books (and the book knowledge) without exception and just remain one with his own essential nature.

Study of scriptures is useful only up to a point, but it is not an end in itself. It is only a means for preparing oneself for the ultimate transformation and the flight into the Infinite. Books and studies have no role in that realm.

One more *śruti (Bṛhadāraṇyaka upaniṣad)* is cited...

तमेव धीरो विज्ञाय प्रज्ञां कुर्वीत ब्राह्मणः ।
नानुध्यायाद्बहूञ्छब्दान्वाचो विग्लापनं हि तत् ।।४७।।

Tam-eva dhīro vijñāya prajñāṁ kurvīta brāhmaṇaḥ
Nānu dhyāyād bahūn chabdān vāco viglāpanaṁ hi tat (47)

धीरः- the wise; ब्राह्मणः- the one wanting to know the Truth; तम् - that *Brahman*; एव - alone; विज्ञाय - having known; प्रज्ञाम् - meditation; कुर्वीत - should practice; बहून् - many; शब्दान् - other worldly readings; न - not; अनुध्यायात् - should contemplate; हि - indeed; तत् - (because) that; वाचो - by the speech; विग्लापनम् - is tiring and wasteful

A wise seeker, after having known the Truth (*Brahman*) should practice meditation. He should desist from indulgence in the worldly themes, because it is indeed tiring and wasteful expenditure of speech. (47)

Dhīraḥ brāhmaṇaḥ : He who has *śraddhā* and patience and who is a seeker of the Truth, the *Paramātmā;*

Tameva vijñāya prajñām kurvīta : He should fix his attention only on the *Paramātmā* and nothing else, and he should again and again practice *dhyānābhyāsa.* This life of every seeker should have *maryādā or niyamam,* so as to maintain vigilance and alertness. By such constant practice, the worldly thoughts get roasted and lose their "germination" value.

Bahūn śabdān na anudhyāyāt: While this *abhyāsa* is being done, one need not read too many books. One needs only one mirror to see one's reflection. Even if one *Upaniṣad* is studied in depth, reflected upon and is put into practice, it can lead one to the goal.

Vācaḥ viglāpanam hi tat : In addition, one should not waste time and energy in speaking too much. Unnecessary involvement in unwanted themes takes one away from the main path (*anyā vāco vimuñcatha...Muṇḍak.*II.2.5)

Now one more quotation is given from *Muṇḍakopaniṣad* and *Kaṭhopaniṣad...*

तमेवैकं विजानीथ ह्यन्या वाचो विमुञ्चथ ।
यच्छेद्वाङ्मनसी प्राज्ञ इत्याद्याः श्रुतयः स्फुटाः ।।४८।।

Tam evaikaṁ vijānītha hyanyā vāco vimuñcatha
Yacched vāṅ manasī prājña ityādyāḥ śrutayaḥ sphuṭāḥ (48)

तम् - to that *Brahman*; एव - only; एकम् - one; विजानीथ - should you know; हि - and; अन्या - other; वाचः- words; विमुञ्चथ - reject; प्राज्ञः- the wise;

वाङ्ग - speech; मनसी - in the mind; यच्छेत् - should absorb; इत्याद्याः- etc.; श्रुतयः- scriptural statements; स्फुटाः- are clear (about).

One should know the *Brahman* alone. All other subjects should be rejected totally. A wise person should absorb his speech in mind. Such scriptural statements are evidently clear about it. (48)

Tam ekaṁ evam vijānītha anyā vācā vimuñcatha : This is the only thing that is worthy of knowing and should be known. All other subjects and discussions should be rejected from one's cognition. Getting involved in worldly affairs of no direct concern is to give importance to *dvaita*m.

Yacchet vāṅg manasi prājñaḥ : Let the speech be absorbed in the mind, let the mind be absorbed in the individual intellect, let the individual intellect be surrendered to the total intellect and the let the total intellect be merged into the Absolute! (K.U.1.3.13)

Ityādyā śrutayaḥ sphuṭāḥ : This is clearly stated in such *upaniṣadic* statements. By keeping a distance from the world, the world will not enter our bosom, although we function in this world. This is called open-eyed meditation. This is practiced by the totality being respected more than the individuality even to the point of surrendering the individuality. The total world will drop away and one comes to the organs, the mind, the intellect and to the *sākṣi bhāva.* From that point, it is the Lord's Grace which lifts one beyond this stage to the realm where efforts die. In the birth of effortless existence is *Amṛtānubhava.*

Now the *aśāstrīya dvaita*, that *dvaita* which is not accepted by the scriptures is dealt with...

अशास्त्रीयमपि द्वैतं तीव्रं मन्दमिति द्विधा ।
कामक्रोधादिकं तीव्रं मनोराज्यं तथेतरत् ।।४९।।

Aśāstrīya mapi dvaitaṁ tīvraṁ mandamiti dvidhā
Kāma krodhā dikaṁ tīvraṁ mano rājyaṁ tathe tarat (49)

अशास्त्रीयम् - not supported by scriptures; द्वैतम् - duality; अपि - also; तीव्रम् - intense; मन्दम् - not intense; इति - thus; द्विधा - is of two kinds; काम क्रोध आदिकम् - the desire, anger etc; तीव्रम् - is intense type; तथा - and; मनोराज्यम् - habit of mental projection; इतरत् - the other.

The *aśāstrīya dvaitam* i.e., the one unacceptable to scriptures is also of two types viz., (i) intense and (ii) mild. The intense type includes the desire, anger etc., while the mild type includes the habit of mental projections and habitual thinking. (49)

Aśāstrīyam dvaitaṁ api tīvraṁ mandam iti dvidhā : The *aśāstrīya dvaitam* also is of two types: 'Intense' and 'not-intense'. The intense *aśāstrīya dvaitam* is that which generates the six modifications (*ṣaḍ vikāra*) such as *kāma, krodha, lobha, moha, mada* and *mātsarya.*

Tathā mano rājyaṁ itarat: The *manda* (non-intense) type of *dvaita*m is in the form of fantasizing, imagining and day- dreaming.

So what should the seeker do about these two types of *aśāstrīya dvaita*?...

उभयं तत्त्वबोधात्प्राङ्निवार्यं बोधसिद्धये ।
शमः समाहितत्त्वं च साधनेषु श्रुतं यतः ।।५०।।

Ubhayaṁ tattva bodhāt prāk nivāryaṁ bodha siddhaye
Śamaḥ samāhitattvaṁ ca sādhaneṣu śrutaṁ yataḥ (50)

उभयम् - both kinds of duality; तत्त्वबोधात् प्राक् - before the knowledge of Truth; बोधसिद्धये - for getting the Self Knowledge; निवार्यम् - is worthy of discarding; यतः- because; शमः- control of mind; समाहितत्त्वम् - single pointedness of mind; साधनेषु - among the means of realization; श्रुतम् - are heard.

These both types of *aśāstrīya dvaitam* should be rejected before the knowledge of the Truth for getting Self-knowledge. Because control of mind and single-pointedness are known to be the means of Self-realisation. (50)

Ubhayaṁ nivārya : Both these types of *dvaita* should be rejected. When?

Tattva bodhāt prāṅg : Before launching on the study of the nature of *Brahman*, it is essential to give up both.

Bodha siddhaye : If one wants to know the Truth, one must have the determination to reject the two *dvaita*-s. While carrying out one's activities correctly and whole-heartedly, every moment should be lived with joy, without a trace of boredom.

Yataḥ śamaḥ samāhita tvaṁ : This *aśāstrīya dvaita* should be totally dropped because only that mind which is not agitated and which is single-pointed is capable of complete involvement or total withdrawal.

Sādhaneṣu śrutaṁ : The *śruti-s* consider such a mind, composed and with full concentration as best qualified for spiritual unfoldment. These two qualities *śama* (absence of desire etc.) and *samāhita* (absence of imagination) are essential pre-requisites.

The essential requirement for a seeker is further emphasized...

बोधादूर्ध्वं च तद्धेयं जीवन्मुक्तिप्रसिद्धये ।
कामादिक्लेशबन्धेन युक्तस्य न हि मुक्तता ।।५१।।

Bodhād ūrdhvaṁ ca taddheyaṁ jīvan mukti prasiddhaye
Kāmādi kleśa bandhena yuktasya na hi muktatā (51)

बोधात् ऊर्ध्वम् - after Self Knowledge; च - also; जीवन्मुक्ति - the state of *jīvanmukti*; प्रसिद्धये - for getting; तत् - these two types of duality; हेयम् - is worthy of discarding; काम आदि - desire etc.; क्लेश - obstacles; बन्धेन -

by bondage; युक्तस्य - of the one associated with; मुक्तता - *jīvanmukti*; न - not; हि - indeed.

Even after the Self-realisation, these two are worthy of rejection for getting firm abidance in *jīvanmukti* state. A person under the influence of the bondage of miseries born out of desires etc., is not meant for *jīvanmukti* indeed! (51)

Bodhāt ūrdhvaṁ ca jīvanmukti prasiddhaye : Even after attaining *tattva jñāna,* for being forever established in that state of oneness with *Brahman* i.e., for being a *jīvanmukta puruṣah*;

Tad heyam : these two types of *dvaita* deserve to be rejected because;

Kāmādi kleśa bandhena yuktasya muktatā na hi : wanting, seeking, planning, undertaking multifarious projects which are only playground of *kāma, krodha* and similar passions, these are not for him who wants to remain stabilised in *jīvan mukta Ānanda.* There is no place for the relative stand point for the *jīvan mukta* even if he is functioning through the relative equipment. He cannot compromise even in the tiniest degree in eschewing scrupulously *kāma, krodha* etc., *manorājyam, saṁkalpa* etc..

A question can be raised : Never mind if one is not liberated in this life, so long as one does not have to be born again?...

जीवन्मुक्तिरियं माभूज्जन्माभावे त्वहं कृती ।
तर्हि जन्मापि तेऽस्त्वेव स्वर्गमात्रात्कृती भवान् ।।५२।।

Jīvan mukti riyaṁ mā bhūt janmā bhāve tvahaṁ kṛtī
Tarhi janmāpi te 'stveva svarga-mātrāt-kṛtī bhavān (52)

इयम् - this; जीवन् मुक्तिः- the liberation while living; मा - not; भूत् - attain; अहम् - I; तु - indeed; जन्म अभावे - in the absence of rebirth; कृती - fulfilled; तर्हि - in that case; ते - your; जन्म - birth; अपि - also; अस्तु - may it happen; एव - certainly; भवान् - your good self; स्वर्गमात्रात् - by attaining heaven only; कृती - may find fulfilment.

If I say that, "I am fulfilled indeed if I do not get rebirth again, although I may not get *jīvanmukti.*" In that case, our reply is, you are certainly to be reborn, for you can attain fulfilment even by going to heavens. (52)

Iyaṁ jīvanmuktiḥ mā bhūt : The student asks, if *jīvan mukti* cannot be attained here in this life, so be it.

Ahaṁ tu janma abhāve kṛti : Once Self-realisation takes place, one will surely get liberation from rebirth after the body is dropped i.e., one will get *videha mukti*? So long as, one is not keen on getting *mukti* in this life itself, it is not necessary to reject *kāma, krodha, manorājyam* etc.!

Tarhi te janma api asti eva : To this question, the teacher responds - Then (i.e., if you want to continue indulging in the *aśāstrīya dvaita i.e., kāma, krodha* etc.), you will have to have rebirths. You cannot hope to have the one and not the other.

Svarga-mātrāt kṛtī bhavān : (At the most) you can expect to go to heaven. Once the reward for the good deeds done in this life is enjoyed, all the dormant desires and *saṁkalpa-s* carried with the *jīva* will propel you back to another birth. It will not be the final emancipation (*mukti*) that is being discussed and which is the goal for the true spiritual seeker.

The limitations of the joys in heaven are stated...

क्षयातिशयदोषेण स्वर्गो हेयो यदा तदा ।
स्वयं दोषतमात्मायं कामादिः किं न हीयते ।।५३।।

Kṣayā tiśaya doṣeṇa svargo heyo yadā tadā
Svayaṁ doṣatam ātmāyaṁ kāmādiḥ kiṁ na hīyate (53)

यदा - when; क्षय - being perishable; अतिशय - specific; दोषेण - by these limitations; स्वर्गः- the heaven; हेयः- is worthy of discarding; तदा - in that case; स्वयम् - oneself; दोषतमात्मा - an abode of blemish; अयम् - this; काम आदि - the desires etc.; किम् न - why not; हीयते - is rejected.

If the heavens are worthy of discarding on account of their association with specific limitation of being perishable; the abode of all blemish, namely desire etc., why one should not reject them? (53)

Yadā svargaḥ heyaḥ : If the heaven is not really worth desiring because it has these two shortcomings;

Kṣaya atiśaya doṣeṇa : These two defects are -

a) that heaven is not eternal, it is also only a relative plane and;

b) that there, one enjoys *bhoga* to the full, but there is really no freedom from *karma.* And because of the extreme enjoyment, the *puṇya* (merit) is exhausted sooner or later, and thereafter the *jīva* has to return to *mṛtyu loka* i.e., mortal's life.

Tadā svayaṁ doṣatamātmā : The nature of the desires etc., is blemish, so they are worthy of rejection. The heaven also deserves to be rejected because of its joy being not stable;

Ayaṁ kāmādiḥ kiṁ na hīyate : Therefore, why do you not discard all these *aśāstrīya dvaita*, instead of rejecting the *jīvan mukti*?

The situation of one who even after knowing the Truth conducts himself without restraint, is described in the next three *śloka-s.*

तत्त्वं बुद्ध्वापि कामादीन् निःशेषं न जहासि चेत् ।
यथेष्टाचरणं ते स्यात् कर्मशास्त्रातिलङ्घिनः ।।५४।।

Tattvaṁ buddhvāpi kāmādīn niḥśeṣaṁ na jahāsi cet
Yatheṣṭā caraṇaṁ te syāt karma-śāstrā tilaṅghinaḥ (54)

तत्त्वम् - The Truth; बुद्ध्वा - having realized; अपि - although; कामादीन् - desire etc.; निःशेषम् - totally; न - not; जहासि - give up; चेत् - then; कर्म शास्त्र अतिलङ्घिनः- you will be disobeying the scriptures and the behaviour (to be like an animal); ते - your; यथेष्ट आचरणम् - uncontrolled behaviour; स्यात् - will result.

If you do not discard the desires etc. fully even after self-realisation, you will end up in disregarding the scriptural injunction and your behaviour will be an uncontrolled one. (54)

Tattvaṁ buddhvā api kāmādīn niḥśeṣaṁ na jahāsi cet: If, even after having known the Truth, you do not want to drop totally the *aśāstrīya dvaita* such as *kāma, krodha, manorājyam* etc., then;

Yatheṣṭā caraṇaṁ syāt: you will slide back into licentious behaviour. *Maryādā* i.e. guarded freedom is very essential in spiritual life. There has to be a very strict discipline imposed on oneself, otherwise a little freedom might easily develop into licentiousness.

Karma śāstra atilaṅghinaḥ: That is called "insulting the scripture". They transgress the discipline laid down in the scriptures.

In his *naiṣkarmya siddhi, Sureśvarācārya* expresses in no uncertain terms, the status of those who claim to be self-realised, but whose conduct (*ācaraṇa*) is not according to the scriptural injunctions (i.e., not *śāstra sammat*)...

बुद्धाद्वैत स्वतत्त्वस्य यथेष्टाचरणं यदि ।
शुनां तत्त्वदृशां चैव को भेदोऽशुचिभक्षणे ।।५५।।

Buddhā dvaita sva tattvasya yatheṣṭ ācaraṇaṁ yadi
Śunāṁ tattva dṛśāṁ caiva ko bhedo-'śuci-bhakṣaṇe (55)

अद्वैत - Non dual; स्वतत्त्वस्य - of one's own self; बुद्ध - he who has known; यदि - if; यथेष्ट आचरणम् - an uncontrolled behaviour; अशुचि - impure; भक्षणे - eating; शुनाम् - of the dogs; तत्त्वदृशाम् - of the man of realization; च - and; एव - certainly; कः- what; भेदः- is the difference?

After the discovery of the non-dual Self to be one's own nature, if one has uncivilized and uncontrolled behaviour such as eating impure things, what is the difference between the dog and a man of wisdom! (55)

Buddha advaita sva tattvasya : If he who has discovered his own essential nature, his *advaita svarūpa*;

Yadi yatheṣṭ ācaraṇaṁ : if he behaves in anyway he wants;

Aśuci bhakṣaṇe śunāṁ tattva dṛśāṁ ca eva kaḥ bhedaḥ : and therefore eating unclean food etc. (as an example of licentious living), then what is the difference between a dog and a man of realization (who also eats unclean food)? In the spiritual path, there can be not a moment's relaxation from absolute self-discipline strictly self-enforced, without exception, on oneself.

Continuing the thought...

बोधात्पुरा मनोदोषमात्रात्क्लिश्नास्यथाधुना ।
अशेषलोकनिन्दा चेत्यहो ते बोधवैभवम् ।।५६।।

Bodhāt purā mano doṣa mātrāt kliśnā syathā dhunā
Aśeṣa loka nindā ceti aho te bodha vaibhavam (56)

बोधात् पुरा - before Self-realization; मनो दोष मात्रात् - on account of defects of mind; क्लिश्नासि - you suffered; अथ - and; अधुना - now after Self-realisation; अशेष लोक निन्दा - the censure done by all; च - and; इति - thus; अहो - Oh! Great one; ते - your; बोध वैभवम् - the glory of your Self-realisation!

You suffered due to the defects of mind before self-realisation, and now after Self-realisation, you are being censured by the world (because of uncontrolled behaviour etc.). Oh! Great one, what a glory of your Self-realisation. (56)

Bodhāt purā mano doṣa mātrāt kliśnāsi : Before self-realisation, before knowing your own essential nature, you were suffering because of *kāma, krodha, lobha, moha* etc..

Atha adhunā aśeṣa loka nindā ca : but now, you also suffer from the censure and condemnation of the world. So your suffering has only doubled.

Not only do you suffer from the consequences of your uncontrolled desires etc., you have also lost the esteem and respect of the society.

Aho te bodha vaibhavam : What a great self-realisation indeed!

By this technique of *pratipakṣa bhāvanā*, the negative points of an argument are shown in such a way that one drops it, out of disgust. Again and again by focussing attention on the drawbacks and shortcomings, one develops *doṣa dṛṣṭi* towards that object.

If therefore, one has to overcome the mental projections of *dvaita* created by the *jīva*, what should be the life-style and what is meant by spiritual unfoldment? This thought is taken up...

विड्वराहादि तुल्यत्वं मा कांक्षीस्तत्त्वविद्भवान् ।
सर्वधीदोषसंत्यागाल्लोकैः पूज्यस्व देववत् ।।५७।।

Viḍ-varāhā ditulya tvaṁ mā kāṁkṣī stattva vidbhavān
Sarva dhī doṣa saṁ tyāgāt lokaiḥ pūjyasva devavat (57)

तत्त्वविद् - Self realized; भवान् - Oh! Great one; विड् वराहादि तुल्यत्वं - similarity of the lowest swine; मा - don't; कांक्षी - desire; सर्व धी दोष - all the defects of the mind; संत्यागात् - by renouncing all fully; लोकैः- by the people; देववत् - like god; पूज्यस्व - become venerable.

Oh! Great one, who wants to realize the Self , don't desire a life similar to that of lowest swine after Self-realisation. On the contrary, renouncing all the defects of mind (desire etc.), become worthy of worship like God by the world. (57)

Very often spirituality is misunderstood to be a mortification of the flesh and therefore, there is an inclination to subject the body to various forms of hardships such as exposure to cold, heat, hunger etc.. Working on the limitations of the body etc., and thereby a sudden experience of going beyond body identification creates abnormal expressions of life...such a notion is a caricature of spirituality.

Therefore, *Tattvavit bhavān* : Oh You, who wants to be self-realised...

Viḍ-varāhādi tulyatvaṁ mā kāṁkṣī : Do not imagine that living like a pig in dirtiness and filth is spirituality.

Importance is given to such physical aspects because one is still at the level of the conditioning called the body.

Therefore, the *tapasyā* in the spiritual practice need not be matter-oriented. Whatever the circumstances we are placed in, to take physical discomforts and shortcomings in the stride constitutes the *tapasyā* i.e., austerities, to remove excessive attention to matter.

Moreover, it is not living in total uncontrolled freedom like a dog (*śloka* 55) that is spiritual unfoldment. Only he who keeps himself under the bondage of discipline, can be freed from all bondages. Then how should spiritual realization be understood?

Sarva dhī doṣa saṁtyāgāt: Let all the shortcomings of the mind be totally and exhaustively rejected. The *dhī doṣa*-s are *kāma, krodha, manorājyam* etc., the *aśāstrīya jīva*-created *dvaita.*

He who has thus ruthlessly thrown all these *doṣa*-s out of his mind; he acquires a great stature, and thereafter – *lokaiḥ pūjyasva devavat,* he becomes worthy of worship by the whole world.

Those who 'want' from the world are not respected; but those who want nothing from the world are respected and worshipped.

In such a realized individual's presence, no one is agitated, nor is he agitated in their presence. In him, there is no excess of happiness, or presence of intolerance or fear. (B.G. XII-15)

This is the goal of spiritual unfoldment.

This thought is now concluded with a blessing...

कामादि दोषदृष्ट्याद्याः कामादित्यागहेतवः ।
प्रसिद्धो मोक्षशास्त्रेषु तानन्विष्य सुखी भव ।।५८।।

Kāmādi-doṣa-dṛṣṭyā dyāḥ kāmādi tyāga hetavaḥ
Prasiddho mokṣa śāstreṣu tān anviṣya sukhī bhava (58)

कामादि दोषदृष्ट्याद्याः- the vision of defects in the desire etc.; काम आदि त्यागहेतवः- are the means of rejecting desires; मोक्ष शास्त्रेषु - in the scriptures of liberation; प्रसिद्धः- are known; तान् - to those; अन्विष्य - having discovered; सुखी - happy; भव - may you be.

The vision of finding defects in the desire of worldly objects etc., is considered as the means of rejecting desires etc. by the scriptures of liberation. Discovering these techniques, may you become happy. (58)

Kāmādi-doṣa-dṛṣṭyā dyāḥ : If one can develop the art of seeing the fallacy, the weakness in every emotion like *kāma, krodha* etc., that rise in the mind, if one can learn a lesson from every experience, the *kāma, krodha* etc., will drop away. Every experience should leave a light of wisdom rather than a dent of anger and frustration. Naciketa had developed a *doṣa dṛṣṭi* to such a high degree that *Yama Rāja* could offer him nothing and was not able to even slightly excite the young boy. (K.U.1.1.26,27).

Kāmādi tyāga hetavaḥ : By such self-education, through vigilant analysis alone will it be possible to reject the *jīva kalpita dvaita* i.e., the duality created by *jīva.*

Mokṣa śāstreṣu prasiddhaḥ : This is very distinctly emphasized in the *mokṣa śāstra* viz., the B.G. (XVI.21) where it is clearly stated that *kāma, krodha* and *lobha* are the gateways to hell. Hell is, being bored, feeling lonely, wanting appreciation, and willingness to purchase that appreciation by any means.

Tān anviṣya sukhī bhava : Discover this truth in your own life, and be happy. It is the only way to true happiness.

In this way, no logic can support the *jīva-kṛta dvaita* (the duality created by *jīva*). They must be rooted out mercilessly at the right time.

A doubt is expressed - That *kāma, krodha* etc. should be rejected is accepted. But as regards the second, *aśāstrīya jīva dvaita,* namely *manorājya* i.e., imaginations and fantasies... why cannot one indulge in it? It is harmless and helps to pass the time pleasantly?...

त्यज्यतामेव कामादिर्मनोराज्ये तु का क्षतिः ।
अशेषदोषबीजत्वात्क्षतिर्भगवतेरिता ।।५९।।

Tyajyatām-eva kāmādiḥ-manorājye tu kā kṣatiḥ
Aśeṣa-doṣa-bījatvāt kṣatir bhagavate ritā (59)

कामादिः- the desires etc.; त्यज्यताम् - should be discarded; एव - certainly; मनोराज्ये - in the mental castle building; तु - indeed; का - what; क्षतिः- is the defect? अशेषदोष बीजत्वात् - being the seed of all the other defects; क्षतिः- are harmful; भगवता - by Lord *Kṛṣṇa*; ईरिता - is said.

The (defects of mind such as) desires etc. should be discarded, we agree. However, what is wrong in mental projections and imagination i.e., *Manorājya*? (To this question the reply is). *Manorājya*, being the seed for all other defects is harmful, so declared Lord *Kṛṣṇa* (In *Gītā*). (59)

Kāmādiḥ tyajyatām eva : It is agreed that *kāma, krodha, lobha* etc. should be rejected certainly.

Manorājye tu kā kṣatiḥ : What is wrong with *manorājya*? *Manorājyam* is a big obstacle on the path of the spiritual seeker. *Manorājyam* is the inability to stay in the present. The mind goes constantly into the future. This monster of habitual, biased thinking is so assiduously nurtured by us throughout our lives, not realizing that, it is a killer-disease. It is not such a harmless thing as it seems. One must be able to say to the mind 'enough is enough' and stop it.

So the teacher says – *Aśeṣa doṣa bījatvāt kṣatiḥ* : It is the final seed of all the miseries in life. It is from this seed alone that the big jungle of *doṣa* grows up in life and it leads to self destruction.

Bhagavata īritā : This is most emphatically stated by Lord *Kṛṣṇa* in the *Bhagavad Gītā*.

The *Bhagavad Gītā* (II-62-63) is now cited in the next two sloka-s...

ध्यायतो विषयान्पुंसः संगस्तेषूपजायते ।
संगात्संजायते कामः कामात्क्रोधोऽभिजायते ।।६०।।

Dhyāyato viṣayān-puṁsaḥ saṁgas-teṣūpa-jāyate
Saṁgāt-saṁjāyate kāmaḥ kāmāt-krodho'bhijāyate (60)

विषयान् - Of the sense objects; ध्यायतः- contemplating; पुंसः- person; तेषु - towards them; संगः- attachment; उपजायते - is born; संगात् - from the attachment; कामः- desire; संजायते - is born; कामात् - from desire; क्रोधः- anger; अभिजायते - is born.

A person contemplating about the sense objects develops attachment towards them. From this attachment is born desire for that object. From the desire comes the anger. (60)

क्रोधाद्भवति सम्मोहः सम्मोहात्स्मृति विभ्रमः ।
स्मृतिभ्रंशात् बुद्धिनाशो बुद्धिनाशात् प्रणश्यति ।।६० अ।।

Krodhād-bhavati sammohaḥ sammohāt-smṛti vibhramaḥ
Smṛti-bhraṁśāt buddhi-nāśo buddhi-nāśāt praṇaśyati (60A)

क्रोधात् - from anger; भवति - comes; सम्मोहः- delusion; सम्मोहात् - from delusion; स्मृति विभ्रमः- loss of memory; स्मृति भ्रंशात् - from loss of memory; बुद्धि नाशः- destruction of discrimination; बुद्धि नाशात् - from the destruction of discrimination; प्रणश्यति - (he) perishes.

From the anger comes delusion, the delusion leads to loss of memory, and from the loss of memory, there is destruction of discrimination. Finally, from the destruction of discrimination, one perishes in life. (60 A)

Viṣayān dhyāyataḥ puṁsaḥ teṣu saṁgaḥ upajāyate : An individual when he goes on building *manorājya* about an object, he begins to give value to that object in his mind. Then begins the chain of events that leads to one's downfall.

Saṁgāt saṁjāyate kāmaḥ : Anything that has been invested with value (it is all only mental) evokes desire, one runs towards the object which has acquired value in the mind; and when that value is negative, one runs away from the object. The "desiring" causes bias. One must protect oneself against both.

Kāmāt krodhaḥ abhijāyate : When the desire cannot be fulfilled, the resulting anger is in direct proportion to the intensity of disappointment. When one likes everything "as is where is", there is neither anger nor frustration. This should become our second nature.

When the desire is fulfilled also, there is trouble, because the mind wants to repeat and multiply that experience. This generates greed or *lobha* and when greed is not satisfied, one becomes angry. In this way, starting from a small desire, one ends up in *krodha*, either directly or via greed.

Krodhāt bhavati sammohaḥ : An angry individual loses discrimination, and is not open to wisdom.

Sammohāt smṛti vibhramaḥ : From lack of discrimination results the loss of balance and loss of memory as to, where one is and what one does and says. *Śaṅkarācārya* says that *moha* can take an individual to such a position where even a disciple dares to insult the *Guru*. Such is the fall.

Smṛti bhraṁśāt buddhi nāśaḥ : From the loss of memory, follows the loss of understanding and wisdom.

Buddhi nāśāt praṇaśyati : With the loss of wisdom, he is totally destroyed.

Thus the total disintegration of the personality is the end of the downfall which commenced from *manorājyam*. Therefore, this *manorājyam* is not to be taken lightly as a small weakness of no consequence but as a terrible curse, to be mercilessly rejected.

A method of rectifying *manorājyam* is recommended by *Ramaṇa Maharṣi*, that is of tracing the path taken by *manorājya* thought back to its source. By constant practice, one will be able to abort the journey of the thought into the future and withdraw it back to one's position.

How to arrest and eliminate *manorājya* is now explained...

शक्यं जेतुं मनोराज्यं निर्विकल्पसमाधितः ।
सुसंपादः क्रमात्सोऽपि सविकल्पसमाधिना ।।६१।।

Śakyaṁ jetuṁ manorājyaṁ nirvikalpa samādhitaḥ
Susaṁpādaḥ kramāt-so'pi savikalpa samādhinā (61)

मनोराज्यम् - The habitual thinking; निर्विकल्प - without any thoughts; समाधितः - through *samādhi*; जेतुं - conquer; शक्यं - is possible; सः- that *samādhi*; अपि - also; सविकल्प - with thought; समाधिना - by *samādhi*; क्रमात् - in stages; सुसंपादः- is attained properly.

Manorājyam i.e., habitual thinking can be conquered by the practice of *nirvikalpa samādhi*. This *nirvikalpa samādhi* can be properly attained in stages though *savikalpa samādhi*. (61)

Manorājyaṁ nirvikalpa samādhitaḥ jetuṁ śakyaṁ : It is possible to control *manorājyam* by *nirvikalpa samādhi*, where thought is suspended without entering into deep sleep. Thus habitual thinking can be controlled by *citta vṛtti nirodha*.

Saḥ api savikalpa samādhinā kramāt susaṁpādaḥ : The *nirvikalpa samādhi* can be gained in gradual stages by the method of *savikalpa samādhi*.

In *savikalpa samādhi*, importance is given to the thoughts that come in the mind, and the trio of the meditator, meditation and meditated upon, is existent. It is from the matter point of view i.e., the thought process.

In *nirvikalpa samādhi*, importance is given to the individual in whose mind the thoughts are appearing. This is from the point of view of the Spirit. In this method, the body is kept still. Gradually, the respiration becomes low and shallow, as if it is moving within the nostrils (B.G. V.27). As a result, the mind which is supported by power of respiration attains relative quietness.

At this point, one must guard against dropping off into deep sleep. This quietened mind is a stepping stone for getting out of the matter aspect of meditation to the Spirit aspect. Up to this point is *savikalpa samādhi*.

To this quiet mind, 'I' the observer gives the order to chant the Lord's name three times, keep quiet. Observe the mind. If thoughts rise again, chant again, stop and watch. By constant *abhyāsa*, one can come to the understanding of the meaning of 'witness' observing the mind, the subject observing the object.

It is at this point that *manorājyam* becomes a problem, the mind playing tyrant and running to distant lands, far into the remote future! So again, we trace it back to the zero point. By this technique of cutting down the thought frequency, in due course (*kramāt*) *nirvikalpa samādhi* is possible.

On replacing habitual thinking by the hobby of thinking i.e., contemplation on Self, by discovering the divine principle in every experience, by devotion, the seeker rises in ever expanding, all-enveloping love. He slowly overcomes *manorājyam.*

Thus through *savikalpa samādhi*, *dhyātā-dhyeya-dhyāna* trio is dissolved, when this matures, one gets absorbed in *Nirvikalpa samādhi*.

Such a mind loses its capacity to create new *manorājyam.* Just as a long unused organ atrophies, so also the mind long exposed to the state of thoughtlessness of *Nirvikalpa samādhi*, loses its habit of unwanted thinking. This is one method of controlling *manorājyam.* The second method is now explained.

The second method is for the student of *Vedānta* who has studied and reflected on : (a) the position of the *jagat* (b) the position of the *jīva* and; (c) the position of *Īśvara*, to help him in conquering *manorājyam...*

बुद्धतत्त्वेन धीदोषशून्येनैकान्तवासिना ।
दीर्घं प्रणवमुच्चार्य मनोराज्यं विजीयते ।।६२।।

Buddha-tattvena dhī-doṣa śūnye naikānta vāsinā
Dīrghaṁ praṇava muccārya manorājyaṁ vijīyate (62)

बुद्ध तत्त्वेन - by the man of Self knowledge; धी दोष - the defects of the mind; शून्येन् - devoid of; एकान्त वासिनः- by he who is living in solitude; दीर्घम् - long; प्रणव - Om; उच्चार्य - chanting; मनोराज्यम् - the habit of thinking; विजीयते - can be conquered.

The habitual thinking can be conquered by a man of Self-knowledge, who is devoid of other defects of mind (such as desire etc.) and who is living in solitude, by prolonged chanting of *Omkar*! (62)

Buddha tattvena : He who has thus discovered that this total world of names and forms, the world of duality and dualism is supported by 'I', the Supreme, that He is the substratum of the whole world, by him who has got rid of the abnormality of thinking and has gained clear understanding;

Dhī doṣa śūnyena : He who is no more under the influence of worldly desires and passions; when these two qualities have been firmly established in him;

Ekānta vāsinā : he starts living all by himself in absolute solitude without a feeling of loneliness. This enjoins the strict adherence to the discipline laid down in the scriptures for each stage of life – *Brahmacarya, gṛhasta, vānaprastha* and *sannyāsa.*

We come alone into this world, and go out all alone. No one holds one's hand. With this knowledge, one should educate the mind again and again to be itself. Alone-ness is the dignity of human existence. *Ekānta vāsi* is one who does not get too much involved in activities, gatherings, discussions which result only in the excitement of the mind.

Eka-anta-vāsi also means the one who lives only in That ONE, the supreme Lord. For him, other than the Lord, nothing else is the Reality. He alone is ever with us in the very core of our personality. He who invokes the Lord, who is the very nature of Bliss, he is the *ekānta vāsi.*

To such an individual, control of *manorājya* is possible instantaneously. How?

Dīrghaṁ praṇavam uccārya manorājyaṁ vijīyate : By the technique of chanting a long *'OM'*, by maintaining the thought on the same theme of the *praṇava* for increasing lengths of time, the frequency of thought is reduced, agitations are also reduced. The content remains the same, just one – *OM.*

In this way, habitual thinking dies away – a natural death. One conquers *manorājyam.* The hobby of thinking takes over and that also culminates in no thinking.

In this state of mind, man-created duality is erased.

After this stage is reached through *savikalpa samādhi* and *OM* chanting, what is the next step?...

जिते तस्मिन्वृत्तिशून्यं मनस्तिष्ठति मूकवत् ।
एतत्पदं वसिष्ठेन रामाय बहुधेरितम् ।।६३।।

Jite tasmin-vṛtti-śūnyaṁ manastiṣ-ṭhati mūkavat
Etat-padaṁ vasiṣṭhena rāmāya bahudhe ritam (63)

तस्मिन् जिते - When the habit of thinking is won over; मनः- the mind; मूकवत् - like a dumb; वृत्तिशून्यम् - devoid of thoughts; तिष्ठति - stays; एतद् - this; पदम् - state; वसिष्ठेन - by the sage *Vasiṣtha*; रामाय - to *Rāma*; बहुधा - in many ways; ईरितम् - is declared.

When the habitual thinking is won over, the mind becomes devoid of thoughts, like a dumb person. This state of mind was explained to Lord *Rāma* by Sage *Vasiṣtha* in many ways. (63)

Tasmin jite vṛtti śūnyaṁ manaḥ mūka vat tiṣṭhati : When the *manorājyam* is conquered, when thoughts are stilled, the mind stays like a dumb person. A dumb does have experiences, only he cannot speak about them. So also, the mind which has conquered *manorājyam*, does experience the world, but does not react. Such a mind is a Divine Mind. It is like a mirror which reflects every object that comes before it, but retains no image. When the mind does not react, the tongue also does not speak, such a divine mind is the one that is soaked in love.

Etat padaṁ vasiṣṭhena rāmāya bahudhā īritam : This state of the Divine Presence without any reaction was explained in many different ways by *Vasiṣtha muni* to *Śri Rāmacandra* (in *Yoga Vāsiṣtha*).

Quotations from *Yoga Vāsiṣtha* follows in the next two *śloka*-s...

दृश्यं नास्तीति बोधेन मनसो दृश्यमार्जनम् ।
संपन्नं चेत्तदुत्पन्ना परा निर्वाणनिर्वृतिः ।।६४।।

Dṛśyaṁ nāstīti bodhena manaso dṛśya mārjanam
Saṁpannaṁ cet tadut panna parā nirvāṇa nirvṛtiḥ (64)

दृश्यम् - the objective world; नास्ति - is nothing but *Brahman*; इति - in this way; बोधेन - by this knowledge; मनसः- from the mind; दृश्यमार्जनम् - removal of the objective thoughts; संपन्नम् चेत् - if achieved; तद् - then; परा निर्वाण - the supreme blissful; निर्वृतिः- state of liberation; उत्पन्ना - is attained.

'Other than Pure *Brahman*, there is nothing like objective world of plurality', by this knowledge, the objective thoughts are removed from the mind. When this state of supreme Bliss is achieved, it is called as liberation. (64)

Dṛśyaṁ na asti iti bodhena : There is nothing like objective perception, there is no duality having reached this *advaita* knowledge (*ekam eva advitīyam nehanānāsti kiñcana*). Rejecting all sense of my, mine and otherness;

Manasaḥ dṛśya mārjanam : the mind will be totally emptied of its contents.

In the mind, there can be thought only of other than oneself. One who has total identity with the total creation, only he can have desireless existence. Only he can have an empty mind, which is non-sleeping, but thought-free.

Saṁpannaṁ cet tat parā nirvāṇa nirvṛtiḥ utpanna : If one is able to attain this particular state, then such an individual will attain a state of Supreme Bliss, where existence carries no purpose, where it has no cause and effect, gain or loss. This state of Absolute Being is *Parā nirvāṇa nirvṛti.* The discovery of this joy of Being is in tune with the Reality, the Supreme Bliss, the Supreme Love; the Love that is quiet and does not have any expression. That Love happens, as a force of existence, as the sun shines helplessly.

The quotation from *Yoga Vāsiṣṭha* continues...

विचारितमलं शास्त्रं चिरमुद्ग्राहितं मिथः ।
संत्यक्तवासनान्मौनादृते नास्त्युत्तमं पदम् ।।६५।।

Vicāritam alaṁ śāstraṁ ciram udgrā hitaṁ mithaḥ
Saṁtyakta vāsanān maunād ṛte nāstyu ttamaṁ padam

शास्त्रम् - the a*dvaita Vedānta*; अलम् - enough; विचारितम् - reflected; मिथः- discussion with teacher and saints; चिरम् - for a long period; उद्ग्राहितम् - thus accepted without doubt; संत्यक्त वासनात् - having rejected all desires; मौनात् - by silence; ऋते - without; उत्तमम् पदम् - the Supreme Truth; न - not; अस्ति - be achieved.

The supreme state is not achieved without the sufficient study of *Vedānta śāstra*, reflection on them, discussion (with the teacher and saints) for a required period of time, thus accepting the knowledge without doubt and (finally) getting established in silence. (65)

How is one to realize this *nirvāṇa nirvṛtiḥ*, this excessively independent absolute existence called *Ānanda*?

Vasiṣṭha Maharṣi explains the step by step *sādhanā* to *Rāmachandraji* :

i) *Śāstraṁ alaṁ vicāritam* : Sufficient reflection on what one has studied. The purpose of reflection or *mananam* is to transfer the knowledge from the book to the brain. Reflection is a process by which all possible doubts are removed by examining the matter from every angle. Truth is examined from the point of view of the *jīva*, the *jagat*, *Īśvara* and *advaita tattva*. Unless the thinking is flawless, meditation cannot happen.

ii) *Mithaḥ* : This reflection is done by the interaction with the teacher in order to get the doubts cleared.

iii) *Ciram udgrāhitaṁ* : Discussion with fellow seekers in respect of those aspects where there appears to be conflicting statements in the scriptures.

iv) *Saṁtyakta vāsanāt* : Giving up all interest in any subject other than *Paramātma tattva*; that is rejecting once and for all, all those thoughts which will precipitate the individuality and which will take one away from the divine core of one's personality.

Maunāt ṛte na asti uttamaṁ padam : There is nothing more to be achieved after attaining the quietitude of mind born out of deep reflection on the one hand, and eschewing of all *un-ātmic* thoughts and *saṁkalpa*-s, desires, *manorājya* etc..

This state where the mind is maintained in shapeless-ness, where individuality has been totally dissolved, where nothing is allowed to agitate the mind, is the one where all the thought knowledge has become thoughtless knowledge. That Knowledge which comes from within is the expression of the Infinite. It is the highest expression of *Paramātmā* which is beyond relative expression of seer and seen.

However, even such a contemplative person can sometimes get disturbed again by desire. What should he do in that case?...

विक्षिप्यते कदाचिद्धीः कर्मणा भोगदायिना ।
पुनः समाहिता सा स्यात्तदैवाभ्यासपाटवात् ।।६६।।

Vikṣipyate kadācid-dhīḥ karmaṇā bhoga-dāyinā
Punaḥ samāhitā sā syāt tadaivā-bhyāsa-pāṭavāt (66)

भोग दायिना - by those experiences (of giving joy and sorrow); कर्मणा - by *karma*; धीः- the intellect; कदाचित् - at times; विक्षिप्यते - disturbed and unstable; सा - that intellect; अभ्यास पाटवात् - by the strength of practice;

तदा - then and there; एव - certainly; पुनः- again; समाहिता - single pointed; स्यात् - can be.

If the intellect gets disturbed and agitated due to our own actions leading to different experiences; at times, it can be again pulled together to be single pointed by the strength of practice, whenever we discover the disturbances in our mind. (66)

Bhoga dāyinā karmaṇā dhīḥ kadācit vikṣipyate : Although one has been doing spiritual *sādhanā* for very long and regularly, yet because of the earlier dormant *karma*, a particular *karma* provokes a new disturbance in the mind. This may cause a fall in the individual in spite of his *sādhanā* and may even cause loss of faith and confidence in himself. Such a fall indicates that consciously or unconsciously, arrogance born out of hardening individuality has raised its ugly head again. And the fall is a reminder to correct oneself that even the smallest progress in the spiritual path is by the grace of the *Guru* and the Lord. This Divine Grace is equivalent to the strength of the *śraddhā* at the feet of the *Guru*. What is *śraddhā* inside (the disciple) is called Divine Grace outside (in *Guru* and God).

Sā punaḥ samāhitā syāt : If such a fall happens, that buddhi can be withdrawn and can again be made single-pointed in contemplation.

Tada eva abhyāsa pāṭavāt : By practising again and again, never forgetting for a moment that every step forward is by His Guiding Hand and not by our effort, one can regain this poise.

Abhyāsa must go hand in hand with *vairāgya*.

The importance of a steadfast mind is stressed...

विक्षेपो यस्य नास्त्यस्य ब्रह्मवित्त्वं न मन्यते ।
ब्रह्मैवायमिति प्राहुर्मुनयः पारदर्शिनः ।।६७।।

Vikṣepo yasya nāsty-asya brahma-vittvaṁ na manyate
Brahmai vāyam iti prāhuḥ munayaḥ pāra darśinaḥ (67)

यस्य - he whose (wise man); विक्षेपः- disturbance and projection; न - not; अस्ति - is; अस्य - to him; ब्रह्मवित्त्वम् - the knower of *Brahman*; न - not; मन्यते - is considered; अयम् - he; ब्रह्म - *Brahman*; एव - indeed; इति - in this way; पारदर्शिनः- the wise *Vedāntin*-s; मुनयः- contemplative ones; प्राहुः - say.

A wise man who does not have any disturbances and projections in his mind is not considered to be merely a knower of *Brahman*, but is considered to be *Brahman* indeed, by contemplative seers of *Vedānta*. (67)

Yasya vikṣepo na asti : He whose mind is not entertaining any *vikṣepa*;

Asya brahma vittvaṁ na manyate : He is not called just a *Brahmavit*, as the knower of *Brahman*. He is *Brahman* Himself! (*'Brahmavit Brahmaiva Bhavati'*, M.U.). In subjective knowledge, the subject-object duality vanishes.

When the seeker wants 'to know himself' (the *Paramātma tattva*), he becomes one with it.

Ayam pāradarśinaḥ munayaḥ brahma iva prāhuḥ : Therefore, the sages who are able to discover Absence in the Presence, say that such an individual is not merely a *Brahmavit* but *Brahman* itself.

This was also said by *Vasiṣṭha Ṛṣi* to Lord *Rāma* (in Mk.U.)...

दर्शनादर्शने हित्वा स्वयं केवलरूपतः ।
यस्तिष्ठति स तु ब्रह्मन् ब्रह्म न ब्रह्मवित्स्वयम् ।।६८।।

Darśanā darśane hitvā svayaṁ kevala rūpataḥ
Yas tiṣṭhati sa tu Brahman brahma na brahma vit svayam (68)

यः - he (wiseman) who; दर्शन अदर्शने - " I know or I do not know " in this way; हित्वा - renouncing; स्वयम् - himself; केवलरूपतः- in his essential Pure Self; तिष्ठति - is established; स - he; तु - indeed; ब्रह्मन् - Oh! Great one; स्वयम् ब्रह्म - himself *Brahman*; न - not; ब्रह्मवित् - knower of *Brahman*.

He who has renounced the language like, " I know *Brahman* or I don't know *Brahman*", and is established in his essential Pure Nature, he is indeed, oh! Great one, not (merely) a knower of *Brahman* but is *Brahman* himself! (68)

Yaḥ darśana adarśane hitvā : He neither says, 'I have seen *Brahman*' nor does he say, 'I have not seen'. Thus;

Svayaṁ kevala rūpataḥ tiṣṭhati : he who remains in the *kevala rūpa* : that is, in which all three types of differences or *bheda*-s (*vijātīya, sajātīya* and *svagata bheda*) are absent. *Brahman* is one in which differences on account of planes of Consciousness; experience-experienced-experiencer trio; and differences of the same experiencer with reference to objects, are absent.

Brahman! Sa tu svayaṁ brahman na brahmavit : Oh! Great one, he is *Brahman*. He is not the knower of *Brahman* as if it is an objective knowledge. It is *Brahman* itself. It is 'Being'.

In this way, the *Dvaita Viveka Prakaraṇa* concludes...

जीवन्मुक्तेः परा काष्ठा जीवद्वैतविवर्जनात् ।
लभ्यतेऽसावतोऽत्रेदमीशद्वैताद्विवेचितम् ।।६९।।

Asau jīvan-mukteḥ parā kāṣṭhā jīva-dvaita-vivarjanāt
Labhyate-'sāvato-'tre dam īśadvaitād vivecitam (69)

असौ - this; जीवन्मुक्तेः- of the *jīvan-mukta*; परा काष्ठाः- acme; जीव द्वैत - duality created by *jīva*; विवर्जनात् - rejecting fully; लभ्यते - is gained; अतः- therefore; इदम् - the duality; अत्र - in the chapter; ईश-द्वैतात् - from the duality created by *Ī*śvara; विवेचितम् - enquired and analysed.

This final abode of *jīvan mukta* is gained by rejecting the duality created by the *jīva*. Therefore, this *jīva dvaita* is enquired and discriminated from the *Īśa dvaita* (in this chapter). (69)

Asau jīvan-mukteḥ parā kāṣṭhā : This is called the acme, the pinnacle of *jīvan mukti* - living in Freedom.

Jīva dvaita vivarjanāt labhyate : It is attained by the renunciation of the *dvaita* created by the *jīva*. Since nothing can be done about *Īśvara sṛṣṭi*, any change is possible for the *jīva* in what he himself has created. So the *jīva* has to renounce the likes and dislikes, friends-foes etc., which are all his own mental creations. Then the Supreme *jīva mukti* is attained.

Ataḥ atra idaṁ Īśa dvaitāt vivecitam : Therefore in this chapter called *Dvaita Viveka Prakaraṇam*, these two *dvaita*-s created by *Ī*śvara and *jīva* have been exhaustively analysed and discussed.

Happiness and misery begin from the *jīva*. It is one's own choice whether to be happy or unhappy. The path to happiness, here and now, always has been indicated in the scriptures. Essentially, it is a matter of changing the vision and understanding the *jīva-jagat-Īśvara* relationship in correct perspective. " In that clear vision, there is an end to all sorrows, there is only serenity, only *prasāda buddhi*" (B.G.II.65).

Once everything that happens to one is accepted as *prasāda* from the Lord, there is nothing but joy in His Grace. One is always *prasanna*, as the Lord Himself is. This is the Supreme state of joyful existence.

OM TAT SAT

Summary

Verse No.	Subject matter covered
	Introduction
1	Topic of *Īśvara* and *jīva dvaita* introduced and purpose of study.
2 - 10	Scriptural authority quoted about *Īśvara*'s creation and *jīva*'s creation.
11 - 13	*Īśvara*'s creation continued, *jīva* defined and the delusion due to *māya*
14 - 16	*Jīva*'s creation.
17 - 23	World is combination of *Īśvara*'s and *jīva*'s creation; their discrimination.
24 - 25	A doubt about *jīva*'s creation raised and replied.
26 - 30	Yet another doubt about *jīva sṛṣṭi* and its reply.
31	Who knows the *Īśvara*'s and *jīva*'s creation?
32 - 35	Bondage is due to *jīva*'s creation - analysis and discrimination.
36 - 37	Are we talking about *Vijñānavāda* of Buddhists? – Replied

38 - 39	Need for *Brahmajñāna* doubted and replied.
40 - 42	Approach to *Brahma jñāna*, the *Īśvara*'s creation is helpful and not a hindrance in Self knowledge.
43 - 48	*Jīva*'s creation that is acceptable to scriptures. Its application in discrimination and limit of practice of *sādhanā*.
49 - 58	*Jīva*'s creation that is unacceptable to scriptures and how to conquer it. Need for overcoming it - doubted and replied.
59 - 66	Importance of conquering the habit of mental projection, the cause for this habit and the technique to achieve it.
67 - 68	The knower of Truth glorified.
69	*Phala śruti* (result) of the study of this chapter.

* * *

5

५

Chapter V

MAHĀVĀKYA VIVEKAḤ

or

ENQUIRY OF THE MEANING OF *MAHĀVĀKYA*

Introduction

Viveka or discrimination means analysis with synthesis in such a way that no doubt is left in the understanding. For e.g. when it is said that smoke appears if there is fire, it does not follow that where there is fire, there should be smoke. So fire is independent of smoke, but smoke is dependent on fire. In this way, in these two variables, fire is the reality and not the smoke. The thought put together makes *viveka*.

Two aspects need to be taken into consideration in discrimination or *viveka* : *vyatireka* and *anvaya*. Independence of cause from the effect is *vyatireka*, and the presence of the cause in the effect is *anvaya*. The two together make a complete analysis, a *viveka*.

Vākya: A *Vākya* or sentence is made up of certain words, and the words have different meanings. The relationship between the words and their meanings gives rise to knowledge which indicates something. Words without meaning is only noise. Therefore, one should be able to put words together into a coherent sentence or *vākya* to make knowledge out of it.

In the process of transfer of knowledge, it is very essential to understand the meaning of the pada or word, the relationship of the words among themselves and the final conclusion indicated by the words in the *vākya*.

Types of *Vākya* : Different types of *vākya*-s are used in the scriptures.

a) Secondary sentence or *gauṇa vākya* : These are sentences which lay down the do's and don'ts for living an ideal life and the consequences if they are not followed (*vidhiniṣedha*). For e.g. if you do not do *sandhyāvandana*, you will suffer the sin of omission (*pratyavāya doṣaḥ*).

b) Sentences that demand action : These are of two categories -

i) Those that delineate the obligatory duties of individuals (*adhikāri nirṇaya*) e.g. if you are a *Brāhmin, Kṣatriya* etc., these are your duties. Such statements demand action in the form of *karma* as in *karma kāṇḍa vidhi*.

ii) The second category of sentences are those that demand action in the form of *upāsanā*. For e.g. if you do so much *japa*, you will go to heaven.

c) The third type of sentence is the statement of facts e.g. this is a temple. What is already there is revealed. Nothing is created. These are called Primary Statements which declare the truth.

Thus, the first two types of sentences bind one with their limitations. e.g. when it says that a *Brāhmin* should do this and this, it also implies that he cannot do those actions which are the prescribed duties of other *varṇa-s*. Therefore, these sentences or statements have the result of throwing the individual into a vortex of do's and don'ts and the whole *Karma Kāṇḍa* begins.

Mahāvākya-s are those statements of facts which tell us what our essential nature is; having known which, nothing remains to be known or done. They constitute *Brahmātmaikya bodhaḥ*.

Ātmā is 'I', whatever one considers this 'I' to be. In reality, *Ātmā* is not a limited being, it is of universal nature, without limitation. But although everyone accepts that *Ātmā* is 'I', the definition of *Ātmā* varies according to one's choice and conviction. To some *Ātmā* means the gross body, to others the near and dear ones, to still other wealth etc..

On the other hand, if one takes the meaning of *Ātmā* to be *Brahma svarūpa*, then it leads to a reassessment and revaluation of the real meaning of *Ātmā*. Then the right enquiry begins, such an enquiry will lead to the conclusion that 'I' is not limited by any limitation. This discovery of the absence of limitations on 'I', the Real One, is called *Brahmātmaikya Bodha*.

All those sentences which reveal the identity of the individuality with the totality are called *Mahāvākya-s*. There are several *Mahāvākya-s* spread throughout the *Upaniṣad-s*. Out of these, the great Masters have selected four *Mahāvākya-s*,one from each of the four veda-s.

This chapter of *Pañcadaśī* discusses these four *Mahāvākya-s* in depth.

The study of the *Mahāvākya-s* leads one on the spiritual path. They are not to be understood objectively and intellectually, and conceived of as concepts. By gaining this knowledge, there is no material gain. Therefore, the study should be carried out as an interaction with the thoughts, without any individuality.

There may seem some repetition of thought in the four *Veda*-s. This kind of repetition is called *Abhyāsa* and is intended to enable the student to remind himself again and again about the Truth, from different angles, and different approaches.

Spirituality is not performance oriented. It is to be lived as naturally as we breathe.

येनेक्षते शृणोतीदं जिघ्रति व्याकरोति च ।
स्वाद्वस्वादू विजानाति तत्प्रज्ञानमुदीरितम् ।।१।।

Yenekṣate śṛṇo-tīdaṁ jighrati vyākaroti ca
Svādva svādū vijānāti tat prajñanam udīritam (1)

येन - that by which; इदम् - this world and objects; ईक्षते - sees; शृणोति - hears; जिघ्रति - smells; व्याकरोति - speaks; स्वादु अस्वादु - tasty and tasteless; विजानाति - knows; च - and; तत् - that; प्रज्ञानम् - Consciousness; उदीरितम् - is called.

That by which one sees, hears, smells this world of objects, and that by which one speaks, tastes the good and bad is called as *Prajñānam* (i.e. Consciousness) in this *Mahāvākya* (1)

The first two *śloka-s* deal with the *mahāvākya - Prajñānam Brahma* from the *Aitereya Upaniṣad* in the Ṛg *Veda*. In this first *śloka,* the meaning of the word *Prajñānam* is defined.

Tat prajñānam īritam : That is called *Prajñānam*; *yena* : by which; *idaṁ īkṣate* : this is seen; (*idaṁ*) *śṛṇoti* : this is heard; (*idaṁ*) *jighrati* :

this is smelt; *vyākaroti* : this or that is spoken; *svādū asvādū vijānāti* : taste or absence of taste is known.

In *Vedānta śāstra*, the word *idaṁ* does not mean just 'this', but refers to all that is known as objects of knowledge (including the relative oneself) through the five sense perceptions of *śabda, sparśa, rūpa, rasa* and *gandha.*

Yena idam īkṣate : That by which colours and forms are seen.

For knowledge in the form of objective perception to take place, colours and forms should be present; they should be bathing in external light because they are not self- illumined; the senses (the eyes) should be operating and the mind should also be bathing in the light of Consciousness. When the Consciousness is withdrawn as in deep sleep, the gross world is not perceptible. Therefore, Consciousness is the reality which is supporting all the colours and forms. If undue importance is given to the names, colours and forms, that which is expressing through them is lost sight of.

If on the other hand, when we look at the world with the perception of the Consciousness in everything that we see; even if the eyes are open, we look within. This is called *Prajñānam.*

Jñānaṁ is that which comes and goes, which is located at the level of the thought, and therefore, likely to be lost. *Prajñānam* is that knowledge which makes every knowledge possible and yet which, in the presence or absence of knowledge, in the memory or absence of memory, is never lost. This 'un-lose-able' Knowledge is *Prajñānam.*

Similarly (*Yena idaṁ*) *śṛnoti* : This is the experience of sound. In silence, the mind is not attracted to any specific sound. Consciousness is manifest without agitation, without specificity. It is present in the sound, as also in the silence, but is beyond sound and silence.

Knowledge of sound is *jñānam* in which the trio of hearer-heard-hearing exists. But that knowledge which is present in all these three factors as well as when the three are absent is *Prajñānam.*

(*Yena idaṁ*) *jighrati*: That which is present in every smell - good and bad; *vyākaroti*: That which expresses as speech; and *svādū asvādū* : that through which experience of good and bad taste is possible.

Vijānāti (viśeṣeṇa jānāti) : that 'general' knowledge or Consciousness by which this objective world of names, forms, sound, smell, speech, taste etc., are known with 'specificity'(specific knowledge); *Tat prajñānam udīritam* : that is called *prajñānam.*

What has been stated in this *śloka* is a guideline to what a spiritual seeker's vision of the world should be; see and yet not see, hear and yet not hear.... Be like a mirror that reflects everything, but react to nothing. Instead of paying attention to what is seen, heard etc., focus attention on how the seeing, hearing etc. happens. This leads to one's own essential being, and to that extent one becomes contemplative.

Experience comes and goes, but Consciousness neither comes nor goes. Consciousness is the one because of which every experience is possible. That pure Consciousness is *Prajñānam.*

चतुर्मुखेन्द्रदेवेषु मनुष्याश्वगवादिषु ।
चैतन्यमेकं ब्रह्मातः प्रज्ञानं ब्रह्म मय्यपि ।।२।।

Catur-mukhendra-deveṣu manuṣyā-śva-gavādiṣu
Caitanya mekaṁ brahmātaḥ prajñānaṁ brahma mayyapi (2)

चतुर्मुख इन्द्र देवेषु - in the *Brahmāji*, Indra and gods; मनुष्य अश्व गवादिषु - in the human beings, horses, cows etc; एकम् - one; चैतन्यम् - Consciousness; ब्रह्म - *Brahma*; अतः- therefore; मयि - in me; अपि - also; प्रज्ञानम् - Consciousness; ब्रह्म - *Brahma.*

There is but one Consciousness in *Brahmāji*, *Indra*, Gods, human beings, horses, cows etc., therefore it is called *Brahma* in this *Mahāvākya*. In me also, the same Consciousness alone is. Hence I am also *Brahma*. (2)

The first *śloka* discussed the meaning of the word *Prajñānam* in the *mahāvākya Prajñānam Brahma*. The second word, *Brahma*, is defined in the second *śloka*.

Brahma (Bṛhatvāt Brahma): That which is bigger than the Biggest. (*aṇoraṇīyān mahato mahīyān*, K.U.) That which is subtler than the subtlest can alone be bigger than the biggest. Just as the space is so small, it can go inside the eyes of the needle, and the same space contains the total cosmos. So depending on the subtlety of the intellect, one perceives the world.

That *Prajñānam* which was explained in *śloka* 1, is of the nature of *Brahman*. The two are not separate. In the sentence, *Prajñānam Brahma*, the verb *asti*, 'is' is understood; meaning that, there is identity between the two.

When Consciousness arises, in the light of this Consciousness, there is knowingness. This knowingness comes and goes. There is another aspect of Consciousness called sentiency or life, which does not come and go.

With 'knowing-ness', the individuality is born. There is no 'knowing-ness' involved in the functioning of the different cells in the body. The differentiation of functions is the natural manifestation called life, and is not done by the knowledge of an individual. This is one part of Consciousness or *Śuddha Cetanā*. The other is the 'knowingness' which differentiates between 'I know' and 'I do not know'.

True knowledge consists in discovering that 'I am this life which manifests' sometimes as knowingness when the waking state is born, and at other, it is able to 'suck in' this knowingness, and what remains then is Pure life which is everywhere.

Caturmukha, Indra, deveṣu, manuṣya, aśva, gau, ādiṣu : The life in *Brahma*, and other lower forms of creations --- human beings, animals etc. is the same. Another way of interpreting this line is : The life which is in everyone, at the individual level and also at the level of the *Antaḥkaraṇa catuṣṭaya*, all the differences because of the mind (*manaḥ*), all the faculties through which we function (*deveṣu*), and all the varieties of expression that come to us, it is the same single principle.

In the initial stage of spiritual *sādhanā*, one tries to be the *Śuddha sākṣi* or witness, one is still holding on to the knowingness aspect of Consciousness; although this is a necessary first step, one has to grow out of it.

One sees the world, but does not participate in it, and thus one develops *dṛṣtā bhāva*. Gradually one acts as if one is with everybody, but in truth one is with nobody. When there is *Āsakti* or attachment, there is love for only one, everyone else is excluded. When love is not for only one, that love includes everyone plus one. It is not the friend that I love, but it is the friendship that manifests in me.

As *Bhagavān Kṛṣṇa* says (B.G. XII-13), the devotee is not the friend of a friend, but one who is friendly with everyone. This friendliness is called expansion or *Brahmatva*. Therefore, the first step to undersand *prajñānam* is to participate in the world in such a way that one does not go too near to or run away from anyone, so that one is not a slave of the world.

The second step is to watch the thoughts that come and go, and develop *sākṣi bhāva* or witness-hood, until gradually the turbulence in the thoughts dies-down. This is the knowing-ness aspect of Consciousness.

Gradually, when the mind is emptied of every thought i.e., every theme of the relative world; a stage is reached when even watching the traffic of thoughts on the road called mind, dies away. A stage of thought-less, object-less, content-less awareness is reached. Slowly, one is able to be, without becoming. There is no otherness left. 'I alone am'.

When this 'I'is discovered, the knower and the known (the thought) have merged. This merger is called sentiency. Knowingness has been absorbed into 'Being'Consciousness. This is ONE. This is the *Caitanya ekam*.

Ataḥ Prajñānam Brahma : Therefore this *Caitanya* is called *Brahma*, ONE without a second.

Mayyapi Brahma : I am not excluded.

There are two types of ONE-s in *vedāntic* thought; One is that ONE which is followed by two; the other is the ONE which is never followed by two. The first ONE can be divided by two; the second ONE cannot be. The second ONE is called infinite; the first is called imagined finitude in the infinite.

Therefore, all mathematical formulae fail in Infinity. Thus, *Ataḥ Brahma* : means, that *Brahma*, where there is no touch of second-ness, no possibility of otherness, where there is nothing other than 'I' the Absolute, and that alone I am.

To be natural is to be without action, without desire, without ignorance. This actionless, Conscious, Blissful Existence---'I am'. This is the meaning of all the *Mahāvākya-s* put together.

Mahāvākya is that which establishes the identity of the part with the whole *jīvātmā-Paramātmā aikya bodha.* When the student listens with faith to the *mahāvākya* from *Guru-mukha*, by the very listening, knowledge takes place, and this knowledge does not require any follow up action.

परिपूर्णः परात्मास्मिन्देहे विद्याधिकारिणि ।
बुद्धेः साक्षितया स्थित्वा स्फुरन्नहमितीर्यते ।।३।।

Paripūrṇaḥ parātmā-smin-dehe vidyā-dhikāriṇi
Buddheḥ sākṣi-tayā sthitvā sphuran-naha mitīr yate (3)

परिपूर्णः- Not limited by time, space, objects; परात्मा - Supreme Self; अस्मिन् - in this *mahāvākya*; विद्याधिकारिणि - fit for getting Self knowledge; देहे - in the body; बुद्धेः- of the intellect; साक्षितया - as witness; स्थित्वा - staying; स्फुरन् - manifests; अहम् - *Aham*; इति - thus; ईर्यते - is called.

The Supreme infinite Self not limited by time, space and object etc.; staying in the human body, that is fit for Self-realisation, as the witnessing Consciousness is called *'Aham'* in the *'Aham Brahma asmi' mahāvākya.* (3)

Asmin dehe Parātmā Paripūrṇaḥ : In this body, the *Paramātmā* is supremely complete i.e., no possibility of limitations or conditionings imposing on the *Paramātmā.*

Limitations are of several types:

a) Those caused by time, space and object (*kālataḥ, deśataḥ* and *vastutaḥ*). These manifest as 'I am this body' thought which gets rooted so strongly that it results in *paricchinnatā,* or acceptance of these three types of limitations as real.

b) Those caused by the trio (*tripuṭi*) of *kartā-karma-karmaphala; jñātā-jñeya-jñānam; bhoktā-bhogya-bhogyam* etc..

c) Those caused by the concern for *Yoga* (to get something) and *kṣema* (to protect something that already is!). Those who are overwhelmed by these two concerns follow the *preyas mārga* referred to in the *Kaṭhopaniṣad,* and fall in the category of *avidyā.* They fall victims to the limitations of doership, to knowership (considering oneself incomplete in knowledge) and of wanting to struggle for happiness, enjoyership.

d) Those caused by *jīva-jagat-Īśvara bheda. Īśvara* is the creator and controller of the world and *jīva*; he presides over the law of *Karma* (*Karmādhyakṣa*) and awards *karma-phala*; *Jīva* is the one who has come into this world to enjoy or to suffer according to his *Karma*; and *jagat* is the field where the *jīva* expresses himself. *Īśvara* is different from *jagat*, and *jagat* is different from *jīva* and so on, one from the other. Thus there are five types of differences between them, limiting each other.

e) Those caused by fear; fear of death and extinction; fear of deception, and fear of unhappiness. These limitations lead to the pursuit of Self-preservation. The opposite of these three fears are *Sat, Cit* and *Ānanda.*

In the *Paramātmā*, all these limitations mentioned above and their ramifications are totally absent. He is therefore *Paripūrṇa*, without *paricchinnatā.*

Where is this *Paramātmā*?

Asmin dehe : In this very body, in this human birth. It is only in the human birth that *mahāvākya Upadeśa* is possible.

Vidyā adhikāriṇi : We are born in this human body for only one thing, for knowing the truth--- nothing else; and nothing short of this is the purpose of this human existence. The *paripūrṇa paramātmā* is abundantly available to us in this very body, where we can discover our own essential nature.

Thus *Paramātmā* has been defined as being without *paricchinnatā* (any limitations) and *Parokṣatā* (otherness).

Now the word *Aham* is being defined. *Paramātmā* was explained as being complete and available in this very body. Where in this body?

Buddheḥ sākṣitayā sthitvā : *Paramātmā* is the witness of all the thought modifications in the mind.

Sphuram aham itīryate: In the *mahāvākya*, '*Aham Brahmāsmi*', the meaning of *Aham* is this *Sākṣi Caitanya* which is illuminating every thought but not coming under the influence of any thought. *'Aham'* does not refer to 'I' as man, woman etc., but the 'I' who is *Anaśnan*, untouched and unswayed by the events around, happy or otherwise.

The total world exists in the dynamic equilibrium of self-cancelling pairs of opposites and the mind per se supports this relative *dvandva*, but itself is neither good or bad. It is totally untouched, uncontaminated (*asaṅgaḥ*).

As *Bhagavān Kṛṣṇa* says (B.G.,V), he who is able to stand apart and not come under the influence of *kāma* and *krodha*, he is already liberated.

Thus this *'Aham'* is the witness of all the turmoil of thoughts in the mind, yet is never influenced by them. This *Aham* is not relative, qualified entity, changing from time to time, but it is *śuddha Aham* not created by effort or by the result of action. When this puny little relative 'I' dies, the real 'I' shines forth in all its fullness-*paripūrṇa Sat* (ref: *Upadeśa Sāram*- 20)

From the above, it follows that one on the spiritual path has to be very disciplined in his contact with the world, avoiding every trace of desire and attachment. Love without attachment is divinity.

स्वतः पूर्णः परात्माऽत्र ब्रह्मशब्देन वर्णितः ।
अस्मीत्यैक्य परामर्शस्तेन ब्रह्म भवाम्यहम् ।।४।।

Svataḥ pūrṇaḥ parātmā'tra brahma-śabdena varṇitaḥ
Asmī tyaikya parāmarśas tena brahma bhavā myaham (4)

स्वतः पूर्णः- Infinite Self independent of anything; परात्मा - the Supreme Self अत्र - in this *mahāvākya*; ब्रह्म शब्देन - by the word *Brahma*; वर्णितः- is described; अस्मि इति - and by word *asmi*; ऐक्य - oneness; परामर्शः - is established; तेन - therefore; अहम् - I; ब्रह्म - *Brahman*; भवामि - am.

The Supreme infinite Self is referred in the *mahāvākya, 'Aham Brahma Asmi'* by the word *Brahma*. The word *asmi* establishes the identity between them. Therefore, 'I am *Brahman*' is the knowledge. (4)

Having defined *'Aham'* in *śloka* 3, the remaining two words in the *mahāvākya, 'Aham Brahma* Asmi' viz., *Brahma* and *Asmi* are defined in this *śloka*.

In the sentence, '*Aham Brahma Asmi*', the word '*Brahma*' is not the adjective of *Aham*, it does not 'qualify'*Aham*, but it establishes the identity between the two i.e., *Aham* is *Brahman*. The two words are in the same case i.e., *Sāmānādikaraṇa* and are defined in terms of the same *Vibhakti pratyaya* or case.

In the last *śloka, Aham* was said to be *paripūrṇaḥ* and *parātmā*. Here it is said : *svataḥ pūrṇaḥ parātmā atra Brahma śabdena varṇitaḥ* - That which is complete in itself, and is the Supreme *Ātmā*, is described as *Brahma*.

The words used to describe *Aham* in the previous verse and *Brahma* in this verse are almost identical, indicating that the object to which both words point is the same. When this knowledge takes place *Aham brahmāsmi anubhūti* results.

Svataḥ Pūrṇaḥ means that complete-ness to which nothing can be added and from which nothing can be subtracted, where there is no dependence on any object or person or circumstance to experience fulfilment. And if *Paramātmā* is *pūrṇa*, the world that is seen is also *Pūrṇa*, because *Pūrṇāt Pūrṇam Udacyate*.

That which is absolutely complete is *Parātmā*. *Ātmā* is 'I', *Parātmā* is the supreme 'I'. That means there are two *Ātmā*-s; one the limited which suffers, enjoys, and the other which is untouched by any of these experiences. This *Parātmā* is indicated by the word *'Brahma'* in this

Mahāvākya. In this way, the evaluation of the description of the two words *'Aham'* and *'Brahma'* established that they are one and the same. The one-ness in the two is indicated by the third word *'Asmi'*.

This word '*Asmi*' is not equivalent to *Asti* in - 'the book is on the table', where the table and the book are two different things. *Asmi* indicates self-asserted existence, independent of everything. *Asmi iti aikya parāmarśaḥ,* when the two words *'Aham'* and '*Brahma*' are analyzed as to their state of being, the conclusion is reached that the two words establish only one name.

Tena Brahma Bhavāmi Aham : *Asmi* indicates that 'I AM', whether I accept it, recognize it or not. It is an 'Am-ness' that has no logic. The Truth is so simple, only we are not available to the Truth. Hence, the need for enquiry, for contemplation.

So, when one contemplates on the *mahāvākya*, it does not mean that we become *Brahman*, as the use of the verb might lead one to think. *Brahman* is already existing as our essential nature, only it is now revealed to us for cognition. That which was lost because of ignorance was never lost, and that which is gained through knowledge is not a real gain because I cannot lose myself (*Aheyam*) nor can I gain myself (*Anupādeyam*).

'I' alone is the important factor. 'I' is the most dear to me (*Ātmanastu kāmāya sarvam priyam bhavati*). It is because of 'I' that the world exists. That which supports this world is this 'I' and this 'I' is *Brahma svarūpa.* The biggest and the most important thing in this world is *Brahman* and this most important thing is 'I' and therefore, *Aham Brahma Bhavāmi.*

Who can do this kind of enquiry? He who is not unduly concerned about worldly things, who can drop the world as dirt. Only then can *Aham Brahmāsmi Vṛtti* take place. Thereafter, the subsequent development is taken care of by the Lord.

एकमेवाद्वितीयं सन्नामरूपविवर्जितम् ।
सृष्टेः पुराधुनाऽप्यस्य तादृक्त्वं तदितीर्यते ।।५।।

Ekameva advitīyaṁ san nāma rūpa vivarjitam
Sṛṣṭeḥ purā-dhunā 'py asya tādṛk tvaṁ tad itīryate (5)

सृष्टेः पुरा - Before creation; एकम् - one; एवम् अद्वितीयम् - without a second; नाम रूप विवर्जितम् - devoid of name and forms; सत् - the pure existence which is referred in scriptures; अस्य - of that sat; अधुना अपि - after creation also; तादृक्त्वं - the same nature; तत् इति - tat in the *tat tvam asi* sentence; ईर्यते - is called.

That one pure Existence which is devoid of all types of differences was before the creation. The pure Existence is without change in its nature even after creation. This pure Existence is referred as *'Tat'* in *'Tat tvam asi' Mahāvākya.* (5)

The third *Mahāvākya, 'Tat tvam asi'* is taken from the *Sāma* Veda (*Chandogya Upaniṣad*).

Śvetaketu spends twelve years in the *Gurukul* and comes back very arrogant and stands before his father with total absence of *bhaya-bhakti.* (*Vidyā vinayena śobhate* : Knowledge shines in humility). The father asks the son, 'What did you study?'. The boy replies proudly, 'Everthing'. The father asks, 'Did you learn that, by which everything becomes known?' 'No, perhaps my teacher did not know it'. The father says, 'Then you know nothing'. *Śvetaketu's* pride receives a jolt and duly humbled, he requests his father to teach him that knowledge. The *upadeśa Vākya* which the Father-*Guru* gives the disciple is *'Tat Tvam Asi'.*

Sṛṣṭeḥ purā : Before the creation, *Ekam eva advitīyam sat* - there was one Truth without a second. *Nāma rūpa vivarjitam* : and this truth had neither names nor form. *Adhunā api* : even after the world was created and in spite of it, *Asya tādṛktvaṁ* : the Truth has not undergone any change.

Tat itīryate : This truth which is immune to change is referred to as *'Tat'* in the *mahāvākya 'Tat Tvam Asi'*.

A doubt can be raised : If *Sat* was before creation, does that mean there was creation at a certain point in time? No, it is like saying in the classic example of the rope and the snake, that before the snake, the rope was. There never was a snake, but it appeared through our wrong perception and therefore, we are made aware of the substratum, the rope. The rope alone is, the snake 'appeared'as an illusion for the time being. The world is an illusion, a *pratīti.* Every illusion must have a substratum, the reality and every illusion must have an appearance. Therefore, if the world is an illusion, there must be a substratum on which it is superimposed and which is 'other'than the illusion. If the illusion, the world consists of name and forms, then the substratum is *nāma rūpa vivarjitam.*

Thus there are two types of visions of the world, one from the point of the substratum and the other from the point of view of what is superimposed on it. A balanced understanding of the two view points gives the meaning of *Sadvastu*.

From the point of view of the ocean, the names and forms that are the waves, are constantly changing and are an illusion. But the wave per se with its content called the ocean is not an illusion. Nevertheless, the birth, existence and death of the wave do not cause disturbance in the mind because one knows the ocean is the substratum of the *Sat*, is *Sad-buddhi*.

Therefore in creation, there is no creation of new matter or energy. There is only conversion or transformation. That *Sat* which never changes but which supports all changes and in which creation and destruction cancel each other is *ekam*, ONE, and it is one without a second. To perceive this Truth, this substratum or *Sat*, is to transcend the limitations of the names and the forms. This *Sat* is *'Tat'* in the *Mahāvākya 'Tat tvam asi'*.

श्रोतुर्देहेन्द्रियातीतं वस्त्वत्र त्वंपदेरितम् ।
एकता ग्राह्यतेऽसीति तदैक्यमनुभूयताम् ।।६।।

Śrotur-dehe indriyā-tītaṁ vastv atra tvaṁ pade ritam
Ekatā grāhyate-'sīti tad aikya manu bhūyatām (6)

श्रोतुः- Of the seeker listening to *Vedāntā*; देह इन्द्रिय अतीतम् - that which is beyond and of different nature than body senses etc.; वस्तु - the thing; अत्र - in this *Mahāvākya*; त्वम् पद - by the word *tvam*; ईरितम् - is meant; असि इति - and the word *asi*; एकता - oneness; ग्राह्यते - is established; तद् ऐक्यम् - this oneness of *tvam* and *tat*; अनुभूयताम् - the seeker should experience.

That which is other than and unlike the body senses etc. of the seeker, 'That' witness is referred by the word *tvam* and the word *asi* establishes the oneness of *tvam* and *tat*. The seeker of Truth should experience this oneness. (6)

In this *śloka*, the remaining two words of the *Mahāvākya 'Tat tvam asi'*, namely, *tvam* and *asi* are explained. *Śrotuḥ,* the one who is listening. How we hear and what we understand out of that hearing depends on the ability of the individual. The type of listener referred to here, to whom the *upadeśa* of the *mahāvākya* will have meaning, is he who is qualified by the nature of his *Śraddhā* and *tapasyā,* he who has withdrawn from the world to know the Truth and has approached the teacher with a calm mind, having burnt all concerns about worldly matters. (M.U. I-2-12). To such a *Śrotuḥ,* the meaning of *tvam pada* will be perceptible.

What does *tvam pada* mean?

Deha indriya atītam vastu atra tvam pada īritam. Tvam pada: indicates that which is beyond the gross body and the subtle body. *Deha atīta vastu* signifies that which is beyond the whole waking state, which begins with the identification of the waker with the gross body.

To understand this *atīta-vastu*, the scriptures suggest several techniques. One is for 'I' as the waker, an individual to withdraw from the world of the waking state to such an extent that the waking experience does not sway him in any way. Only then will it be possible to drop the wakerhood in me and be awakened to that to which everyone else is sleeping. (B.G. II-69)

Taken from another angle, when the Consciousness gets indentified with the gross body, the whole waking world is created with its three components of the waker, the waking experience and the waking world existing simultaneously and being mutually dependent. That which is beyond the system of mutually dependent variables, be it the waking state, dream state or deep sleep state, that entity is indicated by the *'tvam'pada*. (*Deham* refers to the gross world of the waking state; and *indriya* refers to the subtle body which predominantly operates in the dream state).

This enquiry into the contemplation on the correct meaning of *'tvam' pada* is called *tvam pada śodhanam*.

How is the enquiry to be done? *Ādi Śaṅkara* advises : Contemplate on 'You are not the *deham*; you are not the *indriyā-s*; you are not the *prāṇa*, *manas* or *buddhi*.'

That means that, you are dissociated from the *pañca kośa-s*. Why? Because all of them have three qualities - they are subject to modifications (*vikāri*), to destruction (*vināśi*), and they are the objects of knowledge (*dṛśyatvāt*). Therefore, the *'tvam'*, the real 'I' cannot be the *pañca kośa-s* which are three *upādhī-s* of the Subject.

This self analysis and self awareness should be maintained by the spiritual seeker all the time, in every department of his involvement. In that sense, he is always 'awake'.

Now the third word *'Asi'*in the *mahāvākya* is dealt with : *Ekatā grāhyatā asi iti* : The word *'asi'*indicates the oneness between the two words *'tat'* and *'tvam'*. This is the meaning of *Asi pada*. 'That is you.' That and Thou are not two. One should contemplate on this *Tat tvam* (*tat* + *tvam*) to realize that the two words mean one and the same thing.

Tat aikyam anubhūyatām : May you realize this identity between *tat* and *tvam*.

What is the meaning of this identity? What is the *Sādhanā*?

The *Sādhanā* for the *tvam pada śodhanam* is *Vedānta sādhanā*, that for the *tat pada śodhanam* is *Bhakti sādhanā*.

Once the sense of 'otherness'is removed, love manifests. Removing the conditioning of otherness and of limitation leads to the establishment of one-ness between these two words which together constitute *'tat tvam'*.

This oneness needs to be experienced in spite of the many-ness. This *abhyāsa* consists of constant discovery of the common denominator of Life, initially in the three states of Consciousness and gradually extending in ever widening circles to include all the beings (*cara*) and things (*acara*).

This *sārvātmyabhāva* was experienced by *Śuka Brahma Ṛṣi* and by many great Masters.

Once the *parichhinnatā* i.e., sense of being limited and *parokṣatā* i.e., sense of otherness are overcome, and the seeker's attention is focussed on the Life Principle, then the *ekatā* or oneness is established.

स्वप्रकाशापरोक्षत्वमयमित्युक्तितो मतम् ।
अहंकाराऽदिदेहान्तात्प्रत्यगात्मेति गीयते ।।७।।

Svaprakāśa parokṣa tvam ayami tyukti to matam
Ahaṁ kārā 'di dehāntāt pratyag ātmeti gīyate (7)

अयम् इति - The word *ayam*; उक्तितः- by this word; स्वप्रकाश - self effulgent; अपरोक्षत्वम् - direct and immediate; मतम् - is meant; अहंकार आदि - starting from ego; देहान्तात् - up to gross body; प्रत्यक् - is nearer and witness of all these; आत्मा इति - *Ātmā*; गीयते - is called.

The word *Ayam* in the *mahāvākya 'Ayam Ātmā Brahma'* is said to mean self effulgent and immediate self; while the word *Ātmā* is used to declare that self to be nearer than everything starting from ego up to gross body. (7)

This *Mahāvākya, Ayam Ātmā Brahma* is from the *Atharva veda* from *Māṇḍukya Upaniṣad.*

'*Prajñānam Brahma*' is the definition of the Truth; this is followed by the *upadeśa vākya, 'Tat tvam asi'*. Having heard (*Śravaṇam*) this *upadeśa*, the student does *mananam* and *nididhyāsanam* and comes to realize the Truth, '*Aham Brahma Asmi*' (i.e., he has internalized *Tat tvam asi*). As a result of this realization, he goes to the teacher and says, *'Ayam Ātmā Brahma'*. The *Brahmātmaikya bodha* - the identity between the *Jīvātmā* and *Paramātmā* is established.

Sva-prakāśa aparokṣatvam ayam iti uktitaḥ matam : This word *ayam* refers to that which is *sva-prakāśa* and *aparokṣatva.* Three words state that the *Ātmā* is self-existent : *Svayambhū* meaning that which is without cause (*Kārya Kāraṇa rahita vastu*), this refers to the *Sat*, existence aspect of *ātmā*; when the *cit* or the *caitanya* aspect of *ātmā* is referred to, it is expressed as *sva-prakāśa svarūpatvāt* - one's own conscious being; *aparokṣatvam*, that *Jñānaṁ* which does not require the need of any sense organs.

Parokṣa jñānaṁ is what has been heard from someone else in whom we have faith (*āptavākya*). *Pratyakṣa jñānam* is what has been experienced directly with one's own sense organs. *Aparokṣa jñānam* is that which is direct experience without the help of any medium.

The *Śuddha Caitanya* or *Paramātmā* is very much in our bosom - THAT I AM, for that I AM, no third entity is required to know that I AM. Therefore, the two qualities of *sva prakāśa* and *aparokṣatva* put together leaves no doubt that *ayam* refers to the closest thing to us - this is called *Ātmā* (*Brahman*).

The second word in the *mahāvākya* is *Ātmā*. This is most misunderstood word because each one understands it according to his own *buddhi*; to some it is the body, to others it is wealth, to others it is name, fame, popularity and still others, it is how much one has studied etc..

In this *mahāvākya*, however, the correct meaning is given in the words *Ahamkārādi dehāntāt pratyag ātmā iti gīyate* : That which is closer than the closest. As one starts from space and approaches oneself nearer and nearer, through one *kośa* after another, a stage comes when one can go no more closer. After having rejected everything, that which cannot be rejected and therefore cannot be gained, is being said to be *Ātmā*.

दृश्यमानस्य सर्वस्य जगतस्तत्त्वमीर्यते ।
ब्रह्मशब्देन तद्ब्रह्म स्वप्रकाशात्मरूपकम् ।।८।।

Dṛśya mānasya sarvasya jagatas tattva mīryate
Brahma śabdena tadbrahma svaprakāśā-tma-rūpakam (8)

दृश्यमानस्य - that appears; सर्वस्य जगतः- of the whole world; तत्त्वम - substratum; ब्रह्म शब्देन - by the word *Brahma*; ईर्यते - is said; तद् ब्रह्म - that *Brahma*; स्वप्रकाशात्मरूपकम् - is of the nature of self-effulgent Self.

By the word *Brahma*, the substratum (which is Conscious Existence) of the appearance of the Whole world is meant. That *Brahman* is of the nature of Self-effulgent Pure Self. (8)

The third word in the *mahāvākya, 'Ayam Ātmā Brahma'* is *Brahma*. Up to this point, one's efforts can help, beyond this point, efforts cannot help for the reason that the individuality disappears. Disappearance of the individuality is the realization of *'Aham Brahmāsmi'* or *'Ayam Ātmā Brahma' mahāvākya.*

The word *Brahma* is used in different ways with different contexts. In this *mahāvākya,* it means what has been defined in *Dṛg dṛśya viveka* as there are five things associated with every thing in this world. *Asti-* existence, *bhāti-* Consciousness, *priyam-*liking, *nāma-*name and *rūpam-*form. Of these five, the first three refer to the *Brahma* or Substratum, and the last two to the *jagat* or the world.

In the example of the ocean and the wave, *asti-bhāti-priya* is the essence of the ocean; and the *nāma-rūpa* characterize the waves as each wave is born, grows, and dies away. *Asti-bhāti-priya* is never born, nor does it grow, nor dies likewise.

Dṛśyamānasya sarvasya jagataḥ tattvam : All that is perceived, known, experienced in this world, the essence that is supporting the totality of the names and forms;

Brahma śabdena īryate : is referred to by the word *Brahma*;

Tat Brahma svaprakāśa ātma rūpakam : That *Brahma* is the self-illumined *Ātma svarūpam.*

CONCLUSION :

There are two aspects to *ādhyātma sādhanā : Tvam pada śodhanam* and *Tat pada śodhanam.*

Taking the *pañca kośa viveka*, that which I am not, is rejected. The gross body, the *indrīyā-s, prāna,* mind etc., are rejected because they, I am not; they are *asat* and *jaḍa.* By themselves, they have no existence. And they are many; but *Aham* 'I' is one and it is Sat. (ref.: *Ramaṇa Maharṣi's Upadeśa Sāram* 22)

By the technique of *laya* or absorption, all that is more than one is rejected and the seeker slowly migrates from many to the one. And by *dhyāna sādhanā*, the *upādhi-s* are absorbed into one's being. This is only up to the level of the *prakṛti*. One is not yet the *Puruṣa* or the *Ātmā*. After the mind has become quiet and single pointed (but awake), such a mind is made to contemplate on ONE. When this is done, the mind disappears and one comes to one's own source - *Pratyagātmeti gīyate*.

Along with this *tvam pada śodhana*, one should simultaneously do the *Tat pada śodhana*. This is *Asi*. We refuse to see the plurality. In everything and being, we do the *bhāvanā* of My Lord *Kṛṣṇa*, he alone is. We invoke His presence in every moment of our lives, and in that one thought, all other thoughts and problems are dissolved. This constant *abhyāsa* of keeping the Lord's presence on our right side is called *Bhakti sādhanā*.

Thus are the two *sādhanā-s* practiced : When the seeker wants nothing other than his own essential nature, then alone is the *Ātmā* revealed to him in all its glory; and from *Bhakti sādhanā* point of view, it is total surrender to the Lord's will to reveal this glory to the seeker, when He wills.

Paramātmā has no desire, but all the strength; and we have all the desire, but no strength. So let us surrender all the desire at His feet and let us take His strength.

Once this knowledge of the *mahāvākya-s* takes place in the seeker, life becomes lighter and a joyful experience.

OM TAT SAT

Summary

Verse No.	Subject matter covered
	Introduction
1 - 2	*Prajñānam Brahma* from *Aitereya Upaniṣad* of *Ṛg* Veda expounded.
3 - 4	*Aham Brahmāsmi* from *Bṛhadāraṇyaka Upaniṣad* of *Yajurveda* elaborated.
5 - 6	*Tat tvam asi* from *Chāndogya Upaniṣad* of *Sāma veda* analysed.
7 - 8	*Ayam Ātmā Brahma* from *Māṇḍukya Upaniṣad* of *Atharvaṇa veda* explained.

* * *